A Field Guide to Southern
New England Railroad Depots
and Freight Houses

1912

NY·NH&H·RR

NEW ENGLAND RAIL HERITAGE SERIES

A Field Guide to
Southern New England
Railroad Depots
and Freight Houses

JOHN H. ROY, JR.

Branch
Line
Press

PEPPERELL, MASSACHUSETTS

Branch Line Press
30 Elm Street
Pepperell, Massachusetts 01463-1603

Email: books@branchlinepress.com
www.branchlinepress.com

Cover design by Diane B. Karr
Book design by Ronald Dale Karr

Cover photographs, clockwise on front: Worcester, MA, Station (photo by Ron Karr); Colchester, CT, Freight House; Kingston, RI, Station; back: Simsbury, CT, Combination Depot. (photos by the author)

Frontispiece: Detail of the clerestory façade of Westerly, RI, Station, proudly proclaiming the station's origins in the heyday of the New York, New Haven & Hartford Railroad. (photo by the author)

Library of Congress Cataloging-in-Publication Data:

Roy, John H.
    A field guide to southern New England railroad depots and freight
    houses / John H. Roy, Jr.
      p.   cm. – (New England rail heritage series)
    Includes bibliographical references and index.
    ISBN-13: 978-0-942147-08-7 (alk. paper)
    1. Railroad stations–New England–Guidebooks. I. Title. II. Series.

TF302.N48R69 2007
385.3'140974–dc22

                                                      2006100258
10 9 8 7 6 5 4 3 2 1

*To my grandfather, Ameddie Henry Roy (1910-2001).
It was his love for model trains that planted the
railroad seed in my heart so many years ago.*

Contents

Preface

THE IDEA for this book was born around 1990, when I began actively photographing railroad stations. Back then I was intrigued by the various styles, and I often wondered what the buildings were like when they were in their prime. It didn't take long for me to figure out that many stations had vanished and many more were not going to last much longer, so I took pictures of those remaining whenever I had the opportunity. Having been a life-long resident of Connecticut, I quickly became interested in the New York, New Haven & Hartford RR, also affectionately known as the New Haven. My love for stations grew, and by the mid 1990s I was exploring every town that ever had a railroad and photographing the remaining stations throughout New England. I began a simple list of those that survived. This list eventually evolved into an extensive relational database that became the foundation for this book.

This guide would not have been possible without the patience of my wife and children, who have spent countless hours patiently riding in the car while I explored. They often asked if we were ever going to get to our destination. I rarely took the direct route; there was always some structure that needed to be investigated along the way. They tolerated many evenings when I would banish myself to the bedroom to work on the book. As with most projects, things usually take longer than expected, and this book was no exception. To my wife, Chulaluk, and my children, Geoffrey and Amanda, I thank you for your patience and support. I can finally answer the question, "When is it going to be done?" with "It's done!"

This has certainly been a family project, as I also enlisted the help of my father, John Roy. In addition to taking some of the photographs, he scanned and prepared hundreds of 35 mm slide images used in this book. This was no small task, and I am greatly indebted for his assistance. If I

Among hundreds of long lost stations, the Boston & Providence RR's Park Square Station was an outstanding example of Gothic architecture and one of the most elegant of New England's old stations. Opened in 1875, it was converted to commercial use in 1899, when rail service was moved to South Station. It was torn down ten years later following a damaging fire. (Courtesy of the Beverly Historical Society & Museum, Beverly, MA, Walker Transportation Collection)

had had to do it myself, it would likely have added another six months to the project. When he accepted this task he had just retired and did not realize how busy he would be in retirement. Despite this, he found the time to help and even ran around to get some last minute images for the book.

I would also like to thank my friends Ron Gallant, Michael and Jimmy Tylick, and John Mrzak, who have helped with the fieldwork and photography required for this book. Over the years, they have been on many expeditions with me, no one more than Ron Gallant, who knows what it is like to spend a double shift on the road with me. Additionally, Ron Karr, Doug Scott, Matt Cosgro, Deborah Bassett, and my daughter, Amanda Roy, also contributed images for this book.

Over the years, I have exchanged numerous e-mails with Gary LaPointe, the publisher of a very helpful website called Railroad Stations in Massachusetts. He is trying to track down any and all standing railroad structures in Massachusetts. I strongly encourage readers of this book to visit his website: http://www.lightlink.com/sglap3/, where you will find numerous images, both past and present, of Massachusetts stations and freight houses.

Of course I have a great deal of appreciation for the efforts of my editor, Diane Karr, for her assistance with my writing and her encouragement and advice. Also many thanks to Ron Karr for his technical input, spirited debates, and for the fine job he has done on the book layout and the maps, which bring it all together.

In addition I have received a great deal of support and encouragement from the following family and friends: Chanjira Boucher, Jason Boucher, Norman Boucher, Wesley Boucher, Atanu Das, Arnab Das, Auypon McBrien, Christopher Roy, Linda Roy, Theresa Roy, Janet Tylick, and my mother, Yvonne Roy.

Last but not least, I would like to thank the many individuals and organizations that made available a great deal of local historical and background information. It would not have been possible to provide so many details without their help. My sincere thanks go to the following for their assistance: George Frazee Amadon, David Balfour, Emily Bancroft, Dave Bartlett, Wilbur Beckwith, Mary Bernat, Richard J. Bolan, Edith Bosselman, Lisa Bourque, Edward Brown, Donna Bryant, Robert Buck, Silvia G. Buck, Nancy Campbell, William Carroll, Paul L. Chalifour, Betsy Cook, Sharon Coss, Bob Costas, Louise Cowing, Craig Della Penna, Devon Dawson, Ellen Dolan, David Erikson, Sherry Evans, Jane Fischer, May Forlain, Janice Franco, Ruth Gagliardi, Judy Gallerie, Bernie Goldberg, Edward Gorski, Carol Goulet, Catherine Granton, Nancy Haag, Judy Jacobs, William Johnson, Mike Jordan, Laura Katz Smith, Jeffrey Klapes, Arthur W. Knuever, Jr., Karen Kowal, Greg Laing, David

Lambert, Anita Lehto, Alan LePain, Jeannine T. Levesque, Warner Lord, Jay Manewitz, Marge McAvoy, Greg McClay, Patricia Mehrtens, Marie Morrissey, Suzanne Nichelson, Richard Nichols, Joan F. Noonan, John Nurek, Mary O'Connell, Philip Opielowski, Jay Peiler, Margaret Perkins, Jeff Pike, Linda Pinder, Mrs. Preston, Rita Prew, Anne Reilly, Kathleen Remillard, Kathleen Black Reynolds, Meg Royka, Nancy Ryan, Jim Schofield, Irene Silva, Rosalie M. Silva, Rob and Kevin Skaling, Bob Suppicich, George S. Swistak, Peter Thornell, Henry Tragert, Richard Trask, Frank and Robin Vizzacco, Sandra Waxman, Edgar Whitcomb, Leslie Wilson, Dwight Winkley, Bob Wood, Joyce Woodman, Sheila Zanca, as well as staff at the following public libraries: Athol, Auburn, Beaman Memorial (West Boylston), Billerica, Brewster Ladies' Library, Bridgewater, Chicopee, Concord Free, Flint, Groton, Hingham, Holliston, Holyoke, Hyannis, Goodnow Library (Sudbury), Leominster, Lucius Beebe Memorial (Wakefield), Lynn, Lynnfield, Meriden, North Haven Memorial, Palmer, Peabody Institute Library (Danvers), S. White Dickinson Library (Whately), Sherborn, Stoneham, Stoughton, Truro, and Warren; the following town historical societies: Beverly, Brewster, Dedham, Hatfield, Kent, Leominster, Litchfield, Meriden, Naugatuck, Stafford, Swift River Valley, Topsfield, Townsend, and Weston; and the following specialty libraries and organizations: Boston & Maine Railroad Historical Society, Central Vermont Railway Historical Society, Chester Foundation, Emily Williston Memorial Library and Museum, New Haven Railroad Historical & Technical Association, North Attleborough Falls Fire Barn Preservation Society, Thomas J. Dodd Research Center at the University of Connecticut, and Wilmington Town Museum. I sincerely apologize if I have accidentally left anyone off this list.

Although every effort was made to make this book as accurate as possible, it almost certainly contains some errors. I apologize and take full responsibility for my mistakes. I encourage readers who find errors or omissions to contact me about them so I may correct them in future editions of this book. I can be reached via e-mail at jroyjr@comcast.net, or you can reach me through my publisher, Branch Line Press.

Introduction

HAVE YOU ever wondered about the history of a railroad station that houses a business in your town's center, where tracks are long gone and there is little evidence of a railroad ever having run? Have you noticed a home in your town that has the classic architecture of a station from a bygone era, when trains were pulled by large-wheeled locomotives powered by coal and water? Does your town have an old freight house, one with large wooden doors spaced about forty feet apart down one or both sides of the structure, and do you know how that building was used when the steam trains ran? If you are fortunate enough to have an active passenger train station in your community, are you curious to know more about its origins?

With the vast network of rail lines that once served Connecticut, Massachusetts, and Rhode Island, nearly every community had one or more depots and freight houses. From the mid 1800s to the early 1900s, the passenger station was the first or last stop on any journey beyond the local community. Even small towns usually had one or more daily passenger trains to and from their town centers. The stations were the pride of the communities they served. The size, materials, and architectural styles of the depots were talked about and debated at great length by the townspeople. The railroad often rewarded communities that subscribed heavily to railroad stock with larger and more elaborate stations. In later years many towns petitioned the railroads for new and improved facilities to replace worn out or inadequate ones. In some cases towns even funded part of the cost, built new roads, and deeded property to the railroads to ensure their stations would be a source of civic pride. Anyone who collects old postcards knows that railroad station postcards were popular throughout the United States.

The 455 structures contained in the three state chapters in this guide illustrate a large cross-section of American architecture of the last 175 years. From simple board-and-batten Gothic structures to elaborate

The stylish arched glass and aluminum sunrise window at the entrance to Ruggles Modern Station is a creative, contemporary interpretation of an architectural element that has appeared in numerous variations and in diverse building materials on significant stations throughout New England. (Ron Karr)

Beaux Arts/Classical stations made of granite and marble, a multitude of architectural styles is represented, including: Romanesque, Queen Anne, Georgian, Second Empire, Spanish, Colonial, Victorian, Gothic, Greek Revival, Bungalow, Tudor, Stick, Renaissance Revival, Italianate, and Classical Revival.

Each original railroad, and later the consolidated railroads, expressed their own styles and corporate images in their depots and stations. Clearly McDonald's and Starbucks weren't the first corporations to standardize their buildings to reduce cost and project a favorable public image. During prosperous times, the railroads built extravagant stations designed by such famous architects as Henry Hobson Richardson, Cass Gilbert, Henry Bacon, and Bradford Lee Gilbert, and architectural firms such as Sheply, Rutan and Coolidge, and McKim, Mead and White. The Index to Architects provides a convenient cross reference to some of their works in southern New England; many more have already been lost. Although the book identifies some of the prominent architectural features of these buildings, and when known, the architectural style, I am not an architect, nor do I claim to have detailed architectural knowledge. What I have gained in preparing this book is a basic knowledge and a new-found appreciation for the architectural diversity in southern New England railroad structures. I hope this book encourages everyone to explore these wonderful treasures and learn more themselves.

When the railroads were abandoned, the locomotives and rolling stock were sold off to other railroads, and the tracks and bridges were often removed; but the stations, freight houses, and other structures remained. It is through these vestiges of the railroads' past glory that we can imagine what it must have been like in the heyday of rail transportation. The depot was the community's center for the latest news and gossip, and the neighborhood around the depot and freight house developed into the commercial center of most communities, if the station hadn't been built in the commercial center to start with. The railroad employed great numbers of people, many of whom lived and worked in the communities they served.

The smaller railroad stations, depots, and combination depots provided railroad passengers with a place to buy tickets, check baggage, and a room to wait in. More elaborate stations provided rest rooms and separate waiting rooms for ladies and gentlemen. Many stations provided express package service and eventually telegraph and Western Union conveniences. Express package service was available for small parcels and packages, similar to packages handled by today's United Parcel Service (UPS). These packages were dropped off at the station, transported in the baggage cars of passenger trains, and picked up at the destination stations. The express business was usually handled by the station agent under contract to the express company. Where demand warranted, separate facilities or rooms were built by the railroad and used by companies like REA Express and Adams Express to conduct their business, which often included pickup and delivery beyond the station.

Large union stations included extravagant and grand waiting rooms with newsstands, separate baggage rooms, express offices, restaurants, and railroad offices. These structures were constructed at great expense and often had train sheds, passenger subways, and multiple boarding tracks for customer convenience and expedited handling of passengers and their baggage.

Small freight houses and combination depots generally provided space to load and unload crated and boxed shipments that were too large to be handled by passenger trains and too small to fill a freight car. These items were loaded into freight cars in what the railroad called "Less-Than-Carload Lots" (LCL). LCL services were used by hardware stores, general stores, farmers, trolley companies, and small manufactures. Large consignees such as factories, coal dealers, and bulk processing plants had their own private warehouses and sidings.

Occasionally a freight house provided a small office for the freight agent. This was often included in the depot, however, since smaller freight houses lacked modern conveniences, and sometimes the agent handled both freight and passenger duties. The freight agent processed the waybills for all freight handled in the town, including the consignees who had their own sidings, as well as those who used the freight house or the local team track. The team track was owned by the railroad and was available for any customer to transfer goods to or from their off-line location. It was used just like the freight house, but without a loading dock or protection from the elements, and the freight cars were loaded for a single consignee, not in lots.

In addition to small freight houses, the railroads had strategically placed large freight houses. These were distributed throughout the system and used as hubs, much the same way the airlines fly people to their hub airports for connecting flights. These large freight houses were typically made of brick and included substantial office space for the freight agency. LCL was picked up at the small freight houses and brought to the large distribution centers, where it was sorted and loaded onto another freight car heading toward its final destination or another hub. The sorting of LCL was very labor intensive and often required twenty-four-hour-a-day operation to keep the consignee lading moving and to meet tight connecting train schedules. Good examples of these large freight houses can still be seen in Waterbury and Wallingford in Connecticut,

Pawtucket and Westerly in Rhode Island, and Holyoke, Haverhill, and South Lawrence in Massachusetts.

The number of depots has steadily declined since the 1920s, when the railroads began abandoning passenger service on the branch lines because of declining passenger demand and their need to cut costs. LCL freight began to drop off in the late 1920s, but improved after the Great Depression. However, it began a steady decline after World War II, when better roads and pneumatic tires made trucks the preferred method for short-haul transport, moving LCL directly between railroad hubs and off-line customers. After World War II local freight service decreased dramatically as the 1950s and 1960s brought the country and the region a network of improved roads that resulted in increased trucking and reduced need for freight houses. Simultaneously, affordable private automobiles gave more Americans the independence to come and go when and where they wanted to, leading to a rapid decline in passenger trains. Most of the remaining branch lines and the stations on them were closed, and lighter patronized stops on the main lines were discontinued.

With the formation of Amtrak in 1971, New England was left with minimal intercity rail passenger service: Boston to New York via Providence, Boston to Springfield, and New Haven to Springfield, with Springfield to Albany service restored in 1975. Commuter service remained in southeastern Connecticut for passengers destined for New York City, as well as commuter service north, west, and south of Boston.

Stations that had once served towns all across southern New England were no longer needed by the railroads. A few were converted for other purposes, such as freight offices or maintenance of way, but many of the former stations were abandoned, torn down, or sold. Many old freight houses were without modern conveniences such as heat, water, and electricity, so they were less likely to be recycled. They were often purchased by or leased to railroad customers for use as warehouses. In some cases the railroads continued to use them for storage or freight offices. As time marched on, the number of depots and freight houses dwindled. Fortunately, preservation efforts gained momentum in the 1980s, and local groups rallied to purchase and preserve these historic structures. This is evident by the number of stations, and even a few freight houses, that have been placed on the National Register of Historic Places. Many communities now look at these restored buildings with a sense of pride and a better appreciation for the purpose they once served. However, even today many historic stations and freight houses are at risk. Thirty-five structures, identified in Appendix B, have been lost just since I began exploring and researching them.

Connecticut's West Cornwall Combination Depot, with a special excursion train parked alongside, October 2005. Built in 1842, this structure is a very well-preserved example of the standard two-story, gable-roofed depots the Housatonic RR built along its entire line from Bridgeport to Pittsfield.

This book is a guide for readers who want to explore the history and rich architectural heritage of southern New England's remaining train stations and freight houses. Its primary purpose is to identify historical structures that survive today and provide information on their current location and use. Each entry includes a brief historical narrative about the structure, as well as easy-to-use summary information including current address, date built, current use, and which railroad(s) currently operate on the tracks that pass by it, if it is on an active rail line. It is not the purpose of this book to provide a comprehensive history of every single building, but a starting point for discovering all those that are extant. For those readers who wish to explore particular structures more fully, suggestions for further research are provided at the end of this introduction.

Types of Structures Included

This book includes only structures that still survived at the time of publication: 467 stations, related passenger service buildings, and freight houses. There are 143 structures in the Connecticut chapter, 279 in the

Massachusetts chapter, 33 in the Rhode Island chapter, and 12 in Appendix A. Not covered in this guide are other surviving railroad structures, such as round houses, engine houses, turn tables, operator towers, section houses, shop buildings, and private freight facilities built or owned by businesses served by the railroads.

The following criteria were used to determine which structures to include in the entries for each state:

Structures must serve or have served railroad passengers, freight operations, or express service. Buildings that serve or have served trolleys, subways, or light rail are not included unless they also serve or have served railroad passengers.

Structures must be enclosed on at least three sides. Modern commuter stations that are open to the elements, such as concrete platforms and three-sided plexiglass shelters, are not included. A few historically significant shelters and wooden shelters built in an historic style are included, however.

Structures must be visible and recognizable from public property or located where public access is available. Specifically excluded are buildings that have been disassembled or are entirely enclosed within another building; these are mentioned in Appendix A.

In some cases freestanding structures that are part of a station complex have been given separate entries to allow for better illustration of each building. Structures that have received extensive modification, such that they are completely unrecognizable as former stations or freight houses, are not included in the entries but are mentioned in Appendix A, as are replicas of structures that no longer exist, the originals of which served railroad passengers, freight, or express. A few structures that do not strictly meet the above criteria, but are worth mentioning for their historical significance, are also included in that appendix.

The following definitions are provided to clarify the entry names used to classify the structures, as well as other structure types mentioned in the text.

Baggage Office/Room: A physically separate building located near a depot or station used to store passengers' luggage prior to train arrival.

Combination Depot: A passenger depot that includes a separate room or section for the handling of freight. A separate wide freight door and often a freight platform are provided to speed loading and unloading of freight from box cars.

Commuter Platform: Platform with a basic covered but open boarding location. It may provide either high-level or track-level boarding.

Depot: Small to medium-sized passenger station. Depots are typically modest affairs consisting of a ticket office, a waiting room, and sometimes rest rooms. In most cases these buildings are constructed of wood.

Express Office: A physically separate building located near a depot or station used to store and process small packages. Packages were typically loaded into baggage cars of passenger trains. Unlike baggage, these packages were not associated with passengers riding the train. This system predated today's UPS.

Freight House: A building usually located near a station or depot used exclusively for the handling of freight and Less-than-Carload Lots (LCL) to or from local consignees. Some larger freight houses may have contained offices for railroad employees. Where large markets required separate freight facilities for inbound and outbound traffic, freight houses are designated as "Inbound" or "Outbound."

Freight Office: A separate building used by railroad personnel to manage the business end of local freight operations.

Mini-High Platform: A loading platform with a short high-level section, which allows passengers to board trains without stepping up to enter the car. The platforms are usually equipped with ramps to comply with Americans with Disabilities Act (ADA) requirements. New stations built or renovated since the passing of the ADA in 1990 are required to have some form of high-level platform.

Modern Station: Fully enclosed passenger station built by a commuter railroad or Amtrak. Stations may include full amenities such as ticket sales and rest rooms.

Passenger Shelter: Three- or four-sided open passenger station used to provide minimal protection from the elements for railroad patrons. Enclosures are typically made of glass or wood and usually have an unprotected opening to ease congestion when boarding.

Passenger Subway: Passageway under the railroad tracks used by passengers to reach another boarding location safely. These are typically used for the simultaneous boarding of two or more trains on a busy main line.

Railroad Office: Within a complex of buildings that serve as a station, a structure that exclusively provides railroad office space.

Station: Medium- to large-sized passenger station. These structures go beyond the bare necessities and typically include multiple waiting rooms, baggage areas, ticket counters, and railroad offices. They are generally constructed of more expensive materials like brick and granite. On busy main lines where stations were required on both sides of the tracks to support a large amount of passenger traffic, stations are designated as "Station, Eastbound," and "Station, Westbound."

Station Restaurant: A separate building that was built for the purpose of providing meals for railroad passengers.

Union Station: A station built to serve more than one railroad on two or more connecting lines. Large cities that were served by multiple downtown stations often passed legislation requiring the railroads to consolidate their facilities for the convenience of the general public.

Some structures served two purposes simultaneously or were converted from one use to another over time. Entry names for those structures reflect that by including both uses with a slash separating them (e.g., Depot/Freight House or Hotel/Station). The classification of some structures is subjective, particularly in the case of large depots or small stations.

Station Photographs

Each entry in this book is illustrated with a recent image of the structure. With a few exceptions where permission was obtained to enter a property, these images provide views of the structures from publicly accessible land and are intended to aid in locating the structures. Unless otherwise noted, photographs were taken by the author.

How to Use This Book

This book is organized into three major chapters, one for each of the three southern New England states. Within each state entries are alphabetical by the station name; the railroad considers each location on a line a station regardless of the presence or absence of any structures. Most often the stations were named by the railroads for the communities in which they were located. At some locations, multiple structures are still extant. For those locations, depots and related passenger service buildings are listed before freight houses. In several instances, there are duplicate structure types at the same location. For example Haverhill, MA, has three extant freight houses and West Brookfield, MA, has two extant stations. In these cases, the structures are listed chronologically by date and numbered "1 of 2," "2 of 2," etc.

Station Names

Station names generally agree with those identified in Ronald Dale Karr's *Rail Lines of Southern New England* (Branch Line Press, 1995). When necessary, clarifications have been added in brackets following the station name. In most cases the brackets distinguish two structures that were operated by two different railroads in two different locations in the same community. For example, the town of Amherst, MA, was served by two railroads—the former Central Vermont RY (CV) and the former Boston & Maine RR (B&M)—with separate facilities located one-half mile from each other. To clarify which stations the entries describe, the station names are listed as "Amherst [CV]" and "Amherst [B&M]." Even where only one of a pair of such structures is now extant, the railroad clarification is given so railfans who are aware of the demised structure will be clear on which of the two railroads' structures is the extant one. The older railroad names or abbreviations used for such clarifications may be unfamiliar to some readers, but these railroads are mentioned in the text for each structure that uses this convention. For structure names that are ambiguous regarding location, such as Constitution Street Station in Bristol, RI, the community is identified in brackets after the name, i.e., "Constitution St. [Bristol]." In cases where the name of the station is a little-known section of a town or city, the legal name of the community is provided in the address line to assist in locating the structure. In some cases station names have been changed over the years; while this is often mentioned in the text, the station is listed only under its most common name.

Build Dates

This field provides the actual or estimated year of the structure's original period of construction. When available, specific build dates are provided in the station description. Where build dates could not be determined, a range of dates is provided, based on available information such as the construction history of the associated railroad, historical maps, the building's architectural style, old photographs, and the construction material. Where a likely build year could be determined, or a short range of proba-

ble years, I have expressed that with circa (ca.) before the estimated date (e.g., ca. 1835 or ca. 1930-32). Particularly in the case of freight houses, however, readily available source material frequently fails to yield that clear an estimate. Where the period of construction is unknown, I have erred on the side of caution, preferring to be less specific for the sake of accuracy, so wide date ranges are given (e.g., before 1850 or between 1835 & 1875). If a structure was extensively rebuilt, such as after a fire, the re-build date is also provided.

Current Use

This field identifies the current use of the structure. In most cases this is based on observation and signs posted on or near the building, but occasionally it is an educated guess. If the current occupant is known, the text provides more detailed information. Some buildings serve multiple purposes, and in these cases all uses are listed with slashes separating them. Although somewhat subjective, primary uses are listed first, with secondary uses following. The text does not always elaborate on commercial enterprises in multi-use structures; it was not practical or useful to record the names of every coffee shop and newsstand occupying portions of the over 100 active railroad stations in southern New England. Occupants of buildings used for commercial purposes change frequently and with little notice; as for any project covering a large geographical area, it was impossible to verify all current occupants before going to print. I welcome readers with in-depth knowledge of particular structures to inform me of updates and errors in this information for correction in future editions.

Each structure's current use is classified according to the following definitions:

Abandoned: Unused and left to Mother Nature; typically falling down and uninhabitable.

Commercial: Used for business purposes such as retail, restaurant, storage, or office space.

Community: Used as a private community center or by a church, school, or non-profit social/service organization that serves the community.

More suggestive of a mission in the American southwest than a railroad station in Massachusetts, this three-story clock tower is the focal point of Nantasket's Spanish-style station.

Government: Used by regional, county, state, or federal government agencies for offices or facilities.

Historical Society: Used by an historical society, typically to house a collection and/or for meeting space or office space.

Municipal: Used by local government for town/city offices, public works, public safety, senior services, visitors' centers, etc.

Museum: Houses a museum or used as an exhibit in a museum or tourist railroad collection.

Private: Used for non-commercial, non-residential purposes such as a garage or shed, or held by a private party, with use unknown.

Railroad: Used by an active railroad for passenger service, offices, maintenance, storage, etc.

Residential: Used as a private home or as apartments or condominiums.

Transit: Used for non-railroad public transportation services such as buses, subways, trolleys, and Dial-A-Ride.

Vacant: No current occupant; currently unused.

Address

The current address is provided in each entry to help locate the structure. Whenever possible a complete street address, including the street name and number, is given. In many cases the street number was not available, and additional information, such as the nearest intersecting street, has been provided to assist the reader in finding the structure. If the structure has been moved from its original location, the address field includes the current city and state, and the text explains where and when the station was moved. The station name at the top of each entry always reflects the original location.

Current Railroads

Current railroads are provided for stations that are located on active rail lines. Abbreviations for the railroad names are used; a list of these can be found after this introduction. In many cases more than one railroad is listed, since different companies often provide passenger and freight services. Multiple railroads are listed alphabetically (by acronym) and are provided for information only; they were accurate at the time of publication but are subject to change. "N/A" (not applicable) appears in this field for stations that have been moved away from the tracks, and "None" for those where the tracks have been abandoned or are out of service (unused but not legally abandoned).

Material

This field identifies the primary materials used in the construction of the structure. When known, the specific material type, such as terra cotta or granite, is identified. When not known, generic terms such as brick and stone are used.

Narrative

For each structure I have endeavored to provide a brief history of the station or freight house, including predecessor and successor stations if known. I have identified, when available, the architect or architectural firm that designed the station. The Index to Architects provides a convenient cross-reference sorted by architect or architectural firm.

For the reader's convenience, the names of railroads mentioned in the description are spelled out on their first occurrence and abbreviated on subsequent mentions in the same entry. For example the Boston & Maine RR is abbreviated as B&M, the New York, New Haven & Hartford RR as NYNH&H, and the Old Colony RR is abbreviated as OC. The New York, New Haven & Hartford RR was also commonly called the New Haven in the twentieth century, and when appropriate this guide refers to it as the New Haven. The Massachusetts Bay Transportation Authority is always referred to as MBTA. In railroad names, "Railroad" is abbreviated as RR and "Railway" as RY throughout.

Maps

Locator maps for the three southern New England states are provided at the beginning of each chapter. These maps are intended to serve as a quick overview of where the surviving stations are located. Only locations where structures survive are shown on the maps. When more then one structure survives in a community, the total number of structures is shown in parentheses. An asterisk following the location name indicates that the structure for that location can be found in Appendix A rather than in the chapter associated with that map. In cases where there is more than one structure at a location, the asterisk indicates that one of these is located in Appendix A. Stations that have been moved to new locations are shown in light gray print at their original location and in the normal font at their current location. If a station was moved only a short distance, within the same town, it is shown in the normal font. The reader should use the information in the description to identify the exact location of each structure. The text description provides details when a structure has been moved.

In three cases structures have been moved across state boundaries. The first case is the West Wrentham (MA) Freight House, which was moved to nearby Arnold Mills, RI, and appears on the Massachusetts and Rhode Island maps accordingly. East Lynn, MA, Station and Tapleyville, MA, Passenger Shelter, however, were moved outside southern New England, to Durham, NH, and Kennebunk, ME, respectively. Their current locations, therefore, do not appear on any of the three maps.

All current railroad lines that were operated as common carriers are shown in solid black, with those that have been abandoned represented by dashed lines. Lines that were legally abandoned, but now host light rail service, trolleys, or rapid transit are considered abandoned and also indicated with dashed lines. Out-of-service lines—lines not officially abandoned but no longer in service—are represented with light gray solid lines. The majority of the structures are shown on railroad lines, but in cases where a structure has been moved to a location never served by rail, it will appear off line.

The size of the font used in the naming of stations is merely a matter of convenience, dependent on the density of stations that appear on various portions of rail lines, and does not suggest population or relative importance.

Suggestions for Further Research

Since this book covers a large geographical area, it was not possible to perform extensive research on every structure contained herein. For readers desiring more information on particular stations, I offer the following suggestions:

Contact the research librarian at the public library in the town where the structure is located to arrange a visit to the local history room. These rooms often have limited hours or are by appointment only, but they frequently have a wealth of information about local buildings.

Contact and visit local historical societies. Contact information can often be found on the internet, but the local librarian can also help. Sometimes for a modest fee, and if you are patient, the historical society will perform the research and mail the material to you.

Become a member of one of several railroad historical and technical groups. Their periodicals, past and present, offer many articles on railroad stations. Among the largest are:

The New Haven Railroad Historical and Technical Association
The Boston & Maine Railroad Historical Society
The Central Vermont Railway Historical Society
The Railroad Station Historical Society

Visit the New Haven and Boston & Maine Railroad archives.

The railroad history collections of the Thomas J. Dodd Research Center at the University of Connecticut comprise the largest collection of New Haven RR corporate records.

The Boston & Maine Railroad Historical Society Archive at the Center for Lowell History of the University of Massachusetts Lowell maintains a collection of documents, books, photos, and railroad hardware.

Explore internet resources, including web sites for the organizations mentioned above. Among many other sites, the following are particularly useful:

Railroad Stations in New Hampshire and Massachusetts
http://www.lightlink.com/sglap3/
This web site provides past and present images of surviving stations and an extensive collection of old postcards for many non-extant stations.

Railroad Station Historical Society
http://www.rrshs.org/
This site contains listings of extant structures in most of the fifty states and has good links for further research.

Library of Congress Panoramic Map Collection
http://memory.loc.gov/ammem/pmhtml/panhome.html
These maps provide bird's eye views from the late nineteenth and early twentieth centuries. Railroads are usually prominently shown on the maps, and the general arrangement of all facilities and building styles can be seen on them.

Connecticut History On Line
http://www.cthistoryonline.org/
This web site provides an extensive searchable collection of historical station images for Connecticut.

The National Park Service's National Register of Historic Places
http://www.cr.nps.gov/nr/
This database of all structures placed on the National Register of Historic Places can be searched to find out if and when your station was placed on the register.

Contact city and town halls to view assessors' records. Many of these can be viewed on line by going to the community's web site. These records can be helpful in obtaining current information but are not usually helpful in determining build dates and other historical data.

Caution

Railroad structures and the properties on which they sit are more often than not owned by private companies or individuals. This includes active and abandoned railroad right of ways. Going onto private property even to take a picture is trespassing unless you have the owner's permission. Where the track is active, this is extremely dangerous, since a train can approach without warning from either direction. Trespassers can be arrested by railroad, state, or local police. If you are not sure who owns the property or do not have permission from the owner, it is best to view and photograph the structures from the roadside or other public property.

Railroad Abbreviations

AMTK	Amtrak
BCLR	Bay Colony RR
BSRM	Berkshire Scenic Railway Museum
CCCR	Cape Cod Central RR
CNZR	Central New England RR
CSO	Connecticut Southern RR
CSXT	CSX Transportation
GRS	Guilford Rail System
GU	Grafton & Upton RR
HRR	Housatonic RR
MBTA	Massachusetts Bay Transportation Authority
MCER	Massachusetts Central RR
MNR	Metro-North RR
NAUG	Naugatuck RR
NECR	New England Central RR
OCN	Old Colony & Newport RR
PVR	Pioneer Valley RR
PW	Providence & Worcester RR
SLE	Shore Line East
VRR	Valley RR

Connecticut

R. D. Karr 2007

N

Salisbury (2)* Canaan East Canaan
Norfolk
Lake-ville Falls Village Granby
Lime Rock
Winsted New Hartford [NH&N]
W. Cornwall High St. Jct. [Collinsville] Sims-bury [NH&N] (2) Blo
Cornwall Bridge Avon
Torrington Collinsville [NH&N]
Litchfield Unionville (2) Hartford
Kent Newington [HP&F] Newin [H&NI
Plainville
Gaylordsville (2) Forestville
Thomaston Terry-ville (2) Berlin East I
Washington Milldale
New Milford Roxbury
Waterbury (3) Meriden
Brookfield Naugatuck Mid
Wallingford (2)
Danbury (3) Newtown East Wallingf
Mill Plain Seymour (2) Mount Carmel (2) North Haven (2)
Bethel (2) Quinnipiak
Redding Stepney Derby-Shelton New Haven
Ridgefield Shelton
Branchville State St. [New Haven] Stony Creek
Cannondale Milford (2)
Wilton (2) Bridgeport Stratford (2)
New Canaan Fairfield (2)
Stamford Southport (3)
Rowayton Greens Farms
Darien Westport (2)
Old Greenwich E. Norwalk
Riverside S. Norwalk (2)
Cos Cob Noroton Hts. (2)
Greenwich (2)

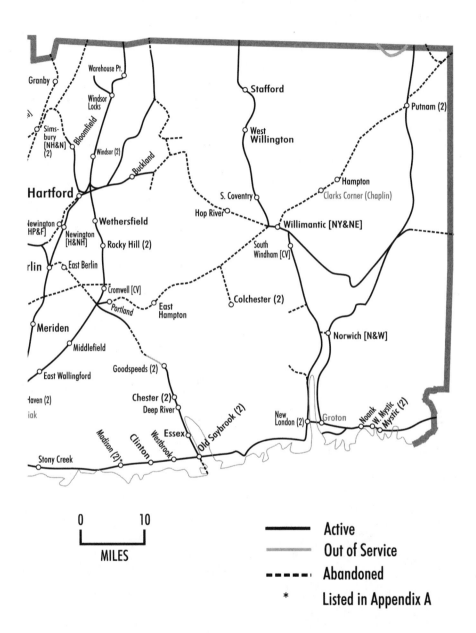

Granby

Warehouse Pt.

Windsor
Locks

Sims-
bury
[NH&N]
(2)

Bloomfield

Windsor (2)

Buckland

Hartford

Newington
[HP&F]

Newington
[H&NH]

Rocky Hill (2)

rlin

East Berlin

Cromwell [CV]

Portland

East
Hampton

Meriden

Middlefield

East Wallingford

Goodspeeds (2)

Haven (2)

iak

Chester (2)

Deep River

Madison (2)*

Clinton

Westbrook

Essex

Old Saybrook (2)

Stony Creek

Wethersfield

Stafford

West
Willington

Putnam (2)

Hampton

Clarks Corner (Chaplin)

S. Coventry

Hop River

Willimantic [NY&NE]

South
Windham [CV]

Colchester (2)

Norwich [N&W]

New
London (2)

Groton

Noank

W. Mystic (2)

Mystic (2)

0   10

MILES

——— Active

——— Out of Service

- - - - - Abandoned

*   Listed in Appendix A

CONNECTICUT 🐛 31

Connecticut

Avon Combination Depot   *136 Simsbury Rd. Bldg. 15 (Rte. 10/202)*

Built: Ca. 1848-50   **Current RR:** N/A   **Material:** Wood
RLSNE: 7-37   **Current Use:** Commercial

AMANDA ROY

Avon's depot was built by the New York & New Haven RR when it leased the line to gain the upper hand in its dealings with the New Haven & Hartford RR. It is similar to other surviving Canal Line stations like Simsbury and Granby. It has been moved about a half mile north of its original location (just north of Route 44) to 15 Riverdale Farms Shopping Center. It is now home to the Hair Loft styling salon.

Berlin Station   *51 Depot Rd.*

Built: 1900   **Current RR:** AMTK, CSO, GRS   **Material:** Brick
RLSNE: 8-26, 8A-0   **Current Use:** Railroad

AMANDA ROY

When rail service to Berlin began in 1839, the ticket office was in a general store located about a half mile south of the current station, with a freight house nearby. Around 1848 the Hartford & New Haven RR erected a wooden station on Depot Road, which the New York, New Ha-

Waterbury Station's unique clock tower soars 240 feet above the city's center. A replica of the Torre del Mangia *of Sienna, Italy's,* Palazzo Publico *(City Hall), it is the centerpiece of McKim, Mead and White's elegant station design. (Ron Karr)*

ven & Hartford RR replaced with three different stations between 1892 and 1900. These stations were all of standard design, similar to ones surviving at South Norwalk and Torrington. The first, a yellow brick structure built in 1892-93, was destroyed by fire and replaced by a red brick building in 1896. Just four years later, the new station was struck by lightning and heavily damaged. It was gutted, but some of the brick structure was used to build the current station, which was completed in December 1900. The interior layout, which survives to this day, includes an express office at the south end, a baggage room at the north end, a large waiting room, and a combined ticket and telegraph office. The station is decorated with butterfly-patterned stained glass windows.

Berlin was a busy junction, at one time boasting two full wyes and an at-grade crossing. Between 1898 and 1920 even trolleys stopped here on their runs between New Britain and Middletown, using the railroad's tracks. Until it burned in the mid 1970s, Berlin's second freight house was located across the tracks from the station, along the south leg of the New Britain wye. Today the New Britain Branch and a short piece of the Middletown Branch still diverge from the main line, but the wyes and at-grade crossing are long gone. The station itself is open and staffed by Amtrak on weekdays.

Bethel Combination Depot   5 Depot Pl.

Built: Ca. 1898   **Current RR:** MNR, PW   **Material:** Wood
RLSNE: 2-21, 2C-0   **Current Use:** Commercial

This former New York, New Haven & Hartford RR station, located between South Street and Greenwood Avenue, was the second depot to serve Bethel residents. It replaced the original 1852 depot, which was destroyed by fire in 1898. It is no longer used by passengers, Metro-North RR having built a new station with increased parking north of here (see Bethel Modern Station). Just north of the station was the junction point for the short branch to Hawleyville. A turntable was once located here between the branch and the main line. The depot has been placed on the National Register of Historic Places and is currently undergoing restoration. It is currently occupied by Bethel Arts Junction, a cooperative gallery.

Bethel Modern Station   *13 Durant Ave.*

Built: 1995-96   **Current RR:** MNR, PW   **Material:** Brick & Granite
RLSNE: 2-21, 2C-0   **Current Use:** Railroad/Commercial

This modern brick station was opened for service in January 1996 to replace the former New Haven RR station located a half mile south of here (see Bethel Combination Depot). This new station was built mainly to provide increased parking capacity over the original. It has a twin station in Danbury. A portion of the station is home to a coffee shop.

Bloomfield Freight House   *Jerome Ave. near Wintonbury Ave.*

Built: Ca. 1871   **Current RR:** CNZR   **Material:** Wood
RLSNE: 17-6   **Current Use:** Vacant

The Bloomfield Freight House was likely built in 1871 when the line was completed. The depot, formerly located across the tracks from the freight house, was removed in 1940. It was a typical Connecticut Western structure with a clipped gable roof similar to the original ones built at Canton, New Hartford, and Norfolk, none of which survive. Today the freight house, which was used for storage by the Bloomfield Farmers Exchange, is vacant.

Branchville Depot
Depot Rd.

Built: 1905   **Current RR:** MNR, PW   **Material:** Wood
RLSNE: 2-13, 2B-0   **Current Use:** Commercial/Railroad

JOHN ROY

The first station here was called Ridgefield, since this was the closest point on the Danbury & Norwalk RR to Ridgefield's village center. In 1870 the railroad built a new four-mile branch to directly serve the citizens of Ridgefield. The new station at the village center (see Ridgefield Depot) was more appropriately named Ridgefield and this one was renamed Branchville by the D&N. The Branchville Depot that survives today was built by the New Haven RR in 1905. It once had tracks on both sides to allow Ridgefield Branch passengers easy access to and from main-line trains. The historic interior of the station was restored in 1982 when the current tenant, the Whistlestop Bakery and Cafe, opened. A high-level platform was constructed south of the station in 1992 to improve passenger boarding and unloading and to reduce station dwell times.

Bridgeport Modern Station
525 Water St.

Built: 1974-75   **Current RR:** AMTK, CSXT, MNR, PW, SLE   **Material:** Concrete
RLSNE: 1-56, 3-0   **Current Use:** Railroad/Commercial

The Housatonic RR was the first railroad to serve Bridgeport in 1842, followed by the New York & New Haven RR in 1849. In 1864 a two-story brick union station was built to serve both companies. This was closed in January 1904. Passengers used a temporary station until 1905, when a new permanent station was completed as part of the grade separation project. The new station was a triangular-shaped granite and brick structure complete with a large tower and four copper gargoyles. Designed by Warren H. Briggs of Bridgeport, this

Romanesque-style station was closed in June 1973. Construction on the current station began the following year and was completed in 1975. Passengers were likely provided minimal alternative accommodations while the contractor, Kepetan, Inc., erected this modern station designed by Antinozzi Associates. On March 20, 1979, the vacant 1905 station was destroyed in a suspicious fire.

Brookfield Combination Depot   *273 Whisconier Rd. (Rte. 25)*

Built: Ca. 1913-14   **Current RR:** HRR   **Material:** Wood
RLSNE: 3-29   **Current Use:** Community

This combination depot and a similar one at Still River, four miles north of here, were built as part of a 1913-14 double tracking and grade crossing elimination project between Berkshire Junction and New Milford. It was erected east of the original station, which was used for freight until it burned. The depot is now home to the Brookfield Craft Center, a non-profit center for crafts education.

Buckland Combination Depot   *41 Depot St.*

Built: Between 1849 & 1875   **Current RR:** CSO   **Material:** Wood
RLSNE: 10-82   **Current Use:** Commercial

Close to Hartford and with convenient highway access, Buckland is best known now for its many shopping malls. Despite an explosion of commercial development all around it in the 1980s and 90s, this former New England RR combination depot still stands alongside an active railroad. It has been modified and given an addition, which encloses the former trackside freight platform. Today the depot is used for commercial office space.

Canaan Station   *7 Main St. (Rte. 7/Rte. 44)*

Built: 1871-72   **Current RR:** HRR   **Material:** Wood
RLSNE: 3-73, 17-55   **Current Use:** Vacant

JOHN ROY

The original Housatonic RR station, completed just in time for the first train, was located on the ground floor of a hotel, a hundred yards north of the present station. The hotel survived until the late 1980s, when it was torn down. With the coming of a second railroad, the Connecticut Western, the original Housatonic station was replaced. Designed by a railroad civil engineer, this Italianate station went under construction in 1871 and was finished the following year. The board-and-batten structure featured two 90-foot-long wings joined in the middle by a three-story tower overlooking the ninety-degree railroad crossing. Each railroad had its own offices in the wing adjacent to its track. Union Station served passengers until April 30, 1971, but continued to be used by successor railroads as a freight office after that. It was added to the National Register of Historic Places the same year passenger service ended.

On October 15, 2001, about 1:30 AM, the historic station was severely damaged by an arson fire. The local fire department, acting on a plan developed ten years earlier, was able to save the north ell of the two-story structure, but the east ell and three-story center tower were lost. Prior to the fire, Union Station was considered by many to be the country's oldest continuously operated railroad station.

Shortly after the fire the remains of the east ell were removed, and the north ell was protected from the elements. The Connecticut Railroad Historical Association has purchased the station, and in summer 2006 restoration began with reconstruction of the east ell. The association plans to use the station for retail space and a museum.

Prior to the devastating fire that laid waste to nearly half of the building in 2001, Canaan Station was a longtime favorite among photographers and rail enthusiasts. In 2006 the Connecticut Railroad Historical Association began the task of restoring the lost portion of the historic structure.

Cannondale Combination Depot   22 Cannon Rd.

Built: Between 1851 & 1900   **Current RR:** MNR, PW   **Material:** Wood
RLSNE: 2-9   **Current Use:** Commercial/Railroad

The Cannondale Combination Depot, with all of its decorative braces, still looks the same as when it was built. Today's passengers board trains using high-level platforms located just north of the depot. The station is home to Café Au Lait, a coffee shop that caters to the morning commuters.

Chester Depot   *22 Bridge St. (Rte. 82), Haddam*

Built: 1871   **Current RR:** VRR   **Material:** Wood
RLSNE: 13-35.5   **Current Use:** Railroad

AMANDA ROY

This small depot was quickly put together when the Connecticut Valley RR was originally opened in 1871. By 1893 it was replaced by a larger wood depot (see Chester Combination Depot). At this time, the original depot was moved to nearby Dock Road, where it became an addition to a house. In the early 1990s the house had become abandoned and derelict, and the local fire department had scheduled a controlled burn to dispose of the structure. Alert members of today's Valley RR saved the depot from destruction and stored it on a flat car in a siding at Chester. In December 2000 the station was moved to Goodspeeds, across the tracks from the freight house (see Goodspeeds Freight House). The restored station was dedicated on July 28, 2001, and now serves as the Valley RR's Goodspeeds yard office.

Chester Combination Depot   *26 Grote Rd.*

Built: 1893   **Current RR:** VRR   **Material:** Wood (Brick Façade)
RLSNE: 13-35.5   **Current Use:** Private

This was the second station to serve Chester; it replaced a small original station in 1893 (see Chester Depot). Passenger service between Old Saybrook and Middletown ended between 1930 and 1931. The unused station was purchased by the Zandari family and moved across the street. The depot was originally a wooden Carpenter Gothic structure. The new owners added brick facing and a stone fireplace.

Clarks Corner (Chaplin) Depot

55 Bridge St., Willimantic

Built: 1872   **Current RR:** N/A   **Material:** Wood
RLSNE: 16-42   **Current Use:** Museum

AMANDA ROY

This tiny depot, built in 1872 and originally called Chaplin, served the Clarks Corner area on the Chaplin-Hampton town line. Replaced by a combination depot in 1901, it was sold to Elmer Jewett, the station master, who moved it for personal use. Outlasting its successor, the structure was moved to the Connecticut Eastern Railroad Museum in 1991, where it has been fully restored.

Clinton Depot

51 West Main St. (Rte. 1)

Built: Ca. 1852   **Current RR:** AMTK, PW, SLE   **Material:** Wood
RLSNE: 12-23   **Current Use:** Vacant

The depot at Clinton was built ca. 1852 to a standard New Haven & New London RR design. It is similar to others built for Stony Creek, Guilford, and Westbrook, of which only Guilford is no longer extant. Around the turn of the last century, the tracks in Clinton were realigned to reduce their curvature; at that time the New Haven RR built a new station just east of here, off Central Avenue. The new station was a typical saltbox-style station similar to one surviving in nearby Madison. The former depot continued to serve the railroad until the 1950s as a freight house. Since then it has served various businesses. Two orthodontists purchased the building and renovated it to its current appearance in 1980. From May 2002 until recently, it was occupied by Malone's Coffee House, but it is now vacant. A commuter platform, erected in 1990 for the then new Shore Line East service, is located east of here, off John Street.

Colchester Depot   *199 Lebanon Ave.*

Built: Ca. 1876-77   **Current RR:** None   **Material:** Wood
RLSNE: 11A-4   **Current Use:** Commercial

In 1876 the Colchester RR was chartered to build a 3.6-mile branch from Turnerville (Amston) on the Air Line RR to Colchester. This was the only depot built on the branch. The depot retains its original gingerbread trim even though a large addition was made to the north end. The addition was decorated with the relocated gingerbread. The depot is now home to the International Package Store.

Colchester Freight House   *187 Lebanon Ave.*

Built: Ca. 1915   **Current RR:** None   **Material:** Wood
RLSNE: 11A-4   **Current Use:** Commercial

After being vacant for many years, as of July 2002 the former Colchester RR freight house received a new lease on life as the Carpet Depot. The interior and exterior are all original, including post-and-beam construction. There is a small office in the south end and a large freight room in the north end. The new owner carefully modified the interior without altering the historic features of the building.

Collinsville [NH&N] Freight House   *3 Depot St.*

Built: Between 1848 & 1875   **Current RR:** None   **Material:** Wood
RLSNE: 7B-8   **Current Use:** Commercial

This freight house was located on the New Haven & Northampton RR's New Hartford Branch. The Collinsville section of Canton was named after the Collins Company, a manufacturer of bladed tools including axes, knives, and plows. The Canton Historical Museum, located nearby at 11 Front Street, has an extensive collection of local history, including an operating HO train layout depicting the town and its railroads. Collinsville was once served by two railroads, the NH&N and the Central New England. The NH&N's station was located just south of the freight house, while the CNE station was located north of here along the banks of the Farmington River. Today the old freight house, which has been enlarged on its north end, is home to the Station House Coffee Bar. The Farmington River Trail, a paved rail-trail, passes within a few feet of it.

Cornwall Bridge Combination Depot   *River Rd. South*

Built: 1886   **Current RR:** HRR   **Material:** Wood
RLSNE: 3-57   **Current Use:** Commercial

Erected by the Housatonic RR in 1886, this is the second station to serve Cornwall Bridge. The original depot once stood a short distance north of the present depot's location, which is near the intersection of Popple Swamp Brook Road. Although dormers have been added and much of the gingerbread trim is gone, this depot retains its original Victorian charm. A similar station once existed at Brookfield Junction. The station, which is located almost underneath a beautiful 700-foot-long concrete arch bridge, has been listed on the National Register of Historic Places since 1972.

Cos Cob Station, Westbound   55 Station Dr.

Built: Ca. 1894   **Current RR:** AMTK, CSXT, MNR, PW   **Material:** Wood
RLSNE: 1-29.5   **Current Use:** Commercial/Railroad

JOHN ROY

The Cos Cob Station, like so many other stations built by the New Haven RR during this time period, was done in the New England saltbox style. It was built when the railroad increased the number of main-line tracks from two to four in the 1890s. The eastbound station, a much smaller wooden structure, once stood opposite this one, and the freight house was west of here, where the highway overpass is now. Today the depot is home to a coffee shop/newsstand. The Metro-North ticket office has been closed, and tickets must be purchased from vending machines on the platform. The depot has been listed on the National Register of Historic Places since 1989.

Cromwell [CV] Freight House   309 Main St. (Rte. 99)

Built: Between 1871 & 1900   **Current RR:** PW   **Material:** Wood
RLSNE: 13-15   **Current Use:** Commercial

The Cromwell Freight House, which may have been built by the Connecticut Valley RR, is similar to structures built at Deep River, Essex, Goodspeeds, Rocky Hill, South Wethersfield, and Wethersfield. With the exception of the latter, all survive today. When originally built, the freight house and depot were located on the main line, but the freight house was moved to its current position on the freight spur in the 1950s. The depot, no longer extant, was located between the freight house and the grade crossing. Located in the grassy area near the parking lot is the only known surviving New Haven RR outhouse. Today the old freight house is the home of the Kit 'n' Caboose Gift Shoppe and Johnson Real Estate.

Danbury Depot   *120 White St.*

Built: Ca. 1881   **Current RR:** HRR, MNR, PW   **Material:** Wood
RLSNE: 2-24, 3B-4, 10C-30   **Current Use:** Commercial

This was the original depot built by the New York & New England RR when the line was opened. It was located across the tracks from the New Haven RR's 1903 station, which replaced it. The depot was moved nearby to Leahy's Fuels, where it is used for storage. The property is fenced off, but the depot can be seen either from the road or from the platform of the 1903 Danbury station.

Danbury Station   *130 White St.*

Built: 1903   **Current RR:** HRR, MNR, PW   **Material:** Brick
RLSNE: 2-24, 3B-4, 10C-30   **Current Use:** Museum

The New York, New Haven & Hartford RR opened this station on July 13, 1903, consolidating two separate wooden stations inherited from its predecessors, the New York & New England and the Danbury & Norwalk. The original D&N station, located on Main Street, was demolished ca. 1915 to make room for the Danbury Post Office. The former NY&NE depot was located on White Street, opposite this station, but has been moved nearby (see Danbury Depot).

The triangle-shaped brick station, which is situated between the tracks of the Maybrook Line and the Danbury Branch, was listed on the National Register of Historic Places in 1986. It underwent a $1.5-million restoration in the mid 1990s that included the rebuilding of the platform canopies, which had been removed in the early 1950s. Owned by the city, the beautifully restored building is now home to the Danbury Railroad Museum. Founded in 1994, the museum is open to the public, and visitors can enjoy exhibits inside the station, explore vintage rolling stock, and see a real working turntable. Metro-North patrons have been using the new station just south of here since 1996.

Danbury Modern Station   *1 Patriot Dr.*

Built: 1996   **Current RR:** MNR, PW   **Material:** Brick & Granite
RLSNE: 2-24, 3B-4, 10C-30   **Current Use:** Railroad/Commercial

Danbury's newest station was opened for service in 1996, the same time as the new Bethel Station (see Bethel Modern Station). It includes an 1,800 square-foot station building that cost $2.5 million, with a high-level boarding platform for easy access to and from trains.

Darien Station, Westbound   *33 West Ave.*

Built: Between 1870 & 1885   **Current RR:** AMTK, CSXT, MNR, PW, SLE
Material: Wood   **RLSNE:** 1-38   **Current Use:** Railroad/Commercial

Long before the railroad was electrified, Darien was served by two saltbox-style stations: this one, located on the westbound side, and a larger similar one on the eastbound side. The eastbound station succumbed to fire in April 1885, but was quickly replaced by a standard brick station similar to those surviving in Fairfield, Southport, and Milford. The brick station was also a victim of fire in the early 1930s. Its replacement, a tiny hip-roofed brick structure, was razed as part of the station renovation project in 2002, which added new steel canopies to both the eastbound and westbound high-level platforms. Having outlasted it eastbound counterparts, the westbound salt-box station, which was also renovated in 2002, continues to serve Metro-North RR patrons and is also home to Darien Taxi.

Deep River Freight House   *152 River St.*

Built: Between 1871 & 1900   **Current RR:** VRR   **Material:** Wood
RLSNE: 13-36   **Current Use:** Commercial

Built to a standard Connecticut Valley design, this freight house was similar to other surviving structures on this line in Essex, Cromwell, Rocky Hill, and Goodspeeds, and one that no longer exists in South Wethersfield. A frame depot of standard Valley RR design was located between the freight house and the Dock Road crossing. Today's Valley RR passengers alight from the train here to take a Connecticut River cruise before returning to Essex on the train. The old freight house now provides office space for the Deep River Navigation Company, the operator of the river cruises. In 1994 the building was added to the National Register of Historic Places.

Overhanging gable roofs supported by brackets were typical of the Connecticut Valley RR's standard wooden freight houses. Similar structures can be found on this line in Rocky Hill and Wethersfield, while large ones of the same design survive in Essex and Goodspeeds. A former Air Line RR freight house in Colchester is very similar to this facility. (Amanda Roy)

Derby-Shelton Station   *1 Main St. (Rte. 34), Derby*

Built: 1903   **Current RR:** GRS, MNR   **Material:** Brick
RLSNE: 6-11   **Current Use:** Railroad/Commercial/Government

The New Haven & Derby RR called this location Birmingham in 1871 because the Naugatuck RR had already named their station, located across the river, Derby. The NH&D and the Naugatuck both came under the control of the New York, New Haven & Hartford RR in 1892. The NYNH&H consolidated the two parallel lines between Derby Junction and Ansonia by routing all Waterbury trains via the NH&D and downgrading the Naugatuck line to an industrial spur. At that time, the NH&D's Birmingham Station was renamed Derby, and the Naugatuck station was renamed East Derby. The NYNH&H realigned and double-tracked the rails in this area in 1903. As a part of the project, the present brick station, with its hip roof and Porte Cohere, was built, as well as a similar one in Ansonia. When passenger service to nearby Shelton was discontinued in 1925, it was renamed Derby-Shelton. Today the station is occupied by the Department of Motor Vehicles Photo License Center, Valley Council of Governments, and the Railroad Cafe.

East Berlin Depot   *406 Berlin Rd.*

Built: Between 1848 & 1900   **Current RR:** None   **Material:** Wood
RLSNE: 8B-4   **Current Use:** Commercial

AMANDA ROY

The East Berlin Depot is similar to other New Haven RR structures in the area (see Cromwell Freight House, Wethersfield Freight House/Depot, and Rocky Hill Freight House and Depot). Although all of its windows have been boarded up, it is used for commercial purposes.

East Canaan Combination Depot   *230 East Canaan Rd. (Rte. 44)*

Built: 1873   **Current RR:** N/A   **Material:** Wood
RLSNE: 17-52   **Current Use:** Residential

The East Canaan Combination Depot was built in 1873 by the Connecticut Western RR. Similar stations once existed at Taconic and Tarrifville. This hip-roofed station once stood near the grade crossing of Route 44, on the south side. In 1938 it was moved west one half mile along Route 44 and converted to a private residence. A two-car garage and enclosed porch have been added to the structure.

East Hampton Depot   *5 Barton Hill Rd.*

Built: Ca. 1910-11   **Current RR:** None   **Material:** Wood
RLSNE: 11-31   **Current Use:** Commercial

RON KARR

This hip-roofed depot replaced an earlier structure located on the opposite side of the tracks. It was built around 1910-11 by the New York, New Haven & Hartford RR. Today the station has been restored and is home to Train Station Motors, an antique auto restoration garage. The Air Line Trail passes directly behind the historic structure.

East Norwalk Depot   *281 East Ave.*

Built: 1980s   **Current RR:** AMTK, CSXT, MNR, PW, SLE   **Material:** Wood
RLSNE: 1-42   **Current Use:** Commercial/Railroad

This attractive little station was formerly a no-frills Metro-North structure that looked more like a tool shed than a depot. It was recently made over with the addition of new windows, doors, clapboard siding, and hip roof extension with small decorative brackets. For good measure Metro-North added classic New Haven RR five-sided eave windows, which were found on all their saltbox-style stations. The cherry on top is the orange and white N-over-H station sign.

Located on the westbound side, the depot is currently occupied by Coffee Creations, a coffee shop and newsstand. Historically speaking, East Norwalk has never been a significant enough stop to warrant a larger station; the 1885 hip-roofed depot, with fancy flared eaves and small decorative dormers, was not much larger than this one.

East Wallingford Combination Depot   *989 East Center St.*

Built: 1870   **Current RR:** PW   **Material:** Wood
RLSNE: 11-11   **Current Use:** Residential

This is the original East Wallingford Combination Depot, built by the New Haven, Middletown & Willimantic RR the same year the line opened. When passenger service to East Wallingford ended in 1930, the combination depot was sold to the owner of the adjacent farm. It was moved back 10-20 feet from the tracks and became a bunk house for migrant workers. Later it was placed on a high foundation and renovated into a residence with a two-car garage underneath.

Essex Freight House/Depot   *1 Railroad Ave.*

Built: Between 1871 & 1900   **Current RR:** VRR   **Material:** Wood
RLSNE: 13-40   **Current Use:** Railroad

The Valley RR began operations in 1971. Prior to that the once busy Essex yard lay abandoned, and the freight house had been boarded up. The current Valley RR enlarged and renovated the freight house to use as a ticket office and gift shop. Today Essex is the departure point for the Valley RR's tourist trains, and passengers can once again board a train here for an exciting ride up the Connecticut River Valley. A wooden depot of standard Valley RR design was located adjacent to the north side of the freight house. In 1994 the freight house was added to the National Register of Historic Places.

Fairfield Station, Eastbound   *333 Carter Henry Dr.*

Built: 1882   **Current RR:** AMTK, CSXT, MNR, PW, SLE   **Material:** Brick
RLSNE: 1-51   **Current Use:** Commercial/Railroad

The eastbound Fairfield Station was completed in the fall of 1882, prior to the mainline improvement project, which increased the number of tracks from two to four. Similar stations survive in Southport and Milford (eastbound station). Today this building is occupied by the Fairfield Cab Company, Station Cleaners, and the Nauti Dolphin Pizza Restaurant. It was added to the National Register of Historic Places in 1989.

Fairfield Station, Westbound
165 Unquowa Rd.

Built: Ca. 1890s   **Current RR:** AMTK, CSXT, MNR, PW, SLE   **Material:** Wood
RLSNE: 1-51   **Current Use:** Commercial/Railroad

The westbound Fairfield Station, like so many others built by the New Haven RR during this time period, was constructed in the New England saltbox style (see Southport, Milford, Cos Cob, and Old Greenwich Stations). It was built when the railroad increased the number of main-line tracks from two to four in the 1890s. Today the station is occupied by Station Cleaners. A small addition has been made trackside, on the west end, to allow customers to drop off their dry cleaning before boarding the train; pick-up is located in the eastbound station across the tracks.

Falls Village Combination Depot
44 Railroad St.

Built: Ca. 1843   **Current RR:** HRR   **Material:** Wood
RLSNE: 3-67   **Current Use:** Residential/Historical Society

This combination depot was built by the Housatonic RR ca. 1843. Named by the railroad, Falls Village was the site of the Ames Iron Works and the Housatonic shops. The interior of the station included separate men's and women's waiting rooms and a ticket office on the north end of the first floor, while the south end was used for freight. There are two apartments on the second floor, the original that served the stationmaster until the 1960s and a second, which was added above the open freight area in the early 1970s, after the railroad sold the building.

The Falls Village Canaan Historical Society now owns the building and uses the passenger service area for their offices. The Historical Society has obtained federal grant money for restoration of the building. Plans include restoration of the exterior, including the platform, and renovation of the old freight area for use as a museum. The second floor continues to serve as apartments. The district of Falls Village, including this combination depot, was placed on the National Register of Historic Places in 1979.

Forestville Depot 171 Central St.

Built: 1881 **Current RR:** GRS **Material:** Wood
RLSNE: 10-105 **Current Use:** Commercial

The New York & New England RR built the Forestville Depot in 1881 to replace the original ca. 1850 station, which was destroyed by fire. Although no longer extant, a similar Queen Anne-style depot was erected in East Hartford. Both depots sported offset, decorative, gable-roofed towers, although Forestville's tower was removed in 1930. Listed on the National Register of Historic Places since 1978, the recently (2000) rehabilitated structure is now home to Roberge Painting.

Gaylordsville Hotel/Station 1 Browns Forge Rd.

Built: Ca. 1837 **Current RR:** HRR **Material:** Wood
RLSNE: 3-42 **Current Use:** Historical Society/Community

Crafty businessman Sylvanus Merwin erected his hotel directly in the path of the Housatonic RR. He negotiated a deal with the railroad that made his hotel the meal stop for passengers between Pittsfield and Bridgeport. He stipulated that the ticket office be in his hotel, that he be the agent, and that the station be called Merwinsville. The ticket office was located in the hotel until 1905, when the New York, New Haven & Hartford RR converted the freight house into a combination station. The hotel then became a private residence and later a warehouse. Fortunately, a 1960s fire was quickly contained. In 1977 the Georgian-style hotel became a registered historical landmark. In the 1970s the owner donated it to Merwinsville Hotel Restoration, which was founded by a handful of town residents to restore the building to its former grandeur. The renovation is ongoing, but a wine cellar and period parlor have been completed, as well as a station waiting room on the north end of the first floor, which is furnished with period railroad memorabilia. The restored rooms occasionally serve as a venue for public events.

Gaylordsville Freight House/Depot   *22 Lime Rock Station Rd., Lime Rock*

Built: Mid to late 1800s   **Current RR:** HRR   **Material:** Wood
RLSNE: 3-42   **Current Use:** Residential

This structure was originally the freight house at Merwinsville (renamed Gaylordsville in 1918). In 1905 it was converted into a combination depot and served Merwinsville for 10 years. In 1914 the original Lime Rock station, built in 1871, was destroyed by fire. The New Haven RR then built a new larger combination depot at Merwinsville and moved the converted freight house to Lime Rock. The New Haven eventually sold the converted freight house, and it was moved across the street. Now a private residence, it has received several additions. (See also Gaylordsville Hotel/Station and Gaylordsville Combination Depot.)

Gaylordsville Combination Depot   *520 River Rd.*

Built: 1915   **Current RR:** HRR   **Material:** Wood
RLSNE: 3-42   **Current Use:** Residential

DEBORAH BASSETTE

This was the third structure to serve as the Gaylordsville station (called Merwinsville until 1918). In 1905 the New Haven RR moved the ticket office from the Merwinsville Hotel to the converted freight house. Ten years later the New Haven built this combination depot to replace the barely adequate former freight house. It is smaller, but similar to the Brookfield Combination Depot built several years earlier. The unused depot was purchased by a private party in 1968 and three years later moved on railroad flat cars a thousand feet south and across the tracks. Today it is serves as a residence. (See also Gaylordsville Hotel/Station, Gaylordsville Freight House/Depot, and Brookfield Combination Depot.)

Goodspeeds Freight House   *22 Bridge Rd. (Rte. 82), Haddam*

Built: Late 1800s   **Current RR:** VRR   **Material:** Wood
RLSNE: 13-32   **Current Use:** Commercial

This former New York, New Haven & Hartford RR freight house, which has received major additions on its north end, is home to Goodspeed's Station, a gift and antique shop. Goodspeeds is the northernmost end of the Valley RR's tourist line. The restored Chester Depot is located directly across the tracks from the freight house, on the site that was once occupied by the Goodspeeds Station. That station was a standard saltbox-style depot common throughout the NYNH&H system.

Granby Combination Depot   *121 Hartford Ave. (Rte. 189)*

Built: Ca. 1853   **Current RR:** None   **Material:** Wood
RLSNE: 7-47   **Current Use:** Commercial

Built ca. 1853 by the New York & New Haven RR, Granby's wooden combination depot closely resembles those surviving at Avon and Simsbury [NH&N] (combination depot). This restored station has been home to a day care center, but is currently occupied by BPD, a roof consulting firm.

Greens Farms Depot   *2 Post Office Ln.*

Built: Between 1849 & 1888   **Current RR:** AMTK, CSXT, MNR, PW, SLE
Material: Wood   **RLSNE:** 1-47   **Current Use:** Railroad

A style enigma along this busy corridor, the Greens Farms Depot looks more like its cousins on the Housatonic RR (see Cornwall Bridge and Housatonic Depots) than like the standard styles used by the New Haven RR when they increased the main line to four tracks. Today this Metro-North RR station retains its Victorian braces and arched eave windows. The part-time ticket office was permanently closed on January 29, 2003. The station is now equipped with multilingual ticket machines. A standard New Haven pagoda-roofed tower is located east of the station.

Greenwich Modern Station
20 Railroad Ave.

Built: 1969-70   **Current RR:** AMTK, CSXT, MNR, PW   **Material:** Stucco & Terra Cotta   **RLSNE:** 1-28   **Current Use:** Commercial/Railroad

Greenwich has had many stations over the years. The original depot was a board-and-batten structure with a cross-gabled roof, similar to the ones surviving at New Canaan and Wilton (original). A second, larger wooden depot, composed of two buildings with simple gable roofs, was constructed between 1870 and 1880. By 1904 Greenwich was served by separate east- and westbound stations. The westbound station was a large saltbox-style structure, and the eastbound was a hip-roofed structure. Today's Greenwich Station, built by the Penn Central RR in 1969-70, is a mini-mall comprising numerous commercial occupants and a Metro-North RR ticket office. The old stations were torn down.

Greenwich Station, Eastbound
Horseneck Ln.

Built: Between 1967-70   **Current RR:** AMTK, CSXT, MNR, PW   **Material:** Stucco & Terra Cotta   **RLSNE:** 1-28   **Current Use:** Commercial/Railroad

The eastbound side of the Greenwich Station, a small enclosure to provide protection from the elements, was built at the same time as the main station. The two buildings are connected via a pedestrian overpass. The eastbound building is now occupied by the Greenwich Taxi Company, and Metro-North passengers have to wait for their trains in three-sided plexiglass shelters.

Groton Freight House
55 *Bridge St., Willimantic*

Built: Ca. 1900   **Current RR:** N/A   **Material:** Wood
RLSNE: 15-0, 19-61   **Current Use:** Museum

AMANDA ROY

The Groton Freight House was moved to the grounds of the Connecticut Eastern Railroad Museum (CERM) in February 1998. It had been located on the New Haven RR's Shore Line, just east of the Thames River bridge and across the tracks from the tower (still standing). Prior to the move Amtrak had used the building for storage, but it had not received any maintenance in years. The volunteers at CERM completely rebuilt the freight house.

Hampton Freight House
72 Kenyon Rd.

Built: Ca. 1872   **Current RR:** N/A   **Material:** Wood
RLSNE: 16-38   **Current Use:** Private

The Hampton Freight House was built ca. 1872, when the Boston, Hartford & Erie RR completed their line from Mechanicsville to Willimantic. Originally located at the Station Road grade crossing, it was moved in the late 1950s to its present location, about a half mile down New Hill Road and 100 feet left on Kenyon Road. Today the structure is adorned with a stunning stained glass window, leading one to believe it is a house of worship, but it actually serves as an artist's studio.

Hartford Station One Union Pl.

Built: 1887 (rebuilt 1914)   **Current RR:** AMTK, CNZR, CSO, GRS
Material: Brownstone   **RLSNE:** 8-37, 10-89, 13-0, 17-0
Current Use: Railroad/Commercial/Transit

The Hartford & New Haven RR built the first Hartford depot in 1839, a tiny facility located on Mulberry Street. With the coming of the Hartford, Providence & Fishkill RR, construction of a union station was begun in 1849. This large Italian Villa-style building was finished the following year, with two tracks passing through the building and several more tracks outside it. In 1871 the Connecticut Western, and the following year the Connecticut Valley RR, began operations from Union Station.

The original Union Station was replaced in 1887 as part of a grade crossing elimination project. The concept for the station was provided by a local architect, George Keller, but the noted Boston architectural firm of Sheply, Rutan and Coolidge was hired to design it. It was constructed by builder Orlando Norcross in the Romanesque style favored by H. H. Richardson, using local Portland Brownstone. The station fell victim to a catastrophic fire on February 21, 1914, leaving only the exterior brownstone walls standing. Railroad architect Fredrick W. Mellor redesigned the station that year, replacing the former gable roof in the center section with a flat roof. Mellor later designed the Pawtucket/Central Falls Station in Rhode Island as well.

Today Union Station is used for commercial and retail purposes, with the Greater Hartford Transit District occupying the majority of the space. Ticket offices for Amtrak and intercity bus services are located in a new section of the building, directly under the tracks. At one time there were as many as four tracks in service through the station, but today only one remains. The beautiful great hall includes a tile mural featuring both steam and electric locomotives of the New Haven.

High Street Jct. [Collinsville] Combination Depot   70 Dyer Ave.

Built: Early 1870s   **Current RR:** None   **Material:** Wood
RLSNE: 17-23, 17B-0   **Current Use:** Municipal

The former Central New England RR combination depot has been moved a short distance south on Dyer Avenue and modified for use as a town garage. Main-line passenger trains used to back the short distance from High Street Junction to Collinsville to provide direct service to the village center and the large Collinsville Axe Company.

Hop River Station   Hop River Rd. (Opposite #850), Columbia

Built: Ca. 1849   **Current RR:** N/A   **Material:** Wood
RLSNE: 10-63   **Current Use:** Private

AMANDA ROY

This station came complete with an upstairs apartment for the stationmaster and his family. It is the original Hop River Station, built in 1849 by the Hartford, Providence & Fishkill RR. Similar stations once served South Windham, CT, and Greene, RI (still extant). The station was moved east one-tenth of a mile in the late 1950s by George W. Johnson, Sr., the grandfather of the current owner. Nature is starting to surround the old building, but it still appears to be structurally sound. The depot was formerly located north of Hop River Road and west of the Hop River State Park Trail, a popular rail-trail established on the HP&F right of way.

Kent Combination Depot   *Rte. 7*

Built: 1872 or 1874   **Current RR:** HRR   **Material:** Wood
RLSNE: 3-48   **Current Use:** Commercial

The large restored combination depot in Kent is little changed from when it was built by the Housatonic RR in the early 1870s. The original Kent Station was located in the Kent Plains Hotel; that building, now gone, was located about 200 feet south of the current depot. Today the old depot is occupied by a doctor's office.

Lakeville Depot   *7 Ethan Allen St.*

Built: 1891   **Current RR:** None   **Material:** Wood
RLSNE: 17-65   **Current Use:** Commercial

JOHN ROY

The Lakeville Depot was built in 1891 by the Central New England & Western RR. It likely replaced the original depot, which was built ca. 1873. The freight house, a board-and-batten, gable-roofed structure, was located west of the station on the opposite side of the tracks. The station, which is owned by the town, has been leased to various commercial tenants over the years, including its current resident, WQQQ, an FM radio station. The building was placed on the National Register of Historic Places in 1996. A similar station still exists in Stanfordville, NY.

Lime Rock Depot

See Gaylordsville Freight House/Depot.

Litchfield Station   *28 A-C Russell St.*

Built: 1871   **Current RR:** None   **Material:** Wood
RLSNE: 4-32   **Current Use:** Commercial

Rail construction in Litchfield began early in 1871 with the relocation of Tannery Brook to make room for this station, an engine house, turntable, freight house, and rail yard. The Shepaug Valley RR completed construction of the line and this Victorian station in late December, with service beginning on January 2, 1872. At the time this was the only station on the line with electric lights, town water, and indoor plumbing. The freight house, engine house, turntable, and rail yard were all located south of the station, along Russell Street. At one time the tracks continued across West Street to serve the J. William Tannery. All maintenance functions were transferred from Litchfield to Hawleyville in 1888, when the Shepaug, Litchfield & Northern RR completed construction of a new four-stall roundhouse.

Between 1937 and 1948 the station was abbreviated to approximately one-third its former size. This small portion has since been turned ninety degrees and received an addition on the south end. The combined structure is now roughly the same size as it was when built. Over the years it has been home to an auto parts store, a luncheonette, and an oil company office. Today it is used for office space.

Madison Station   *107 A-D Bradley Rd.*

Built: Between 1900 & 1910   **Current RR:** AMTK, PW, SLE   **Material:** Wood
RLSNE: 12-19   **Current Use:** Commercial

Similar to other New York, New Haven & Hartford RR saltbox-style stations, Madison Station was built in the early 1900s. It replaced the original ca. 1850 wooden station, which was then converted to a freight house. The Shore Line East commuter shelter is located just east of here. Today the old station has been eclipsed by a recent addition, the depot being the section of the building nearest the tracks. The complex provides office space for several small businesses.

Prior to the 1980s the original ca. 1850 depot was moved a short distance to a temporary location east of Wall Street, with hopes of finding a use for the historical structure. One consideration was use of the building as the local senior center. Unfortunately, after many years sitting on blocks, the building was deemed unsuitable and later demolished. The Depot Meeting Center/Madison Senior Center, located nearby on Old Route 79, was eventually built to resemble the former freight house (see Appendix A, Madison Freight House).

Meriden Station   60 State St.

Built: 1970   **Current RR:** AMTK, CSO   **Material:** Brick
RLSNE: 8-19   **Current Use:** Railroad/Transit

The first train station in Meriden was located in Conklin's Hotel in 1840. Two years later it was moved across Main Street to the Rogers Building. It wasn't until 1854 that the Hartford & New Haven RR built its first station in Meriden. Ten years later it was heavily damaged in a terrific fire that devastated a whole block of buildings; the station was repaired, but Conklin's Hotel was lost. After nearby Wallingford opened its new station, Meriden residents petitioned the New York, New Haven & Hartford RR for a new station. Persistence paid off, and in September 1882 the new Meriden Station opened. It was a large Second Empire-style structure with a mansard roof, similar to the one surviving in Wallingford. The H&NH station was torn down shortly thereafter.

The city of Meriden and the railroad have had a long history of disputes, going back to the 1870s, over the condition of the station's inside comfort facilities. Unlike today, nineteenth- and early twentieth-century cities had few restrooms and many sanitary issues to contend with. In 1940 the public health officer permanently closed the problematic public sanitary facilities in the 1882 station. Negotiations between the railroad and the city resulted in a new station, built in 1942. The station cost $75,000 to build, but the city contributed $20,000 to defer the cost of the public comfort station included in the building. The single-story, Colonial-style brick station was designed by railroad engineer F. J. Pitcher. It was similar to the one surviving at Sharon, MA. Demolition of the remaining portion of the 1882 station, of which half had already been demolished to construct the new one, was completed that year to make room for parking.

The current station, a non-descript, flat-roofed brick structure, was built by the city of Meriden for the Penn Central RR in 1970 as part of a project that rerouted State Street. The 1942 station was demolished as part of this project. Today a sign on the outside of the building proclaims this as the Meriden Transit Center, serving Amtrak patrons as well as providing local bus service.

Middlefield Combination Depot   *24 West St. Building. 1*

Built: Ca. 1870   **Current RR:** PW   **Material:** Wood
RLSNE: 11-17   **Current Use:** Commercial

This building is the freight portion of the former Middlefield Combination Depot. It was built ca. 1870 by the New Haven, Middletown & Willimantic RR. The depot was an imposing two-story structure with this single-story freight section on the south side. In 1910 the freight area was enlarged to its current size, the half closest to West Street having been added. The former freight house is now home to Country Depot Antiques. A restored Erie caboose is located nearby.

Milford Station, Eastbound   *40 Railroad Ave. South*

Built: Ca. 1881   **Current RR:** AMTK, CSXT, MNR, PW, SLE   **Material:** Brick
RLSNE: 1-63   **Current Use:** Community/Railroad

The well-maintained, brick eastbound station at Milford was built to a standard New York, New Haven & Hartford RR design, similar to those surviving elsewhere (see Southport and Fairfield Eastbound Stations). This station predates its wooden westbound counterpart, having been built ca. 1881 prior to the main line's four-track upgrade. Today it is home to the Milford Center for the Arts.

The New York, New Haven & Hartford RR built several large brick stations to a standard design, which featured numerous windows and a large flat overhang on the first floor, supported by oversized brackets which extended halfway down the walls of the building. The gable-roofed second stories of these stations gave the buildings a distinctive layered appearance. Other examples of this unusual design survive in Fairfield and Southport.

Milford Station, Westbound

1 Railroad Ave. North

Built: 1896   **Current RR:** AMTK, CSXT, MNR, PW, SLE   **Material:** Wood
RLSNE: 1-63   **Current Use:** Commercial/Railroad

This standard New York, New Haven & Hartford RR saltbox-style station was built in 1896 when the main line was expanded to four tracks. A wooden freight house, extant until at least the mid 1980s, was located west of here. Today only three tracks remain, and the station has been equipped with a high-level platform where the fourth track once lay. The station is now occupied by a coffee shop.

Mill Plain Depot   *110 Mill Plain Rd.*

Built: Ca. 1885   **Current RR:** N/A   **Material:** Wood
RLSNE: 10C-35   **Current Use:** Commercial

The Mill Plain Depot was built by the Hartford, Providence & Fishkill RR ca. 1885. The depot was once located at the former Mill Plain Road grade crossing, just west of the current highway overpass. The depot has been moved about one-tenth of a mile east and is now occupied by Best Round Golf Car Repair. It has received several additions over the years; the central hip-roofed portion is the original depot.

Milldale Combination Depot   *Canal St. (opposite #450)*

Built: 1894   **Current RR:** None   **Material:** Wood
RLSNE: 7-20   **Current Use:** Commercial

This combination depot, which is currently used by the E&W Construction Company, was built by the New York, New Haven & Hartford RR in 1894. On February 4, 1928, the station was heavily damaged by fire. It was rebuilt in June of that year, although the north end of the structure, where the freight area and freight platform were located, was not rebuilt; freight functions were moved into the remaining portion. The depot is similar to other NYNH&H structures (see Rocky Hill Depot, Wethersfield Freight House/Depot, and Cromwell [CV] Freight House).

This station was renamed Holgate for a cameo appearance in the movie *It Happened to Jane*. The rails were recently removed, and this portion of the former New Haven & Northampton will be developed as a rail-trail.

Mount Carmel Station   *Sherman Ave.*

Built: 1880   **Current RR:** None   **Material:** Brick
RLSNE: 7-8   **Current Use:** Commercial

The Mount Carmel station was built by the New Haven & Northampton RR in 1880. The "Canal Line" had many Italianate brick stations; others in Connecticut included Cheshire, Plantsville, Plainville, Farmington, Unionville, Pine Meadow [NH&N], New Hartford [NH&N], and Simsbury [NH&N], of which only Simsbury and Unionville survive. Although no longer used by passengers, a second story was added to this station when it was rebuilt after a fire in the 1950s. The station originally featured a cross-gabled roof with decorative dentils and attractive arched windows. Close examination of the brickwork reveals the drastic changes made to the structure. The station is now home to E.C.L. Construction. Today's trackside passers-by are users of the extremely popular Farmington Canal Greenway Rail-trail.

Mount Carmel Freight House   *3342 Sherman Ave.*

Built: 1883   **Current RR:** None   **Material:** Brick
RLSNE: 7-8   **Current Use:** Commercial

This Italianate brick freight house is particularly ornate for its size, with arched doorways and decorative dentils. The building once had a large wooden platform, which extended along two sides. Similar structures were built at New Hartford, CT (see New Hartford [NH&N] Freight House), Williamsburg, and West Springfield, MA. Today the freight house is home to Hair by Toni.

Mystic Combination Depot   *2 Roosevelt Ave. (Rte. 1)*

Built: Ca. 1905-07   **Current RR:** AMTK, PW   **Material:** Wood & Brick
RLSNE: 19-53   **Current Use:** Community/Railroad

This attractive depot, located in the author's hometown, was built ca. 1905-07 by the New York, New Haven & Hartford RR. It replaced the original wooden depot built ca. 1858-59, which was similar to the ones surviving at West Mystic and Noank. That station and the freight house were located on the opposite side of Broadway Avenue, where the B. F. Hoxie Fire Department is now. Although damaged in the hurricane of 1938, the Mystic Depot fared better than nearby Stonington and other Shore Line stations, which were completely destroyed. Similar to the one surviving in Franklin, MA, the Mystic Depot features paneled doors with transoms, elaborate window glazing, and a large Palladian window.

Over the years the station's canopy was shortened to a fraction of its former length and a small roof dormer removed. In the late 1970s Mystic Depot, Inc., renovated the building and has been in charge of its care since. As part of their agreement, Amtrak leases it to the group for $1.00 per year. The depot has hosted several businesses in the past, but since summer 2001 it has served as the local tourist information center. Although it may appear that the station was moved from its original location, it was the tracks that were moved to a new alignment in 1981, when the old Mystic River Bridge was replaced.

This station was modeled by the A. C. Gilbert Company's American Flyer Trains for over 50 years. A granite memorial erected nearby is dedicated to Louis B. Palmer in recognition of his efforts to renovate and restore the station. It is adorned with the bell from New Haven steam locomotive #3249.

Mystic Passenger Shelter   *2 Roosevelt Ave. (Rte. 1)*

Built: Ca. 1986   **Current RR:** AMTK, PW   **Material:** Wood
RLSNE: 19-53   **Current Use:** Railroad

Located on the eastbound side of the tracks, this simple wooden structure provides limited shelter for patrons waiting for eastbound trains.

Naugatuck Station   *195 Water St.*

Built: 1908-10   **Current RR:** GRS, MNR   **Material:** Stucco & Brick
RLSNE: 5-22   **Current Use:** Historical Society/Museum

JOHN ROY

John H. Whittemore, Naugatuck's most influential citizen and a director of the New York, New Haven & Hartford RR, offered to pay for a new station if he could choose the architect. He commissioned Henry Bacon, who would later design the Lincoln Memorial in Washington, DC, to design the station. Construction of the Spanish Colonial Revival-style station began in 1908 and was completed in 1910. It replaced a short-lived structure built on the same site when the NYNH&H relocated the line along the Naugatuck River through the center of town. This was the third station to serve Naugatuck, the other having been located on the original alignment about a tenth of a mile east of the current Maple Street railroad overpass. For many years, the Naugatuck Daily News used the old station. Today it is home to the Naugatuck Historical Society Museum.

New Canaan Station   *198 Elm St.*

Built: 1868   **Current RR:** MNR   **Material:** Wood
RLSNE: 1A-8   **Current Use:** Railroad/Commercial

JOHN ROY

This beautiful Victorian station, which was built by the New Canaan RR, was opened on the Fourth of July 1868. It is similar to the original Wilton Depot. The freight house was located across the tracks. In 1999 the building and surrounding area were raised to allow high-level loading without the unsightly mini-platforms that had been used for many years. A coffee shop/newsstand and a Metro-North RR ticket office now occupy the station.

New Hartford [NH&N] Freight House   *Greenwoods Rd.*

Built: 1877   **Current RR:** None   **Material:** Brick
RLSNE: 7B-14   **Current Use:** Municipal

When originally built in 1850, the New Hartford Branch only went as far as Collinsville. Twenty years later it was extended to Pine Meadow. A new depot and freight house were built by the New Haven & Northampton RR in 1877, when the Farmington River was bridged and the railroad finally reached New Hartford. At one time there were also an engine house and turntable here, neither of which remain today. The freight house was sold in 1957 to the New Hartford Village Fire District. A large ell was added, and today it houses the town's ambulance corps.

New Haven Station   *50 Union Ave.*

Built: 1920   **Current RR:** AMTK, CSXT, MNR, PW, SLE
Material: Brick & Cast Concrete   **RLSNE:** 1-72, 6-0, 7-0, 8-0
Current Use: Railroad/Commercial

New Haven's first union station, designed by Henry Austin, was built in 1848. The large pagoda-style building, located on Chapel Street, was the first station in America with a Campanile (Italian-style bell tower with arches). This short- lived station was closed in 1871, when a second brick station with a mansard roof was opened. (See State Street Station [New Haven] for more information.) That station was severely damaged by fire on March 19, 1892. The fire, which started in the third floor offices, broke out in the evening after the workers had gone home. The new station was rebuilt, although most of the third floor was removed.

Today's Union Station was completed in 1920, replacing its 1871 predecessor, which was destroyed by a second fire on May 8, 1918. Union Station was designed by Cass Gilbert, best known for his Gothic skyscraper,

New Haven's impressive Union Station was designed by presitgious architect Cass Gilbert. Restored to its original grandeur in 1985, its tall windows give it the same kind of sleek lines that are featured in his Woolworth Building in New York, which was the world's tallest skyscraper when it was completed in 1913. Elements of Gilbert's incorporation of classic historical features into his designs are seen in the station's arched center windows and the Classical-style trim above and below the upper story.

the Woolworth Building in Manhattan, which was the world's tallest building when built in 1912. Gilbert, who began his career with the firm McKim, Mead and White, later designed the U.S. Supreme Court Building in Washington, DC, which opened in 1935.

Gilbert's Union Station, made of brick and cast stone, employs a simple symmetric design. It features five three-story-high arched windows on the central portion of the building, while the wings have narrower, rectangular three-story openings. The building also has a short attic story. The attractive station interior features a three-story-high center section with spherical light fixtures suspended from a gold and white coffered ceiling, and balconies at each end.

Union Station was restored in 1985 as part of the Northeast Corridor Improvement Project, funded by the U.S. and Connecticut Departments of Transportation and the Federal Railroad Administration. Today Amtrak, Metro-North, and Shore Line East passengers are treated to the beautifully restored great hall with its thirty-five-foot ceiling, marble floors, and old-fashioned wooden benches. Union Station was added to the National Register of Historic Places in 1975.

New London Station   27 Water St.

Built: 1886-87   **Current RR:** AMTK, NECR, PW, SLE   **Material:** Brick
RLSNE: 12-49, 14-0, 19-62   **Current Use:** Railroad

New London's first real railroad station was built in 1852 by the New London, Willimantic & Palmer RR; from 1848-52 patrons had used a previously existing structure that was converted to serve passengers. After just thirty-three years of service, the two-story Greek Revival station was destroyed by fire in 1885.

The New London Northern RR, then leased by the Central Vermont, hired the famous architect Henry Hobson Richardson to design a replacement station. Construction of New London's Union Station began in 1886 and finished the following year. Union Station was located on a sharp curve along New London's waterfront; to account for this, it was designed with a long curved canopy that had a unique eyebrow-styled raised portion over the grade crossing to allow access to the pier. The

Entryway arch and brick relief lettering on New London station. The sleek lines and solid brick façade of this station are a striking departure from H. H. Richardson's earlier granite and brownstone Romanesque-style stations in Massachusetts.

large brick building was a departure from the typical Romanesque-style stations Richardson had designed previously. With its Colonial influence, it was considered by many to be one of his finest designs and a forerunner of twentieth-century design. Unfortunately it was also his last; Richardson died in 1887 before Union Station was completed.

It is often overlooked that the CV, whose predecessor first brought the rails to New London, actually built and owned this station. The New Haven RR always had far more service to New London than the CV, and both railroads had offices on the second floor until 1937, when the CV moved its division headquarters to a new building at nearby State Pier. By 1949 the CV had discontinued passenger service to New London altogether.

After nearly becoming a victim of urban renewal, the station was completely renovated 1976-77 under the direction of Anderson, Notter, Finegold, Inc., of Boston. As of 2003 the station is again undergoing a multi-phase historic renovation. In continuous service since 1887, the station today serves both Amtrak and Shore Line East passengers. Looking carefully, one can still see the words "Union Railroad Station" on the street side of the building. Union Station was placed on the National Register of Historic Places in 1971.

New London Baggage/Express Office 45 Water St.

Built: 1886-87 **Current RR:** AMTK, NECR, PW, SLE **Material:** Brick
RLSNE: 12-49, 14-0, 19-62 **Current Use:** Transit

RON GALLANT

Built at the same time as Union Station, the former baggage and express office now serves as the local bus station; both Greyhound and Peter Pan provide bus service from here. In later days the New Haven RR moved the baggage services to the east end of the station.

New Milford Depot 11 Railroad St.

Built: 1886 **Current RR:** HRR **Material:** Wood
RLSNE: 3-36 **Current Use:** Municipal/Community

This station replaced the original ca. 1840 structure. When built by the Housatonic RR in 1886, it cost $15,000. A wooden gable-roofed freight house stood north of here in the small yard area. The station is now occupied by the Greater New Milford Chamber of Commerce and a New Milford Police Department sub-station. The depot was placed on the National Register of Historic Places in 1984.

Newington [HP&F] Depot   *162 Willard Ave.*

Built: Between 1850 & 1870   **Current RR:** AMTK, CSO, GRS
Material: Wood & Brick   **RLSNE:** 10-95   **Current Use:** Commercial

RON KARR

Until the late 1890s, when the New York, New Haven & Hartford RR took control, there were two different railroads serving Newington; the Hartford & New Haven RR began service in 1839, and it was joined by the Hartford, Providence & Fishkill in 1850. At one time there were four main tracks between this depot and the H&NH freight house (see Newington [H&NH] Freight House). The tiny Newington Depot had only a waiting room and a ticket office. The two tracks nearest the depot were those of the former HP&F. Today the station has been enlarged slightly and appears to be used for commercial purposes. It was added to the National Register of Historic Places in 1986.

Newington [H&NH] Freight House   *200 South Francis Ave.*

Built: Between 1850 & 1874   **Current RR:** AMTK, CSO, GRS   **Material:** Wood
RLSNE: 8-32   **Current Use:** Commercial

RON KARR

The Hartford & New Haven RR built this former freight house, which was listed on the National Register of Historic Places in 1986. Into the 1990s Cashway Lumber used the building for storage, but it is currently occupied by the Newington Nursery. In addition to the former Hartford, Providence & Fishkill RR depot surviving across the tracks, there was a wooden H&NH depot located just west of this freight house.

Newtown Depot   57 Church Hill Rd. (Rte. 6)

Built: 1890   **Current RR:** HRR, PW   **Material:** Wood
RLSNE: 3-19   **Current Use:** Commercial

This former Housatonic RR depot is the third station to serve Newtown. It was constructed in 1890 to replace the previous station, built in 1880, which had burned to the ground. The two stations were built to the same plans, with only minor differences. Although its passenger canopy is gone, the depot still maintains much of its original charm; the decorative braces and much of its gingerbread trim (replaced in the 1950s) still survive. The station has served various commercial interests over the years and is currently the home of Cave Comics and Burgerittoville.

Noank Depot   102A Front St.

Built: Ca. 1858-59   **Current RR:** AMTK, PW   **Material:** Wood
RLSNE: 19-55   **Current Use:** Commercial

The Noank Depot was built to a standard design used by the New Haven, New London & Stonington RR on its stations between Stonington and Groton. The depot, which was retired in June 1939, has been moved a short distance from its original location, raised on a foundation, and given a walk-around deck and a garage underneath. It is currently occupied by a real estate agency. Other similar stations survive, including the twin station located less than one mile east of here in West Mystic. This building still bears the distinctive, compass-like decorative element present on many of the New York, Providence & Boston RR stations. A small wooden gable-roofed freight house was formerly located east of the depot.

Norfolk Station   *10 Station Pl.*

Built: 1898   **Current RR:** None   **Material:** Stone
RLSNE: 17-46   **Current Use:** Commercial

This attractive stone station was built in 1898 by the Central New England RR with generous contributions from local residents. It replaced a smaller wooden structure of standard design. Today the building is used for commercial purposes.

Noroton Heights Station, Westbound   *Heights Rd.*

Built: 1890s   **Current RR:** AMTK, CSXT, MNR, PW, SLE   **Material:** Wood
RLSNE: 1-37   **Current Use:** Community

Noroton Heights is another typical New Haven RR saltbox-style station. Buildings of this type could be found throughout the system, but were very prevalent on the main line between New York and New Haven. The eastbound station, formerly located across the track, was little more than a partially enclosed canopy. Saved from demolition by parents and high school students in 1989, the neatly kept station currently houses the Depot, a substance-free center for Darien teenagers. Metro-North patrons use the nearby modern station with high-level commuter platforms to board their trains.

Noroton Heights Modern Station   *325 Heights Rd.*

Built: Early 1970s   **Current RR:** AMTK, CSXT, MNR, PW, SLE
Material: Concrete & Glass   **RLSNE:** 1-37   **Current Use:** Railroad/Commercial

This small modern Metro-North station, located on the westbound side of the tracks, was built by the Penn Central RR in the early 1970s. It includes a weekday-mornings-only ticket office and a coffee shop. The 1890s westbound station is located at the far east end of the parking lot.

North Haven Station   *81A Old Broadway*

Built: 1860   **Current RR:** AMTK, CSO   **Material:** Brick
RLSNE: 8-7   **Current Use:** Commercial

The original North Haven Depot was located in the front room of a private dwelling that was built in 1840. That dwelling, formerly located on the east side of the tracks at Broadway, was demolished long ago. The Hartford & New Haven RR built this Italianate station, the second and final depot to serve North Haven, in 1860. It once sported four brick chimneys and a canopy that projected from the sides of the building beneath its circular windows. Old Broadway Mason Supply currently occupies the building.

North Haven Freight House   *81B Old Broadway*

Built: Between 1872 & 1899   **Current RR:** AMTK, CSO   **Material:** Wood
RLSNE: 8-7   **Current Use:** Commercial

The North Haven Freight House was built by the New York, New Haven & Hartford RR. It is similar to the combination depot extant at East Wallingford. Today it serves commercial interests.

Norwich [N&W] Station   *10 Railroad Ave.*

Built: 1899-1900   **Current RR:** PW   **Material:** Brick & Wood
RLSNE: 15-12, 15A-0   **Current Use:** Community

The Norwich & Worcester RR built the first depot in Norwich in 1840 at the foot of Ferry Street, about 200 feet west of the current station. Across town, the original New London, Willimantic & Palmer RR depot was built on North Thames Street. It was barely adequate for a dozen passengers and was replaced in 1863 by a larger structure built by the New London Northern RR.

Local citizens felt that neither of the railroads provided worthy facilities for their growing city. After much criticism by the local newspaper, a petition by local residents, and an act of the General Assembly, the two railroads built a new granite and brownstone Romanesque-style union station in 1892. The famous architectural firm of Sheply, Rutan and Coolidge designed that station. The N&W's Ferry Street station was initially closed, except for boat train passengers, but a year later, after renovations, it was reopened and used in conjunction with Union Station. The old NLN depot was razed in 1893.

In 1899 the N&W, under the control of the New York, New Haven & Hartford RR, extended its line to Groton and the new Thames River

Bridge. This allowed an all NYNH&H route to New London, obviating N&W service to Union Station. The station continued to be used by the Central Vermont RY until it was destroyed by the 1938 hurricane along with the former N&W freight house.

In conjunction with the extension to Groton, the NYNH&H started construction of the present station in 1899 on the site of the former car house; it was completed the following year. A similar station once existed at nearby Jewett City, and others could be found throughout their system. Subsequent to the loss of the freight house in the 1938 hurricane, a small addition was made to the west end of the station to handle freight; this has since been removed. The station was last used for passenger service on April 30, 1971. It is now occupied by St. Vincent de Paul Place, a soup kitchen. A monument commemorating the 100th anniversary of the N&W is located on Railroad Avenue. It is made of granite from a sill of the 1839 freight house.

Old Greenwich Station, Westbound   *160 Sound Beach Ave.*

Built: 1891-92   **Current RR:** AMTK, CSXT, MNR, PW   **Material:** Wood
RLSNE: 1-31   **Current Use:** Railroad/Commercial

This standard New York, New Haven & Hartford RR New England saltbox station was built in 1892, replacing an earlier structure. The depot was

This station is a well-preserved example of the New York, New Haven & Hartford's typical saltbox-style stations, which were numerous throughout Connecticut. The only ones that survive are in Cos Cob, Darien, Fairfield, Madison, Southport, and a pair on either side of the tracks in Westport.

moved to its present location in 1895, when the NYNH&H eliminated grade crossings and increased the main line from two to four tracks. In 1931 the name was changed from Sound Beach to Old Greenwich. Metro-North RR currently uses the station.

In the early morning hours of August 19, 2002, an arson fire damaged this historic building. Quick response by local firefighters helped minimize the smoke and water damage to the station's interior. The building has been restored and looks better than before the fire. The depot has been listed on the National Register of Historic Places since 1989.

Old Saybrook Station   *455 Boston Post Rd. (Rte. 1)*

Built: 1873   **Current RR:** AMTK, PW, SLE   **Material:** Wood
RLSNE: 12-31, 13-44   **Current Use:** Railroad

This Victorian-style station was built in 1873 by the New York, New Haven & Hartford RR and served as a union station with the Connecticut Valley RR, which had extended its line from Old Saybrook to Fenwick. The station's shape and location in the southwest corner of the former grade crossing provided travelers of both railroads with easy access to its facilities. New high-level platforms were completed and opened on November 1, 2002. Today the station is used by both Amtrak and Shore Line East riders.

Old Saybrook Freight House   *455 Boston Post Rd. (Rte. 1)*

Built: 1873   **Current RR:** AMTK, PW, SLE   **Material:** Wood
RLSNE: 12-31, 13-44   **Current Use:** Commercial

Old Saybrook's saltbox-style freight house was originally located in the southeast quadrant of the diamond, but has been moved several times and currently abuts the west end of the station. It is now home to the Pizza Works restaurant. Although it has received an addition, much of the interior is original, and the décor is all railroadiana, including operating model railroads with realistic scenery.

Plainville Freight House   70 Neal Ct.

Built: Between 1875 & 1900   **Current RR:** GRS   **Material:** Wood
RLSNE: 7-27, 10-103   **Current Use:** Railroad

Plainville was the former junction of the New Haven & Northampton and the Hartford, Providence & Fishkill RRs. This freight house, located in the northeast quadrant of the diamond, was the second freight house. The first was located opposite this one on the south side of the HP&F's track. The station, razed in the 1980s, was an L-shaped brick structure with a hip roof. It was located right at the junction, in the southeast quadrant of the diamond. Today the freight house is used by Guilford RY System (GRS) as a base for its Connecticut operations.

Portland Combination Depot   Rte. 17/66 near Airline Ave.

Built: Between 1870 & 1899   **Current RR:** PW   **Material:** Wood
RLSNE: 11-24   **Current Use:** Government

This former combination depot was abbreviated sometime after 1931, perhaps because of fire. The passenger section—roughly the easternmost two-thirds of the building—was removed. The state-owned building was in poor shape as recently as March 1996, but has since been restored. Portland, famous for its brownstone quarries, was where the stone for Hartford's Union Station was quarried.

Putnam Station   *Next to 35 Main St.*

Built: 1907   **Current RR:** PW   **Material:** Brick
RLSNE: 15-45, 16-25   **Current Use:** Vacant

This Putnam station was completed in 1907 by the New Haven RR. It replaced a two-story wooden structure with a mansard roof that was built ca. 1875. The previous station was located in the center of the New England RR and Norwich & Worcester RR tracks, exposing passengers and pedestrians to obvious dangers. The new arrangement consolidated the tracks east of the station and provided fencing and an elaborate subway to control access to far-side tracks. The north end of the station, originally open, was enclosed sometime after February 1970. Today the station is being renovated into a restaurant, and the old passenger subway is being reused as a wine cellar.

Putnam Express Office   *35 Main St.*

Built: Between 1877 & 1899   **Current RR:** PW   **Material:** Wood
RLSNE: 15-45, 16-25   **Current Use:** Commercial

Located just south of the station, this express building was operated by the Adams Express Company. It was moved a short distance to its current location when the 1907 station was built. For many years it was the home of Nikki's Dog House, but they have moved nearby and Jessica Tuesday's Market & Deli recently took their place.

Quinnipiak Depot   *Grote Rd. near Railroad Ave., Chester*

Built: Between 1838 & 1872   **Current RR:** VRR   **Material:** Wood
RLSNE: 8-4   **Current Use:** Railroad

AMANDA ROY

Despite the fact that the local area is called "Quinnipiac," this station was called "Quinnipiak." The tiny Hartford & New Haven RR depot was moved to Hamden, CT, in the 1920s for private use. In 1975 it was donated to the Connecticut Valley Railroad Museum (now called the Railroad Museum of New England) and moved again to Chester. Restored in 1976 and renamed "Chester," today it resides on the former site of the Chester Depot (see Chester Combination Depot).

Redding General Store/Station   *3 Sidecut Rd.*

Built: Before 1852   **Current RR:** MNR, PW   **Material:** Wood
RLSNE: 2-17   **Current Use:** Commercial/Community

Redding never really had its own station; the building here served as a general store, post office, and train station combined. The building was modified for use by the Danbury & Norwalk RR. The railroad and its patrons were provided a separate portion of the building near the tracks. The arrangement lasted until 1952, when the railroad erected a no-frills concrete block passenger shelter between the depot and Long Ridge Road. In 1999 Metro-North relocated the station south of Long Ridge Road, where passengers are afforded a new high-level platform, and more importantly, a large commuter parking lot. The former depot is home to the Station House Cafe and the Calvary Independent Baptist Church.

Ridgefield Depot   *27 Prospect St.*

Built: Ca. 1870   **Current RR:** None   **Material:** Wood
RLSNE: 2B-4   **Current Use:** Commercial

The Danbury & Norwalk RR built this depot ca. 1870 when the short branch was opened. It has a unique roof design that consists of eaves on both ends with a flat roof in between. A catchwater system funnels water into a cistern above the waiting room. Last used for passenger service on August 8, 1925, the structure has been boarded up and the canopies enclosed. The station was purchased by the Ridgefield Supply Company in 1946, and today they use the main building for storage; the enclosed canopy portion is occupied by their Renaissance Kitchens showroom.

Riverside Depot   *Corrona Dr., Greenwich*

Built: Between 1945 & 1965   **Current RR:** AMTK, CSXT, MNR, PW
Material: Brick   **RLSNE:** 1-30   **Current Use:** Railroad

This simple brick depot was built by the New Haven RR in the mid 1900s. It replaced one of the New Haven's typical saltbox-style stations, which was built in the mid 1890s when the line was upgraded from two tracks to four.

Rocky Hill Depot   *240 Meadow Rd.*

Built: 1892   **Current RR:** PW   **Material:** Wood
RLSNE: 13-9   **Current Use:** Commercial

The Rocky Hill Depot was built in 1892 by the New York, New Haven & Hartford RR. With the exception of a concrete block addition in the rear, it looks much the same as when it was built. Today it is the home of Tapestry Rose.

Rocky Hill Freight House   *262 Meadow Rd.*

Built: Between 1871 & 1899   **Current RR:** PW   **Material:** Wood
RLSNE: 13-9   **Current Use:** Commercial

This former New York, New Haven & Hartford RR freight house is occupied by the Wilderness Connection, a taxidermist's studio. The tracks in this area were abandoned in 1972 but have been rehabilitated by the Providence & Worcester RR, which reinstated freight service on July 10, 2003.

Rowayton Depot   *299 Rowayton Ave.*

Built: Ca. 1909-10   **Current RR:** AMTK, CSXT, MNR, PW, SLE
Material: Wood & Stucco   **RLSNE:** 1-39   **Current Use:** Railroad

Like many other New York, New Haven & Hartford RR stations built around 1910, this one was designed in the Spanish style. Today only the stucco walls tell of its original style, the terra cotta on the hip roof having been removed and replaced with ordinary roofing shingles. There is no longer a staffed ticket office at this station.

Roxbury Combination Depot   *Mine Hill Rd.*

Built: Ca. 1871   **Current RR:** None   **Material:** Wood
RLSNE: 4-12   **Current Use:** Commercial

Built ca. 1871 by the Shepaug Valley RR, the Roxbury Combination Depot was a busy location for freight. A nearby brass foundry, a granite quarry, and a high-grade iron ore mine must have kept the local agent busy. The Mine Hill Quarry had its own counterbalanced inclined plane to bring granite down the hill to the railroad siding. The remains of the old iron blast furnace can be seen close by, off Hodge Road. The depot is now home to a woodworking firm.

Salisbury Depot   *15 Library St.*

Built: Ca. 1889-1892   **Current RR:** None   **Material:** Wood
RLSNE: 17-63   **Current Use:** Residential

The original Salisbury Depot burned to the ground around the turn of the last century. This replacement station was brought in from Berea, NY (3.5 miles east of Maybrook), on a flat car via the Poughkeepsie Bridge. The Berea Depot was similar to other stations on the Philadelphia, Reading & New England RR main line west of the Hudson River, such as Modena, Clintondale, Loyd, and Highland Station. These stations were all built within a few years of the line's opening in 1889. The imported structure served Salisbury until the end of passenger service in 1927. The depot has been turned ninety degrees and moved 150 feet west of the right of way; it is now a private residence. The Railroad Ramble, a short rail-trail, passes along the right of way behind the old depot.

Seymour Passenger Shelter   *Main St. near Bank St.*

Built: Between 1980 & 1999   **Current RR:** GRS, MNR   **Material:** Brick
RLSNE: 5-15   **Current Use:** Railroad

Prior to 1898, Seymour was served by a wooden station with a large hip roof. That station was replaced by a buff brick station similar to the one surviving at Torrington. The brick station was torn down on February 30, 1953. Today's Metro-North passengers are provided only this small enclosed brick depot to protect them from the elements.

Seymour Freight House   *Washington Ave.*

Built: Ca. 1909-10   **Current RR:** GRS, MNR   **Material:** Wood
RLSNE: 5-15   **Current Use:** Commercial

This former New York, New Haven & Hartford RR freight house was built ca. 1909-10. It replaced an earlier wooden structure, which was located opposite this one. Similar flat-roofed freight houses survive at Lee, MA, and Franklin Junction, MA. Today the freight house is used by the Kerite Company, a manufacturer of High Voltage Cable.

Shelton Freight House   *White St. Ext.*

Built: Between 1889 & 1896   **Current RR:** HRR, PW   **Material:** Wood
RLSNE: 3A-13   **Current Use:** Commercial

This former New Haven RR freight house is now home to the New England Stair Company. The station, which was located just east of here along the canal, was torn down in the 1970s. Passenger service had ended in 1925 (see Derby-Shelton Station).

Simsbury [NH&N] Combination Depot   *736 Hopmeadow St.*

Built: Ca. 1847-50   **Current RR:** None   **Material:** Wood
RLSNE: 7-42, 7F-0   **Current Use:** Commercial

The Simsbury Combination Depot was originally built by the New York & New Haven RR while they controlled the New Haven & Northampton RR. The structure was converted to a freight house when a replacement brick station was built in 1874. It is similar to nearby depots surviving at Avon and Granby. The former station has been restored and moved several hundred feet south of the 1874 station (see Simsbury [NH&N] Depot) and is now the home of an architectural firm. The depot cannot be seen from Hopmeadow Street; the best way to access the station is from Mall Way.

Simsbury [NH&N] Depot   *4 Railroad St.*

Built: 1874   **Current RR:** None   **Material:** Brick
RLSNE: 7-42, 7F-0   **Current Use:** Commercial

This standard Canal Line Italianate depot, with its distinctive circular eave windows, was built in 1874 by the New Haven & Northampton RR to replace an earlier wooden combination depot (see Simsbury [NH&N] Combination Depot). By 1913 the Central New England RR was sharing the depot with the NH&N. A similar depot survives at Unionville. The attractive brick building is now home to the One Way Fare restaurant. The restaurant is a popular eatery, which is attractively decorated with railroad memorabilia, including a caboose outside. The building was placed on the National Register of Historic Places in 1976.

South Coventry Combination Depot   *525 Coventry Rd.*

Built: Ca. 1850   **Current RR:** NECR   **Material:** Brick
RLSNE: 14-35   **Current Use:** Commercial

This former Central Vermont RY combination depot is similar to the one still surviving at South Windham. It was built ca. 1850 when the New London, Willimantic & Palmer RR opened their line from Willimantic to Stafford. A garage door has been added to the freight section, and it is now home to an auto body repair business.

South Norwalk Station, Eastbound   *1 Chestnut St.*

Built: Ca. 1895   **Current RR:** AMTK, CSXT, MNR, PW, SLE   **Material:** Brick
RLSNE: 1-41, 2-0, 2A-0   **Current Use:** Railroad/Commercial/Municipal

The original Norwalk station was a wooden Victorian-style depot similar to the one surviving at New Canaan. The depot was replaced around 1860 with a large, attractive, two-story mansard-roofed brick building with a clock tower and twenty chimneys. When the New York, New Haven & Hartford RR upgraded the line between New Rochelle and New Haven in the mid 1890s, they eliminated all grade crossings and added two tracks for a total of four main-line tracks. This project required that the NYNH&H replace its stations with new and separate eastbound and westbound stations.

As part of this project, the NYNH&H erected twin stations at South Norwalk to replace the large, at-grade brick station. Today only the eastbound station survives, the westbound having been razed in the mid 1990s to make way for a much needed parking garage. The station was refurbished and modernized in 1994 with the help of the architectural firm of Sullivan/Jamieson. Today it is home to a dry cleaning service and the South Norwalk Community Police Center. Metro-North RR patrons are treated to a climate controlled waiting room with lots of railroad character.

South Norwalk Station, Westbound   *29 Monroe St.*

Built: 1996   **Current RR:** AMTK, CSXT, MNR, PW, SLE   **Material:** Concrete & Steel   **RLSNE:** 1-41, 2-0, 2A-0   **Current Use:** Railroad/Commercial/Muncipal

The Connecticut Department of Transportation and the Norwalk Transit District built the South Norwalk Railroad Station and Commuter Garage in 1996. Sadly, it was necessary to demolish the 1890s brick station to make room for a much needed parking garage. Fortunately, the nearly identical eastbound station was maintained and renovated as part of the project. This new station is still connected to its older eastbound counterpart via the 1890s pedestrian tunnel under the tracks. Metro-North commuters enjoy the convenience of a full service ticket office and a coffee shop inside. The station is also home to the South Norwalk Electric and Water business office.

South Windham [CV] Combination Depot   *Rte. 203 near Rte. 32*

Built: Ca. 1849   **Current RR:** NECR   **Material:** Brick
RLSNE: 14-26   **Current Use:** Vacant

South Windham was once a busy place on the New London, Willimantic & Palmer RR, predecessor to the Central Vermont RY. Wood-burning steam locomotives once stopped here for both water and wood. The station agent's house, now gone, was located on the opposite side of Windham Center Road. Built ca. 1849 by the NLW&P, the station originally had a four-column portico on the north end. It is similar to ones built at South Coventry, CT, and Monson, MA (see South Coventry Combination Depot). Vacant for years, the station was formerly used by the Windham Lumber Company.

Southport Station, Eastbound   *96 Station St.*

Built: 1884   **Current RR:** AMTK, CSXT, MNR, PW, SLE   **Material:** Brick
RLSNE: 1-49   **Current Use:** Commercial/Railroad

Now the home of Paci Restaurant, this former New York, New Haven & Hartford RR station is similar to other surviving stations on this line (see Fairfield and Milford Eastbound Stations). It replaced the original station, which was built in 1859 by the New York & New Haven RR. That station, built to a standard plan, was a small Gothic-style, board-and-batten structure with a cross-gabled roof. The current brick station was quickly erected between June and August of 1884, after fire destroyed its predecessor on May 17th of that year. The attractive structure, which is still decorated with gingerbread trim, was built by a local contractor for $6,500. It was added to the National Register of Historic Places in 1989.

Southport Station, Westbound   400 Center St.

Built: Between 1875 & 1899   **Current RR:** AMTK, CSXT, MNR, PW, SLE
Material: Wood   **RLSNE:** 1-49   **Current Use:** Railroad/Community

This station was built by the New York New Haven & Hartford RR in their standard saltbox style. It was erected for the convenience of westbound commuters so they would not be required to cross the busy tracks to board their morning trains. Since January 1982 the station has been the home of the Art Place, a well-known non-profit artists' cooperative. The station has an open waiting room with restrooms for Metro-North patrons. It was added to the National Register of Historic Places in 1989.

Southport Freight House   54 Old Post Rd.

Built: 1870   **Current RR:** AMTK, CSXT, MNR, PW, SLE   **Material:** Wood
RLSNE: 1-49   **Current Use:** Commercial

This charming Victorian freight house was saved from demolition and restored by the Southport Conservancy between 1988 and 1993. It is the only surviving freight house on the old New York and New Haven RR. It is currently home for a commercial design studio. The structure was listed on the State Register of Historic Places in 1989.

Stafford Station   *2 Main St.*

Built: 1893   **Current RR:** NECR   **Material:** Brick
RLSNE: 14-50   **Current Use:** Municipal

The Stafford Station was built in 1893 by the Central Vermont RY. It replaced the original depot, a small wooden gable-roofed structure located about 100 yards west on the corner of Main and Spring Streets; it was similar to those in Lebanon and Montville. When the new station was built, the original depot was retained for other purposes; however, it no longer survives today. The current station once had a carriage way on the street side. This old depot is currently owned by the town and occupied by the town of Stafford Police, Department of Public Safety.

Stamford Modern Station   *30 South State St.*

Built: 1985-87   **Current RR:** AMTK, CSXT, MNR, PW, SLE
Material: Aluminum & Concrete   **RLSNE:** 1-33, 1A-0   **Current Use:** Railroad/Commercial

The New York & New Haven RR's 1867 Stamford Station was an ornate, two-story, mansard-roofed brick structure similar to one in South Norwalk. It was located at ground level between the east- and westbound tracks. In 1893 this station was demolished as part of a grade separation project and the expansion of the line to four tracks. To replace it, the New York, New Haven & Hartford RR built two nearly identical brick stations, one for each direction. These were similar to the pair built at South Norwalk (see South Norwalk Eastbound Station).

Stamford was, and still is, the busiest station between New Haven and New York's Grand Central Terminal. By 1980 plans were being drawn up for a new $40-million transportation center that included a replacement station and an 850-car parking garage. Construction began in March 1983 and included the demolition of the ninety-year-old westbound station. The following year inspections revealed serious structural problems with the five-story parking garage and, later, with the new station itself. Corrections were made to the parking garage, but analysis and tests conducted on the station revealed that it could barely support its own weight. After much investigation and legal maneuvering, it was determined that the eighty-five-percent-completed station had to be demolished. The original architect, Wilbur Smith & Associates of Columbia, SC, hired Lev Zetlin Associates of Manhattan to redesign the station.

Demolition of the unfinished station began in 1985, and construction was resumed by December of that year. The transportation center, although not quite complete, was opened in November 1987. One week later the remaining eastbound station was demolished. The heavily used Stewart B. McKinney Transportation Center was named for the late U.S. Representative from Connecticut who died of Acquired Immune Deficiency Syndrome (AIDS) while in office; he had been a very vocal supporter of the project.

State Street Station [New Haven] Modern Station   259 State St.

Built: 2001-02   **Current RR:** AMTK, CSXT, MNR, PW, SLE
Material: Glass & Steel   **RLSNE:** 7-0.4, 8-0.4   **Current Use:** Railroad

This Shore Line East station was opened on June 7, 2002. It is intended to lure drivers off the overcrowded interstate by providing better access to downtown New Haven. State Street Station was built just one block east of where the New Haven RR's first union station was located. That station was built in 1848 by the New York & New Haven and the New Haven & Hartford RRs. It was replaced in 1875 and converted to the City Market. Ironically on July 4, 1894, the former station was destroyed by a fire that started in a fireworks vendor's stall inside the market.

Stepney Combination Depot   55 Maple Dr.

Built: Ca. 1905-06   **Current RR:** None   **Material:** Wood
RLSNE: 3-10   **Current Use:** Commercial

This structure is the second hip-roofed combination depot to serve Stepney. Although both were built by the New York, New Haven & Hartford RR, this one is slightly larger, having been erected ca. 1905-06 to replace a short-lived but smaller structure built around the turn of the century. A similar station was located just five miles south of here at Trumbull, and a large water tank was once located about 300 feet south of the station. The combination depot was last used for passenger service around 1931-32. A large garage door has been added, and today Monroe Septic uses the old station. Just north of here, in Wolf Park, the old railbed serves as the Housatonic Rail-Trail.

Stony Creek Depot   48 School St.

Built: Ca. 1852   **Current RR:** AMTK, PW, SLE   **Material:** Wood
RLSNE: 12-10   **Current Use:** Private

This former Shore Line RR station was built ca. 1852 across the street from its present location. It was replaced by a standard New York, New Haven & Hartford RR saltbox-style station around the turn of the last century. The depot is currently situated on the old Stony Creek Quarry spur, but it is on private property and difficult to see from the road. This spur served the same quarry that provided the granite for New York's Grand Central Terminal and Boston's South Station. Owned by the New York, Providence & Boston RR between 1858 and 1862, this building still bears the distinctive, compass-like decorative element present on many of its stations. This depot is very similar to those surviving at Noank, West Mystic, Clinton, and Westbrook.

Stratford Station, Eastbound   *2480 Main St. (Rte. 113)*

Built: Between 1853 & 1880   **Current RR:** AMTK, CSXT, MNR, PW, SLE
Material: Wood   **RLSNE:** 1-59   **Current Use:** Museum/Railroad

This station replaced the original 1849 depot, which was converted to a freight house and is now gone. The building was moved on railroad flat cars from Linden Avenue (just west of here) in 1894 when the railroad was widened to four tracks. The original depot, also moved from Linden Avenue, was located just east of here in what is now the station parking lot.

In 1973 the station was closed. It is now home to the National Helicopter Museum. Founded in 1983, this modest museum chronicles the development of the helicopter and the life of aviation pioneer Igor Sikorsky. Stratford is the home of Sikorsky Aircraft, maker of the famous Blackhawk Helicopter. Metro-North passengers now board their trains on high-level platforms located directly behind the museum.

Stratford Station, Westbound   *Main St. (Rte. 113)*

Built: Ca. 1894   **Current RR:** AMTK, CSXT, MNR, PW, SLE   **Material:** Wood
RLSNE: 1-59   **Current Use:** Railroad/Commercial

The westbound Stratford Station was built by the New Haven RR ca. 1894 as part of the expansion of the main line to four tracks. The station is now home to the Shell Station Restaurant and the Reality Cafe. Passengers are offered shelter in the eastern end of the building, but tickets must be purchased on the train.

Terryville Depot   *96 East Washington Rd.*

Built: Ca. 1850   **Current RR:** GRS   **Material:** Wood
RLSNE: 10-112   **Current Use:** Commercial

This was the original Terryville Depot built by the Hartford, Providence & Fishkill RR ca. 1850. The depot is now located on an active freight spur, which, prior to the completion of the Terryville Tunnel in 1910, was the main line. The New York, New Haven & Hartford RR replaced this building with a Spanish-style station on the new alignment just east of the Terryville Tunnel. The older depot was originally located directly across the track from where it now stands. Because it has the same width and roof pitch as the old freight house, it was easily added to the west end of that building (see Terryville Freight House). The depot has lost its small bay window and the gable over it, but is otherwise in reasonably good shape. Oddly enough a railroad-style passenger canopy has been added to the south end of the depot, a luxury this station never had during its half century of service. The depot and freight house are located in the Pequabuck Industrial Park and are currently used by the Worhunsky Corporation, operators of the local school buses.

Terryville Freight House   *96 East Washington Rd.*

Built: Ca. 1850   **Current RR:** GRS   **Material:** Wood
RLSNE: 10-112   **Current Use:** Commercial

The Terryville Freight House was built by the Hartford, Providence & Fishkill RR ca. 1850. The original Terryville Depot has been relocated adjacent to the freight house (see Terryville Depot). The track here still sees regular use by Guilford Rail System freight trains serving several customers in an industrial park located at the end of this two-mile freight spur. This section of the freight track has the distinction of being the highest elevation in Connecticut served by rail. The freight house is located in the Pequabuck Industrial Park and is currently used by the Worhunsky Corporation, operators of the local school buses.

Thomaston Station   *East Main St.*

Built: 1881   **Current RR:** NAUG   **Material:** Brick
RLSNE: 5-36   **Current Use:** Railroad

JOHN ROY

This brick station was built in 1881 by the original Naugatuck RR to replace a wooden combination depot, which was located directly across the tracks until 1994, when it collapsed under heavy snow. Thomaston's brick depot was very similar to the one built in 1877 for Winsted. The Winsted Station was razed in 1966 to make way for a service station. In 1993 the Thomaston Station was heavily damaged by an arson fire. The Railroad Museum of New England (RMNE) purchased the building and, with the support of the local community, has been restoring it since 1997. Today it is used by the RMNE's Naugatuck RR as a passenger boarding point for their seasonal tourist trains.

Torrington Station   *Railroad Sq. near Water St.*

Built: 1898   **Current RR:** NAUG   **Material:** Brick
RLSNE: 5-47   **Current Use:** Vacant

Built in 1898 by the New York, New Haven & Hartford RR, this station was the third and final station to serve Torrington. Its predecessor was an 1870 Victorian station. The original depot, a small wood structure, was destroyed by fire. Similar stations were once located in Seymour and Ansonia. The station is currently vacant and in poor shape, but the city, with help from the state, is planning to purchase it from the Kelly Bus Company and restore it for public use.

Unionville Depot
1 Depot Pl.

Built: 1874   **Current RR:** None   **Material:** Brick
RLSNE: 7B-3   **Current Use:** Commercial

This Italianate depot was erected in 1874 by the New Haven & Northampton RR. Similar stations were built in New Hartford, Pine Meadow, and Simsbury (see Simsbury [NH&N] Depot). It is the last remaining station on the NH&N's New Hartford Branch. The station is now home to Flea Market at the Depot, an antique dealer. It was placed on the Connecticut Register of Historic Places in 1997. The Farmington Canal Heritage Trail passes the rear of the depot on the old right of way.

Unionville Freight House
108-110 South Main St. (Rte. 177)

Built: 1915   **Current RR:** None   **Material:** Wood
RLSNE: 7B-3   **Current Use:** Commercial

This former New York, New Haven & Hartford RR freight house, now called "Depot West," is used by various retail and commercial establishments, including a coffee shop located in an addition. It was built in 1915 to replace an earlier structure.

Wallingford Station   *51 Quinnipiac St. (37 Hall Ave.)*

Built: 1871   **Current RR:** AMTK, CSO, CSXT   **Material:** Brick
RLSNE: 8-12, 10C-0   **Current Use:** Railroad/Community

Built in 1871 by the Hartford & New Haven RR, this mansard-roofed Second Empire-style station was saved from being razed in 1969 thanks to the efforts of a local man, David Peters. In the 1970s the Wallingford Station was renovated, including modifications to the interior and the entrance to provide better handicapped access, but it wasn't until 1993 that a $400,000 historical restoration was completed. The handsomely restored station was placed on the National Register of Historic Places in 1993 and is now home to the Adult Learning Center and the Spanish Community Center.

A large freight house, built by the New York, New Haven & Hartford RR in 1910 and similar to Waterbury's outbound freight house, was located across the tracks from the station.

Wallingford Freight House   *105 N. Cherry St*

Built: Between 1905 & 1930   **Current RR:** AMTK, CSO   **Material:** Brick
RLSNE: 8-12, 10C-0   **Current Use:** Commercial

The Wallingford Freight House, now a private warehouse, is occupied by Central Connecticut Acoustics. It was built to replace an 1870s mansard-roofed building that was located across the tracks from the Wallingford Station. It is similar to the surviving outbound freight house in Waterbury, which also has a two-story office section and a one-story warehouse area.

Warehouse Point Freight House · *4 Old Depot Hill Rd.*

Built: Between 1838 & 1872   **Current RR:** AMTK, CSO, GRS
Material: Wood & Metal Siding   **RLSNE:** 8-50   **Current Use:** Commercial

This former New York & New Haven RR freight house is now home to Criscitelli Enterprises, a landscape service company. Located just east of the Connecticut River, it appears to be unusually far from the tracks; this is because the track alignment was shifted slightly northward when the current bridge over the Connecticut River was built in 1904-05.

The Warehouse Point Station, which was located between the freight house and the Connecticut River Bridge, was a well-kept brick structure built in 1872 by the New York, New Haven & Hartford RR. Severely damaged by the 1938 hurricane, the depot was torn down in 1939.

Washington Combination Depot · *Main St.*

Built: 1895   **Current RR:** None   **Material:** Wood
RLSNE: 4-19   **Current Use:** Community

This combination depot was built in 1895 by the Shepaug, Litchfield & Northern RR to replace the original depot, which was destroyed by fire. The original village center is about a mile up the hill, where the Gunnery School is located. The depot was moved nearby, with an assist from Mother Nature in the 1955 floods, and is now the local American Legion hall.

Waterbury Station 389 Meadow St.

Built: 1908-09   **Current RR:** GRS, MNR, NAUG   **Material:** Brick & Terra Cotta   **RLSNE:** 5-27, 9-0, 10-122, 10C-0   **Current Use:** Commercial/Railroad

RON KARR

Waterbury, the "Brass City," was a hub of railroad activity. Its first station, that of the Naugatuck RR, was completed shortly after the railroad opened to Waterbury on June 11, 1849. The Hartford, Providence & Fishkill RR was next, reaching Waterbury from Hartford in 1855. Their station, a single-story wooden structure, was located on West Main Street, east of the track and north of the then at-grade crossing of the Naugatuck's line.

In June 1867 the Naugatuck began construction of a new station west of the tracks, off Meadow Street and just north of the intersection of Bank Street. The stone-trimmed brick structure, which opened on January 22, 1868, had a two-story, mansard-roofed head house with an attractive cupola.

On November 1, 1870, the Watertown & Waterbury RR became the third railroad to serve Waterbury. The line, which was a little less than five miles long, connected with the Naugatuck in Waterbury. Just seven years later, the Naugatuck and the former W&W, by then a branch of the Naugatuck, were leased by the New York, New Haven & Hartford RR.

In 1878 the New York & New England RR leased the financially plagued HP&F. The NY&NE finally connected Waterbury to Fishkill in 1882. In the summer of 1888 the Meriden, Waterbury & Cromwell RR opened its line from Meriden to Waterbury. Called the spite line, it connected with the NY&NE to provide its namesake cities with an alternative to the NYNH&H's high rates.

In 1903 the aggressive NYNH&H, having gained control of all of Waterbury's railroads, began planning a major reconfiguration of the city's railroad facilities. Due to difficulties in obtaining the required land (through condemnation hearings), construction was delayed until 1907. The old station was closed on March 29, 1908, and a temporary station was erected at West Main Street.

The reconstruction project included the consolidation of the former Naugatuck and NY&NE main line between West Main Street and Bank Street, new freight and passenger facilities, an engine house, new signaling, control towers, and a large freight yard. The crowning jewel of the project was this elegant station designed by the prestigious firm of McKim, Mead and White, the architects of New York's Pennsylvania Station and Boston's Symphony Hall. Interestingly, Stanford White and Charles McKim both worked under H. H. Richardson, himself a designer of many New England stations. The station's 240-foot clock tower is a replica of the often copied *Torre del Mangia, Palazzo Publico* (City Hall), in Sienna Italy. The station opened on July 1, 1909. It also served as the NYNH&H's Western Division Headquarters.

The station, which was purchased from the New Haven RR by the Republican-American newspaper in the late 1940s or early 1950s, is still occupied by the newspaper. A large addition on the north end houses the newspaper's printing press and includes an area where inbound newsprint arrives by rail. Metro-North uses the former express office for a train crew room. Ironically, their passengers no longer have access to the station; they use a small enclosed shelter just south of it. The station was placed on the National Register of Historic Places in 1978.

Waterbury Freight House, Inbound   43 Freight St.

Built: Ca. 1907   **Current RR:** GRS, MNR, NAUG   **Material:** Brick & Wood
RLSNE: 5-27, 9-0, 10-122, 10C-0   **Current Use:** Commercial

This former New York, New Haven & Hartford RR freight house was used for Waterbury's inbound freight. It was built as part of a project that consolidated the former Naugatuck and New York & New England main line between West Main Street and Bank Street (see Waterbury Station). It replaced an earlier freight house, which was removed in 1907. Today it no longer receives freight cars. The outbound freight house is located next door.

Waterbury Freight House, Outbound
45 Freight St.

Built: Ca. 1909   **Current RR:** GRS, MNR, NAUG   **Material:** Brick
RLSNE: 5-27, 9-0, 10-122, 10C-0   **Current Use:** Commercial

Built as part of a project that consolidated the former Naugatuck and New York & New England main lines between West Main Street and Bank Street, this former New York, New Haven & Hartford RR freight house was used for Waterbury's outbound freight. The freight office was located in the large two-story portion of the building. The inbound freight house is located next door. A similar freight house, built in 1912, existed in Wallingford directly across from the station. This building is now used for commercial purposes.

West Cornwall Combination Depot
6 Railroad St.

Built: Ca. 1842   **Current RR:** HRR   **Material:** Wood
RLSNE: 3-61   **Current Use:** Community

This station was built to a standard Housatonic RR design. It was almost identical to the original Lime Rock station and similar to Falls Village, Kent, and the original New Milford stations. At one time a large wooden water tank was located just south of the depot. Today the Little Benefit Shop occupies the depot.

West Mystic Depot
105 School St.

Built: Ca. 1858-59 **Current RR:** AMTK, PW **Material:** Wood
RLSNE: 19-54 **Current Use:** Commercial

This former New Haven RR depot was built ca. 1858-59 by the New Haven, New London & Stonington RR. It was moved from the opposite side of School Street ca. 1938, possibly with a little help from nature via the 1938 hurricane. The depot, now perpendicular to the track, is home to Haugland Engineering. Similar stations still exist at Clinton, Noank, Stony Creek, and Westbrook, while others, like the original Mystic and Stonington depots, are long gone. This building still bears the distinctive compass-like decorative element present on many of the New York, Providence & Boston RR stations.

West Willington Combination Depot
14 Tolland Turnpike (Rte. 74)

Built: Between 1890 & 1919 **Current RR:** NECR **Material:** Wood
RLSNE: 14-44 **Current Use:** Commercial

Tolland, the shire town (county seat), had no direct rail service; West Willington was the closest the rail line came to Tolland center. Attempting to gain favor with county officials, the New London, Willimantic & Palmer RR built the station here and called it Tolland. The name was later changed to Tolland & Willington, and eventually it became known as West Willington. This wooden structure, built by the Central Vermont RY, succeeded an earlier brick combination depot. A branch office of the Savings Bank of Tolland was opened here in 1976, and more recently the combination depot has been home to an antique jewelry store.

Westbrook Combination Depot   *Essex Rd. (Rte 153)*

Built: Ca. 1852   **Current RR:** AMTK, PW, SLE   **Material:** Wood
RLSNE: 12-27   **Current Use:** Commercial

This is the original Westbrook Combination Depot, built by the Shore Line RR ca. 1852. It was used until ca. 1905-06, when the New York, New Haven & Hartford RR replaced it with a standard hip-roofed station similar to the one surviving in Mystic. That station was located on the south side of the tracks. The depot has been moved back from the tracks and turned forty-five degrees from its original location. Owned by the New York, Providence & Boston RR between 1858 and 1862, this building still bears the distinctive, compass-like decorative element present on many of its stations. It is slightly larger than similar depots surviving at Noank, West Mystic, Clinton, and Stony Creek. Ironically the old depot has outlasted its replacement.

Westport Station, Eastbound   *Ferry Ln.*

Built: 1891   **Current RR:** AMTK, CSXT, MNR, PW, SLE   **Material:** Wood
RLSNE: 1-44   **Current Use:** Railroad/Commercial

Westport's eastbound station was built by the New York, New Haven & Hartford RR in 1891 as part of the main-line expansion to four tracks. It is typical of the New England saltbox-style stations found throughout the NYNH&H system. The westbound station located across the tracks is very similar to this one. In 2003-04 this station and its westbound counterpart were upgraded for compliance with the Americans with Disabilities Act (ADA). This was part of a $7.8-million improvement project, which included the installation of a new elevator-equipped pedestrian tunnel between the two station parking lots. Today this station is home to Westport Taxi Cab Company, Avis, and Lilis Fine Food Takeout and Catering.

Westport Station, Westbound
1 Railroad Pl.

Built: 1890s   **Current RR:** AMTK, CSXT, MNR, PW, SLE   **Material:** Wood
RLSNE: 1-44   **Current Use:** Railroad

Similar to its eastbound counterpart, this station was built by the New York, New Haven & Hartford RR in the 1890s as part of the main-line expansion to four tracks. A Metro-North RR ticket office occupies the station today.

Wethersfield Freight House/Depot
212 Church St.

Built: Between 1871 & 1900   **Current RR:** PW   **Material:** Wood
RLSNE: 13-6   **Current Use:** Commercial

RON KARR

The original Wethersfield Depot was destroyed by fire prior to the mid 1920s. This former freight house was then converted to a combination depot, serving passengers until 1933. Today it is the home of Wethersfield Bicycle.

Willimantic [NY&NE] Express Office
Bridge St.

Built: 1870s   **Current RR:** NECR   **Material:** Brick
RLSNE: 10-58, 14-30, 16-50   **Current Use:** Commercial

This Second Empire-style railway express office was built by the New York & New England RR. It is located in the rear of a small shopping mall near the entrance to the Connecticut Eastern Railroad Museum. The freight house, no longer extant, was located on the south side of the express office. The privately-owned building was added to the National Register of Historic Places in 1982.

Wilton Combination Depot   *146 Norwalk Danbury Rd. (Rte. 7)*

Built: 1851   **Current RR:** N/A   **Material:** Wood
RLSNE: 2-7.5   **Current Use:** Commercial

This former combination depot, which once stood opposite the current depot, has been moved south on Route 7 in Wilton. This station was similar to other original Danbury & Norwalk RR depots, but today it is the only survivor. It has been carefully restored and retains much of its original charm. The depot served the railroad for 87 years prior to being replaced in 1939. It is now home to the office of Pearson, Ceppi and Associates.

Wilton Depot   *7 Station Rd.*

Built: 1939   **Current RR:** MNR, PW   **Material:** Wood
RLSNE: 2-7.5   **Current Use:** Railroad/Commercial

This depot was built in 1939 by the New Haven RR to replace the original depot. It originally had a portico on the north end to offer patrons cover when the station was closed. The portico has since been enclosed. Metro-North patrons still board trains here. A portion of the station is home to the Fast Track Coffee Shop. A similar depot existed five miles north of here at Georgetown.

Windsor Station   *35 Central St.*

Built: 1871   **Current RR:** AMTK, CSO, GRS   **Material:** Brick
RLSNE: 8-43   **Current Use:** Community/Railroad

This Second Empire-style station was built by the Hartford & New Haven RR in 1871, replacing the original station. The mansard-roofed depot had separate gentlemen's and ladies' waiting rooms with a centrally located ticket office. It also had an express room, baggage room, and telegraph office; however, there were no bathrooms. The station is occupied by the Rideshare Company, and although unstaffed, it is also an Amtrak station. The beautifully restored structure was placed on the National Register of Historic Places in 1988.

Windsor Freight House   *50 Central St.*

Built: Ca. 1871   **Current RR:** AMTK, CSO, GRS   **Material:** Brick & Brownstone
RLSNE: 8-43   **Current Use:** Community

This freight house was built by the New York, New Haven & Hartford RR ca. 1871. Like the station across the tracks, the Rideshare Company now occupies this building. The beautifully restored structure, with its round eave windows and three cupolas, was placed on the National Register of Historic Places in 1988.

Windsor Locks Station — *North Main St. (Rte. 159) near Oak St.*

Built: 1875   **Current RR:** AMTK, CSO, GRS   **Material:** Brick
RLSNE: 8-49, 8C-0   **Current Use:** Vacant

This station was built by the New York, New Haven & Hartford RR in 1875, replacing an earlier depot built by the Hartford & New Haven RR. The facilities included a large waiting room, express room, baggage room, ticket office, telegraph office, and rest rooms. To serve the industries separated from the railroad by the Windsor Locks Canal, the railroad built a substantial brick freight house. Located adjacent to and north of the Windsor Locks Station, it was similar to the one still extant in neighboring Windsor.

Today, the Windsor Locks Station stands vacant and forlorn, bearing a label that states, "This building unsafe for human occupancy." Fortunately, the Windsor Locks Preservation Association has launched a grass roots campaign to restore the old station. Perhaps someday passengers will again use the old depot instead of Amtrak's bus stop-like mini-high platform, located just south of the interstate highway. The station was added to the National Register of Historic Places in 1975.

Winsted Freight House — *140 Willow St.*

Built: Ca. 1906   **Current RR:** None   **Material:** Wood
RLSNE: 5-56, 17-35.5   **Current Use:** Commercial

This former New York, New Haven & Hartford RR freight house was closed in 1963. Since then it has been used for various commercial purposes, including a nightclub. When originally constructed ca. 1906, it was a single-story structure with a head house on the north side that served as the freight office. In the late 1990s it was substantially altered for use as a professional office building, the second floor and dormers having been added at that time.

Massachusetts

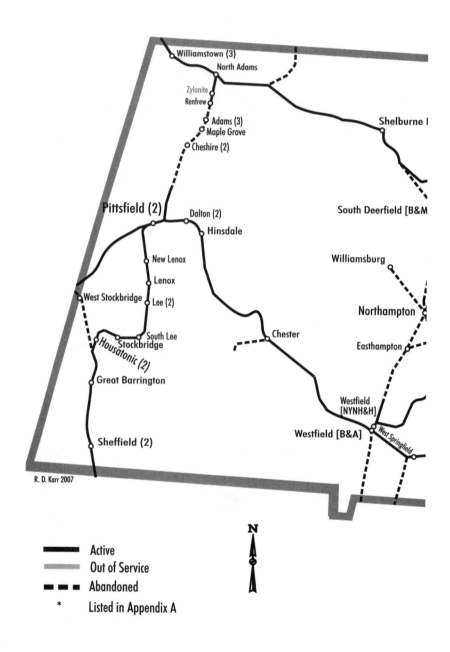

Williamstown (3)
North Adams
Zylonite
Renfrew
Adams (3)
Maple Grove
Cheshire (2)
Shelburne I
Pittsfield (2)
Dalton (2)
Hinsdale
South Deerfield [B&M
New Lenox
Lenox
Williamsburg
West Stockbridge
Lee (2)
Northampton
South Lee
Chester
Housatonic (2)
Stockbridge
Easthampton
Great Barrington
Westfield
[NYNH&H]
Sheffield (2)
Westfield [B&A]
West Springfield

R. D. Karr 2007

━━━━━ Active
━━━━━ Out of Service
■ ■ ■ Abandoned
* Listed in Appendix A

N

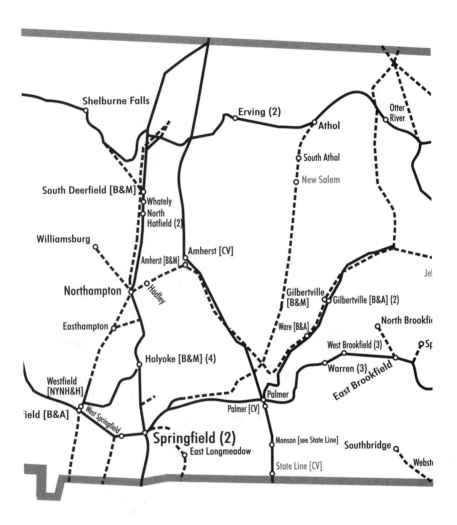

Shelburne Falls

Erving (2)

Otter River

Athol

South Athol

New Salem

South Deerfield [B&M]

Whately

North Hatfield (2)

Williamsburg

Amherst [CV]

Amherst [B&M]

Northampton

Hadley

Gilbertville [B&M]

Gilbertville [B&A] (2)

Je

Easthampton

Ware [B&A]

North Brookfi

West Brookfield (3)

Sp

Holyoke [B&M] (4)

Warren (3)

East Brookfield

Westfield [NYNH&H]

West Springfield

Palmer

field [B&A]

Palmer [CV]

Springfield (2)

East Longmeadow

Monson [see State Line]

Southbridge

Webst

State Line [CV]

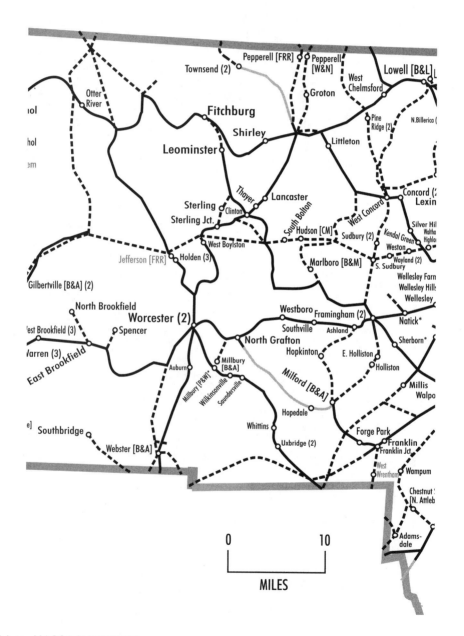

Pepperell [FRR]
Pepperell [W&N]
Townsend (2)
West Chelmsford
Lowell [B&L]
Groton
Otter River
Pine Ridge (2)
N.Billerica
iol
Fitchburg
Shirley
hol
Littleton
Leominster
em
Thayer
Lancaster
Concord (
Lexin
Sterling
Clinton
West Concord
Sterling Jct.
South Bolton
Silver Hil
Waltha
Highla
Kendal Green
Hudson [CM]
Sudbury (2)
West Boylston
Weston
Jefferson [FRR]
Holden (3)
Wayland (2)
S. Sudbury
Marlboro [B&M]
Wellesley Farn
Gilbertville [B&A] (2)
Wellesley Hill:
North Brookfield
Wellesley
Westboro
Framingham (2)
Worcester (2)
Natick*
'est Brookfield (3)
Spencer
Southville
Ashland
North Grafton
Sherborn*
Hopkinton
E. Holliston
Varren (3)
Auburn
Millbury [B&A]
Holliston
East Brookfield
Milford [B&A]
Millis
Millbury [P&W]*
Walpo
Wilkinsonville
Saundersville
Hopedale
Southbridge
e]
Whittins
Forge Park
Franklin
Webster [B&A]
Uxbridge (2)
Franklin Jct.
West Wrentham
Wampum
Chestnut :
N. Attleb
Adams-
dale

0   10

MILES

Amesbury (2)
Salisbury Pt.
Newburyport
Rosemont
Bradford
Haverhill (3)
Methuen (2)
Lawrence (2)
S. Lawrence
North Andover (2)
E. Boxford (2)
Ipswich
Shawsheen
Andover (2)
Ballard-
vale
Lowell [B&L]
Lowell [B&M]
Topsfield (3)
Conomo
Essex
West
Chelmsford
Tewksbury
Center
Pine
Ridge (2)
N.Billerica (2)
Tapleyville (to Kennebunkport, ME)
S. Middleton
N. Reading
Middleton (2)
Howes*
Danvers
[NRR]
Danvers
East
Manchester
Prides Crossing
Beverly Farms
eton
Wilmington (3)
Lynnfield Centre
Reading
Ander-
son RTC
Beverly
Salem
Bedford (2)
Wakefield (3)
Stoneham
Farm Hill
Winchester
Wakefield Centre
Concord (2)
Lexington
Wedgemere
Malden (2)
Cliftondale
Saugus
Swampscott
East Lynn (to Durham, NH)
Lynn
West Concord
Silver Hill
Waltham
Highlands
Park St.
[Medford]
udbury (2)
Kendal Green
Weston
Wayland (2)
S. Sudbury
Belmont (2)
Porter Sq.
Allston
Back Bay
North Sta.(2)*
B&M]
Newton
Highlands Newton Ctr. (2)
South Sta.
BOSTON
Wellesley Farms
Wellesley Hills
Wellesley
Woodland
Newton Uppper Falls
Ruggles
Forest Hills
Allerton
Nantasket
am (2)
Natick*
Needham
Needham Jct.
Mattapan
Black Rock"
Cohasset
Hingham (2)
North Scituate
Sherborn*
Dover
E. Holliston
Holliston
Rte. 128 [Westwood]
Beechwood*
South Weymouth
Millis
Walpole
Norwood
Central
Canton Jct.
East
Walpole
Stoughton
Avon
North Abington
Rockland
Forge Park
Franklin
Franklin Jct.
South
Walpole
Sharon (2)
North
Easton
South Hanson
Kingston (2)
West
Wrentham
Wampum
Mansfield
Chestnut St.
[N. Attleboro]
Norton
Silver Lake*
Bridgewater
Attleboro (3)
Adams-
dale
Barrowsville
Dean St. [Taunton]
Middleboro
Lakeville

MASSACHUSETTS ❧ 115

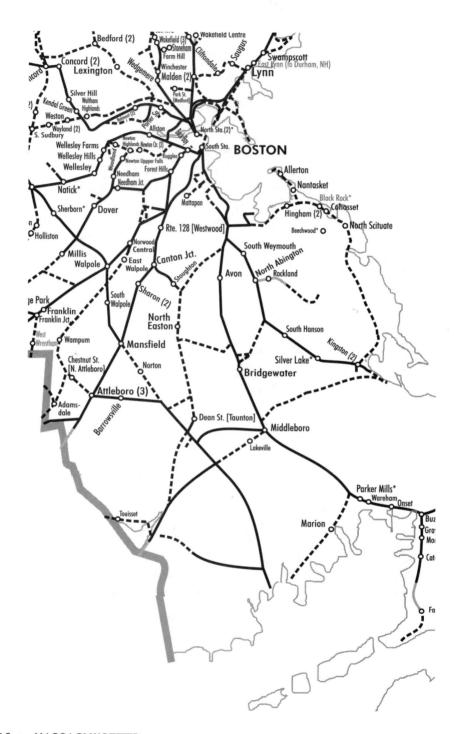

Bedford (2)

Wakefield (3)
Wakefield Centre
Stoneham
Farm Hill
Winchester

Concord (2)
Lexington
Wedgemere
Malden (2)
Clifondale
Saugus
Swampscott
East Lynn (to Durham, NH)
Lynn

Silver Hill
Waltham
Highlands
Park St.
[Medford]

Kendal Green
Weston
Belmont (2)
Porter Sq.
North Sta. (2)*

Wayland (2)
S. Sudbury
Allston
Berkley

Wellesley Farms
Newton
Highlands
Newton Cr. (2)
Ruggles
South Sta.
BOSTON

Wellesley Hills
Wellesley
Woodland
Needham
Newton Uppper Falls
Forest Hills

Allerton
Nantasket

Natick*
Needham Jct.
Black Rock*
Cohasset

Sherborn*
Dover
Mattapan
Hingham (2)
North Scituate

Holliston
Rte. 128 [Westwood]
Beechwood*

Norwood
Central
South Weymouth

Millis
Walpole
East
Walpole
Canton Jct.
Stoughton
Avon
North Abington
Rockland

ge Park
South
Walpole
Sharon (2)
South Hanson

Franklin
Franklin Jct.
North
Easton
Kingston (2)

West
Wrentham
Wampum
Mansfield
Silver Lake*

Chestnut St.
[N. Attleboro]
Norton
Bridgewater

Attleboro (3)
Adams-
dale
Barrowsville
Dean St. [Taunton]
Middleboro

Lakeville

Touisset
Parker Mills*
Wareham
Onset
Buz

Marion
Gra
Mo

Cat

Fa

tuate

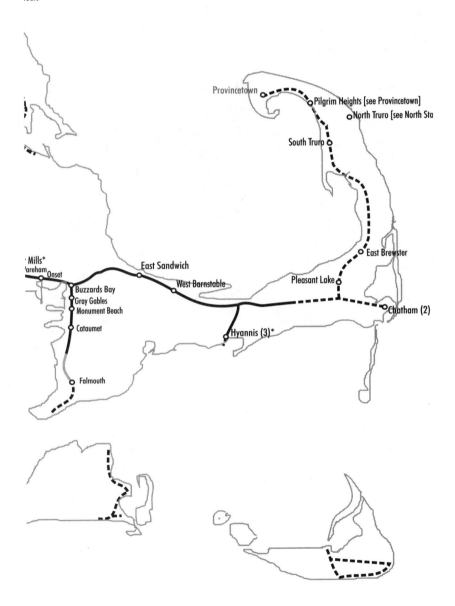

Provincetown
Pilgrim Heights [see Provincetown]
North Truro [see North Sta
South Truro
East Brewster
Mills*
Wareham
Onset
East Sandwich
West Barnstable
Buzzards Bay
Gray Gables
Monument Beach
Cataumet
Pleasant Lake
Chatham (2)
Hyannis (3)*
Falmouth

Sheply, Rutan and Coolidge's ornate Classical Revival main entrance was the centerpiece of the Boston & Maine and Fitchburg RRs' 1894 North Union Station. This block-long multi-building station consolidated the former Boston & Lowell RR station with adjacent new facilities built to replace the former Eastern RR's station, the Fitchburg's old stone station, and the B&M's Haymarket Square station. This massive edifice was torn down, along with the whole consolidated station, less than thirty-five years later. (Courtesy of the Beverly Historical Society & Museum, Beverly, MA, Walker Transportation Collection)

Massachusetts

Adams Station   *10 Pleasant St.*

Built: 1884   **Current RR:** None   **Material:** Brick
RLSNE: 30-13   **Current Use:** Commercial

This station and the adjacent express office were built by the Boston & Albany RR in 1884. They replaced the original wooden depot built ca. 1846 by the Western RR. That station, which looked similar to the one surviving at Cheshire, was located across the tracks from the current one.

Home to CJ's Pub since 1999, this brick station was added to the National Register of Historic places in 1982. The popular Ashuwillticook Rail Trail, which opened in the fall of 2003, follows the old right of way by the station and ends just north of here.

Adams Express Office   *10 Pleasant St.*

Built: 1884   **Current RR:** None   **Material:** Wood
RLSNE: 30-13   **Current Use:** Commercial

The Adams Express Office was built by the Boston & Albany RR in 1884. The wooden structure is located adjacent to the north end of the station and is currently used for storage. It was placed on the National Register of Historic Places in 1982.

Adamsdale Depot
78 Depot St.

Built: Ca. 1877 **Current RR:** None **Material:** Wood
RLSNE: 67B-12 **Current Use:** Private

The Adamsdale Depot was likely built in 1877, when the New York & New England RR opened its Valley Falls Branch. It was moved across the street and 100 yards east in the 1930s, to a farm owned by the grandfather of its current owner. The gable-roofed depot has been modified for use as a garage.

Allerton Freight House
Y St.

Built: 1916 **Current RR:** None **Material:** Wood & Aluminum
RLSNE: 74A-5 **Current Use:** Commercial

This simple lean-to-style freight house was built by the New York, New Haven & Hartford RR in 1916. It was likely built to serve its current occupant, Daley & Wanzer, Inc., a family-owned moving and storage company since 1916. It is their trucks that can still be seen in the lot surrounding the small freight house. A garage door has been added to the east end of the structure.

Allston Station · 553 Cambridge St.

Built: 1887 **Current RR:** AMTK, CSXT, MBTA **Material:** Stone
RLSNE: 63-0, 64-4 **Current Use:** Commercial

Between 1886 and 1894, the Boston & Albany RR commissioned the Boston firm of Sheply, Rutan and Coolidge to design twenty-three stations. Eight of these stations survive today in Massachusetts, with another in nearby Chatham, NY. Construction of this station was performed by Norcross Brothers of Worcester between May and October 1887. At a cost of $21,109, it was the only Sheply, Rutan and Coolidge station designed with a gable roof. Although no longer evident, the station's original landscaping was designed by Fredrick Law Olmsted. This Richardson-inspired station is now home to Captain Fishbones Restaurant.

Amesbury Station · 32 Elm St.

Built: 1872 **Current RR:** None **Material:** Wood
RLSNE: 58G-4 **Current Use:** Commercial/Residential

RON KARR

Amesbury was famous for the manufacture of carriages, wagons, and sleighs. The Eastern RR built this station in 1872, just east of the Black River trestle, in the heart of the carriage district. By 1885 business was booming, and the railroad expanded the freight yard and built a four-stall roundhouse. Two years later the station was moved from the carriage district across the river to its current location. This unique move was accomplished with four flat cars in a two-by-two arrangement on parallel tracks.

Passenger service ended in 1936, and the Boston & Maine RR sold the building. The station had been home to J. S. Auto Parts for forty years, but the store closed in 2003. The building, which was renovated in 2004, is currently used for apartments and the Riverwalk Bead Shop and Gallery. Similar Victorian-style stations exist at Bradford and Danvers East.

Amherst [B&M] Depot   *320 South Pleasant St.*

Built: Ca. 1886-87   **Current RR:** None   **Material:** Wood
RLSNE: 34-93   **Current Use:** Commercial

RON KARR

The stations built by the Central Massachusetts RR, later part of the Boston & Maine RR, all conformed to the Victorian style of architecture, which was at its height of popularity in the 1870s and 80s. They were characterized by oversized roofs with significant overhangs to protect the public from the elements. These roofs required numerous knee braces to support the weight of the overhangs and any snow that might accumulate on them. The braces lent themselves naturally to the kind of decorative trim that characterized the Victorian style. Cost being an issue, there were three basic designs employed by the CM. The more important stations used either a hip or gabled-hip roof, while the subordinate stations used a simple gable roof.

The hip-roofed station at Amherst was built during the time the Boston & Lowell RR controlled the CM. It is currently used as a warehouse by the Amherst Farmers Supply. Today's users of the popular Norwottuck Rail Trail are reminded of travel in a bygone era as they pass by the old station.

Amherst [CV] Depot   *13 Railroad St.*

Built: 1853   **Current RR:** NECR   **Material:** Brick
RLSNE: 14-85   **Current Use:** Commercial/Railroad

This attractive brick depot was built in 1853 for the Amherst & Belchertown RR, a predecessor to the Central Vermont RY. The terminus of the railroad until 1866, Amherst was the only original station constructed of brick, the others being made of wood. It once had a separate wooden baggage room on the south end of the platform. The depot was restored in 1992 and today is the home of Plouffe Corporation, a design and consulting firm. A small portion of the depot serves as a waiting room for patrons of the two Amtrak trains that stop here daily.

Anderson RTC Modern Station   *100 Atlantic Ave., Woburn*

Built: 2001   **Current RR:** AMTK, GRS, MBTA   **Material:** Brick
RLSNE: 51-12.9   **Current Use:** Railroad/Commercial/Transit

Although an early twenty-first-century building, the MBTA station in Woburn is reminiscent of the Victorian period. It stands in sharp contrast to its modern peers in Lynn, Forest Hills, and Ruggles Street in Boston.

This eight-thousand-square-foot MBTA station includes a clock tower and plenty of nineteenth-century charm. Opened on May 16, 2001, it was designed by Meyer and Meyer Architecture and Interiors, the same firm that designed the Charles Gallagher Terminal in Lowell, MA (see Lowell [B&L] Modern Station) and the JFK/UMass Subway Station in Dorchester, MA. In addition to MBTA commuter trains, the Anderson Regional Transportation Center began serving the Amtrak *Downeaster* on July 1, 2002, and also provides Woburn-to-Logan express bus service.

The station is named in memory of Jimmy Anderson, who lived in Woburn in the 1970s. He fought a long and courageous battle with leukemia, but died January 18, 1981, at the age of 12. The station is built on the Superfund Site that was depicted in the movie *A Civil Action*, which is based on the lawsuit his mother, Anne Anderson, won against W. R. Grace & Company

Andover Station   *100 School St.*

Built: 1907   **Current RR:** AMTK, GRS, MBTA   **Material:** Yellow Brick &
Brownstone   **RLSNE:** 52-23   **Current Use:** Commercial

The original Andover Station was a Greek Revival-style wooden structure located on the 1836 alignment of the Andover & Wilmington RR at Essex Street, near the Memorial Hall Library. In 1848 the Boston & Maine RR relocated the line to directly serve the new industrial city of Lawrence and abandoned seven miles of track through Andover and North Andover. To serve the new alignment, a small home was purchased in 1848 and converted into a station. This temporary station was replaced with an L-shaped wooden structure with a run-through train shed, a large cupola, and a Palladian window over the main entrance.

As was the case with train sheds all over the country, the local citizens began to complain about the soot and smoke from the steam locomotives inside. The Boston & Maine RR capitulated, and on September 1, 1907, this yellow brick and brownstone station opened on the site of the old station. Although built ten years later, it is a copy of the Bradford Lee Gilbert-designed station still surviving in Beverly. Today Carriage House Studios and Main Line Creamery occupy the station.

Andover Freight House   *15 Railroad St.*

Built: Between 1848 & 1875   **Current RR:** AMTK, GRS, MBTA
Material: Brick   **RLSNE:** 52-23   **Current Use:** Commercial

This former Boston & Maine RR brick freight house is now occupied by the Andover Insurance Agency, the Financial Advisors, and Moontone, a Japanese restaurant. It has been home to several commercial tenants over the years. Today's MBTA patrons board their trains behind the freight house.

Ashland Station   *Homer St. near Main St.*

Built: 1887   **Current RR:** AMTK, CSXT, MBTA   **Material:** Granite & Brownstone   **RLSNE:** 64-24, 71-20   **Current Use:** Commercial

This station was another of those designed by Sheply, Rutan and Coolidge for the Boston & Albany RR. It was built by Norcross Brothers between June and October 1887. The pink granite used in the station was quarried at nearby Milford, MA.

Ashland Station was very similar to one that existed in Newton Lower Falls. It cost $12,793, about $2,000 more than the simpler Newton Lower Falls Station. The differences were primarily in the addition of a decorative horizontal brownstone belt and different fenestration on the Ashland Station. The building currently serves as a doctor's office.

Athol Station   *South St. near Exchange St.*

Built: 1872-73 (rebuilt 1892)   **Current RR:** GRS   **Material:** Brick & Stone
RLSNE: 31-32, 35-45   **Current Use:** Transit

The first regular train service from Boston to Athol commenced on January 1, 1848, with service from Athol to Brattleboro and Greenfield starting in 1849 and 1850 respectively. The station at that time was a wooden clapboard-sided structure with arched windows and a cross-gabled roof. It was built by the Vermont & Massachusetts RR in 1847 and served as the station until 1872, when it was moved to the south side of the tracks to make room for its successor. The old depot was used for commercial purposes for many years but was destroyed by fire in 1935.

The second station, designed by H. M. Francis, was a spacious Second Empire structure, which was built 1872-73 by the V&M at a cost of nearly $30,000. The two-story building was made of brick with stone trim and had a mansard slate roof with a three-story, four-sided clock tower in the center and four smaller corner towers. The second story was intended to serve as the V&M's general offices, but before the station was completed the Fitchburg had absorbed the V&M. The Fitchburg, which had its offices in the much larger Fitchburg Station, decided to turn the Athol Station's second story into a restaurant. In the days before dining cars, most trains scheduled a twenty-minute refreshment stop at Athol. As traffic increased, a sizeable kitchen (made of wood) was attached to the corner of the depot. Unfortunately, on July 22, 1892, an accident in the kitchen started a devastating fire which destroyed the station's entire second story and all five of its decorative towers.

A temporary station was set up in an old passenger car, the restaurant moved to Greenfield, and work began immediately to rebuild the station. The Fitchburg engaged architect Alden Frink to redesign the station into its present form. The now single-story, hip-roofed structure with a narrow clock tower is similar to other Fitchburg stations surviving at Concord, MA, and Milford, NH. At the peak of service in 1919, twenty-four trains a day stopped at this station. A decline in passenger service led to the station being closed in 1959. It has since been used as a post office annex, warehouse, shoe factory, youth center, and night club. Community Transit Services bought it in January 2001. Today it is home to the region's Dial-A-Ride service.

Attleboro Station, Eastbound   *1 Mill St.*

Built: 1906   **Current RR:** AMTK, CSXT, MBTA   **Material:** Brick
RLSNE: 27-32, 27C-0, 77A-9   **Current Use:** Railroad/Commercial/Transit

In 1891 Attleboro petitioned the New York, New Haven & Hartford RR to eliminate a number of dangerous grade crossings in the downtown area. Construction was delayed, and it wasn't until 1905 that the railroad began the massive project, which eliminated thirteen grade crossings and included the construction of four granite arch bridges and two new stations. This station, which was designed by the railroad's own staff, was built in 1906 as part of this project. It replaced an earlier Boston & Providence RR station, an ornate Victorian Gothic brick structure with multiple towers and gables, that was located at grade north of Mill Street.

The Greater Attleboro-Taunton Regional Transit Authority (GATRTA) and Tony's Whistle Stop, a shop that caters to commuters, occupy this old depot. The Romanesque-style station with its terra cotta roof was added to the National Register of Historic Places in 1989.

Attleboro Station, Westbound   3 Mill St.

Built: 1908   **Current RR:** AMTK, CSXT, MBTA   **Material:** Brick & Granite
RLSNE: 27-32, 27C-0, 77A-9   **Current Use:** Commercial

This was the second of two new stations designed and built by the New York, New Haven & Hartford RR as part of a 1905-08 grade elimination project. This two-story structure is larger than its cross-track counterpart, and it featured an express office with a freight elevator. It was erected on the site of the old grade-level freight house, which was relocated south of South Main Street but is no longer extant.

Amtrak does not stop in Attleboro, and MBTA Boston commuters use a platform just south of here to disembark from their trains. The Romanesque-style station, currently used for office and retail space, was added to the National Register of Historic Places in 1989.

Attleboro Freight House   65 South Main St.

Built: Between 1834 & 1888   **Current RR:** AMTK, CSXT, MBTA
Material: Wood   **RLSNE:** 27-32, 27C-0, 77A-9   **Current Use:** Commercial

Attleboro once had two freight houses to serve the many local but off-rail industries. This freight house was once served by tracks from an extensive yard located where the MBTA commuter parking lot is now. The other Attleboro Freight House was located just south of this one, having been moved here as part of the 1905-08 grade elimination project (see Attleboro Westbound Station). That freight house, a large single-story frame structure with a gabled-hip roof, is no longer extant. The surviving freight house is now home to Attleboro's Old Barn, a feed store.

Auburn Combination Depot
20 Auburn St.

Built: Ca. 1839-40 **Current RR:** PW **Material:** Wood
RLSNE: 15-66 **Current Use:** Commercial

The Norwich & Worcester RR built this combination depot ca. 1839-40, shortly after the line was completed to Worcester. The New York, New Haven & Hartford RR discontinued passenger service on the Norwich & Worcester Branch in 1946, but restored it six years later. Passenger service at Auburn ended for good, however, in the fall of 1964, and by 1971 all service on the line was discontinued. Similarly, less-than-carload freight service was transferred to Worcester ca. 1964-65. The freight dock, added to the south end of the building in the 1920s, continued to be used at a decreasing rate for carload freight service.

By 1975 the vacant station had become an eyesore, and the town wanted it taken down. That same year the proprietors of the Wooden Apple, a maker of carved wooden signs, leased the building from the Providence & Worcester RR. The following year they purchased it and began restoring it. Since the Wooden Apple moved out in the early 1990s, the station has been home to several businesses, including a musical instrument dealer and the current occupant, Golden Pizza.

Avon Station
271 East High St.

Built: Between 1865 & 1875 **Current RR:** CSXT, MBTA **Material:** Granite
RLSNE: 78-6 **Current Use:** Commercial/Residential

This station was originally called East Stoughton, but the name was changed to Avon in 1888 when the village of East Stoughton seceded from Stoughton to form the town of Avon. The station was erected around the same time as its twin, the Quincy Adams Station (built 1869 but no longer extant). Constructed of granite, it replaced an earlier wooden structure. It has received additions and is currently occupied by Cycle Performance Auto Body with apartments upstairs.

Back Bay Station

145 Dartmouth St., Boston

Built: 1986-87   **Current RR:** AMTK, CSXT, MBTA   **Material:** Concrete & Brick
RLSNE: 27-1   **Current Use:** Railroad/Transit/Commercial

The original Back Bay Station was built ca. 1901. Part of the South Station project, it was also designed by the prestigious firm of Sheply, Rutan, and Coolidge. The New Haven RR's Boston & Providence trains used to terminate nearby at the Park Square Station, located north of the Boston & Albany RR's tracks. This short section of track and the station were abandoned when the New Haven opened the station in Back Bay. Back Bay Station burned in 1928 and was replaced by a second in 1929. The B&A trains used two of their own stations, Trinity Place (westbound) and Huntington Avenue (eastbound), until 1964, when they were demolished. At that time the New Haven RR cut a hole in the north wall of Back Bay for the B&A passengers. The 1929 station was demolished and the current station was completed in 1987. Some of the decorative concrete trim from the 1929 station was reused on the new station. Most notable is the large rectangular concrete station sign which reads "N.Y.N.H.&H.R.R. BACK BAY STATION," considering that railroad ceased to exist as of January 1, 1969. Today the station serves Amtrak, MBTA commuter trains, and the MBTA Orange Line subway.

Ballardvale Station   *174-176 Andover St.*

Built: 1849   **Current RR:** AMTK, GRS, MBTA   **Material:** Wood
RLSNE: 52-20.5   **Current Use:** Residential

The Boston & Maine RR built this large two-story Italianate frame station in 1849, when the main line was relocated; the original 1836 alignment of the Andover & Wilmington RR was located one-half mile east of here (see Andover Station). The station was formerly located at the north side of the Andover Street grade crossing. In 1950 it was turned ninety degrees, moved 150 feet, and converted to a residence. At the time of the move, the small baggage room extension (added ca. 1893) was detached and used for the waiting room. Ballardvale is still an MBTA stop; however, patrons are only provided a mini-high platform.

Barrowsville Depot   *205 South Worcester St.*

Built: 1880   **Current RR:** CSXT   **Material:** Wood
RLSNE: 77A-5   **Current Use:** Residential

RON KARR

This small gable-roofed depot was built by the Old Colony RR in 1880. It has been moved south and turned ninety degrees. With some minor alterations, it serves today as a private residence.

Bedford Depot   *South Rd. near Loomis St.*

Built: Ca. 1874   **Current RR:** None   **Material:** Wood
RLSNE: 49-0, 49A-0   **Current Use:** Commercial

The Victorian-style Bedford Depot was built ca. 1874 by the Boston & Lowell RR. It is located in between what was the junction of the Billerica & Bedford and the Lexington & Arlington RRs. Passenger service to Bedford ended on January 10, 1977, when a large snowstorm stranded the rail diesel car at the depot. The MBTA officially suspended all service on the Lexington Branch several days later.

The town purchased the depot and the nearby freight house in 1999 for eventual inclusion in the Bedford Depot Park. The park was recently added to the National Register of Historic Places. The station, which received a new second story in the 1960s, is currently occupied by James F. Sullivan, Jr., a plumbing and heating contractor.

Bedford Engine House/Freight House   *120 South Rd.*

Built: 1877   **Current RR:** None   **Material:** Wood
RLSNE: 49-0, 49A-0   **Current Use:** Museum

This former Boston & Maine RR freight house began life in 1877 as the engine house for the two-foot-gauge Billerica & Bedford RR. The unsuccessful narrow gauge line was abandoned the following year, making a short career for the engine house. It was eventually converted to a freight house.

The building was purchased by the town in 1999 for inclusion in the Bedford Depot Park. It was occupied by Friends of Bedford Depot Park, who used it for a museum building until early 2006, when it was closed for a $350,000 renovation. The Minuteman Bikeway, one of the most popular and successful rail-trails in the United States, terminates alongside this historic structure. The Bedford Depot Park has recently been added to the National Register of Historic Places.

Belmont Depot   *Common St. near Concord Ave.*

Built: 1840s   **Current RR:** GRS, MBTA   **Material:** Wood
RLSNE: 34-2, 42-6   **Current Use:** Historical Society

Originally called Wellington Hill, the Fitchburg RR added this stop ca. 1852-55. This unique octagon-shaped structure, which was built in the early 1840s as part of a private school, was moved here to serve as the depot. Around 1879 the Fitchburg RR replaced it with a new two-story wooden station. The old depot was then moved to the grounds of the nearby Underwood Estate, where it was used as a summer house and art studio. In 1975 it was given to the Belmont Historical Society, and it was moved to its current location in 1980.

Belmont Station   *1 Common St.*

Built: Ca. 1908   **Current RR:** GRS, MBTA   **Material:** Fieldstone
RLSNE: 34-2, 42-6   **Current Use:** Community/Railroad

The Boston & Maine RR built this unique Bungalow-style station ca. 1908 as part of the Concord Avenue grade crossing elimination project. Constructed of 365 tons of fieldstone dug and hauled from Belmont Hill by a local farmer, it replaced an earlier two-story framed station built around 1879.

Passenger service was terminated by the Boston & Maine RR in 1958 and then reinstated in 1974 by the MBTA. The station was added to the National Register of Historic Places in 1998. It is owned today by the Belmont Lions Club, which convinced the railroad to sell them the station instead of demolishing it. MBTA patrons can still catch a train here, but only the platforms are open to the public.

Beverly Station   *10 Park St.*

Built: Ca. 1896-97   **Current RR:** GRS, MBTA   **Material:** Yellow Brick & Brownstone   **RLSNE:** 58-18   **Current Use:** Commercial

The first depot in Beverly was built by the Eastern RR in 1839 and located opposite the Essex Bridge. That depot was replaced around 1855 by a second larger wooden depot with a Quonset-style train shed. The train shed was torn down to make room for construction of the current station on the opposite side of the tracks. The old station was closed ca. 1897, when the new one opened. The Boston & Maine RR commissioned architect Bradford Lee Gilbert to design Beverly's third station. Gilbert, who became famous for his work enlarging New York's first Grand Central Terminal and the Illinois Central's Chicago station, had already designed the B&M stations at Concord, Laconia, and Amoskeag, NH. The station is constructed of yellow brick and trimmed in brownstone, with the baggage room of red brick. The waiting room included a fireplace and a marble fountain.

The ticket office was closed in 1965, and the station was later sold. On February 15, 1971, it was damaged by fire. The building was soon renovated, and on December 2, the new Beverly Depot Restaurant and Saloon opened and today continues to be a popular restaurant. An identical station was built ten years later at Andover.

Beverly Farms Depot   *3 Oak St.*

Built: Ca. 1897-98   **Current RR:** GRS, MBTA   **Material:** Wood   **RLSNE:** 59-4.5   **Current Use:** Commercial

Then called West's Beach, the original station was located about one-half mile east of here near the intersection of Hale and West Streets. This was a flag stop established by David A. Neal, then president of the Eastern RR, to serve his seaside residence. By 1852 the Eastern

had erected a new depot, located on Oak Street, which featured a hip roof with flared eaves.

The Boston & Maine RR erected the present hip-roofed station in 1897-98, replacing the much smaller Eastern predecessor. In 1952 the station agency was discontinued and the freight house closed. The unused freight house, formerly located just east of the depot, was demolished the following year. The station building was sold in 1958 and remodeled into a retail store.

Today, the station's trackside windows have all been covered and shingled over, and the canopy has been shortened to about twenty percent of its original length. In recent years the building has been home to various commercial enterprises and is now occupied by Coast, a retail store, and by Townsend Oil Company.

Bradford Depot   *Railroad Ave.*

Built: Ca. 1870s   **Current RR:** AMTK, GRS, MBTA   **Material:** Wood
RLSNE: 52-32.5   **Current Use:** Commercial

The Andover & Haverhill RR came to town in 1837 as an extension of the Andover & Wilmington RR. Bradford was the terminal until several years later, when the Merrimac River Bridge was completed. This station was likely built as part of a curve reduction and double-tracking project undertaken by the Boston & Maine RR in the 1870s. The depot, which once had a central cupola, is similar to stations that survive in Danvers East, Amesbury, and Swampscott. The railroad sold the building in the 1960s, and it has served as a laundromat ever since. Today it is home to Bradford Depot Laundromat and Dry Cleaning. The trackside windows have been shingled over.

Bridgewater Station   *115 Broad St.*

Built: 1894   **Current RR:** CSXT, MBTA   **Material:** Granite & Brownstone
RLSNE: 78-16   **Current Use:** Commercial

The Romanesque-style Bridgewater Station was designed by noted architect Bradford Lee Gilbert and built in 1894 by the New York, New Haven & Hartford RR. Built of rough-faced Milford granite and brownstone, the structure was one of many such stations on the former Old Colony RR, in-

Well-known architect Bradford Lee Gilbert designed some twenty railroad stations in Massachusetts, New Hampshire, and New York, of which at least thirteen survive. The station in Bridgewater, with its stone construction, large overhanging roof, and prominent dormers, is a typical example. Other survivors in Massachusetts are Andover, Beverly, Canton Junction, and North Attleboro Stations.

cluding North Easton, Stoughton, North Abington, Brockton, Dedham, and Fall River, of which only the first three survive.

This is at least the third station to serve Bridgewater; it replaced a wooden hip-roofed station with slightly flared eaves. That structure was located between the current station and Broad Street; the new one was erected before the old one was removed. The freight house, a small wooden gable-roofed structure, was located across the tracks from the old station.

The Gilbert station is now home to a Burger King restaurant, and the former carriage port is used to serve drive-thru customers. Its interior has been preserved, including a tile fireplace and beautiful wood ceilings. It is decorated with old railroad photos and is worthy of a visit.

When the Old Colony commuter service was restored in 1997, none of the old stations were used. The MBTA's new Bridgewater Station is located a half mile south on the campus of Bridgewater State College. Today's passengers are afforded only a high-level platform and canopy.

Buzzards Bay Station   *70 Main St.*

Built: 1912   **Current RR:** BCLR, CCCR   **Material:** Stucco & Brick
RLSNE: 80-20, 80B-0   **Current Use:** Community

Originally called Cohasset Narrows, the station here was renamed Buzzards Bay on August 1, 1879. This station, completed in 1912, replaced an earlier hip-roofed one that was built in 1870. The construction of the original Cape Cod Canal between 1909 and 1914 required the New York, New Haven & Hartford RR to relocate its main line between Buzzards Bay and Sagamore as well as a small portion of the Woods Hole Branch east of Buzzards Bay. This Spanish-style station was erected on the new alignment. Similar stations were built at Sagamore, Pocasset, and West Barnstable, the latter still extant. The west end of the curved canopy was shortened in the 1970s to make room for Academy Drive, which now passes just west of the station. Today the building is occupied by the Cape Cod Canal Region Chamber of Commerce.

In the first quarter of the twentieth century, the New York, New Haven & Hartford RR built a number of stations in the Spanish Mission style, which featured stucco exteriors and red tile roofs, some with large overhangs supported by columns. The station at Buzzards Bay is a fine example of this style, as are the more elaborate stations in Westerly, RI. Other examples of the Spanish style survive in Cataumet, Nantasket, North Scituate, Southbridge, and West Barnstable, MA.

Canton Junction Station   *Sherman St.*

Built: 1892-93   **Current RR:** AMTK, CSXT, MBTA   **Material:** Granite &
Brownstone   **RLSNE:** 27-15, 27B-0   **Current Use:** Railroad

RON KARR

The original station at Canton (Canton Junction after 1879) was a flat-roofed Italianate structure with a cupola built ca. 1834 by the Boston & Providence RR. By 1845 the Stoughton Branch RR was opened, and Canton was served by two railroads. The current station was built by the Old Colony RR and was opened by the New York, New Haven & Hartford RR on April 19, 1893, a little over a month after they leased the Old Colony. The original depot was torn down.

The station was designed by Bradford Lee Gilbert, a prominent New York City architect best known for his remodeling of the old Grand Central Terminal. It is one of five Gilbert-designed stations still surviving in Massachusetts; the other four are Andover, North Abington, Beverly, and Bridgewater. Built at a cost of $12,000, it features local Milford granite with a rough face and is trimmed with brownstone.

On April 10, 2000, the station was reopened after being moved sixty-five feet south and forty feet back from the main line. This was done to permit Stoughton Branch trains to stop here without fouling the high-speed main line. The station is located just north of the famous Canton Viaduct. Built in 1834-35, the multi-arch granite viaduct is 615 feet across and 70 feet above the water.

Cataumet Depot   *Scraggy Neck Rd.*

Built: 1926   **Current RR:** BCLR   **Material:** Stucco & Brick
RLSNE: 80B-6   **Current Use:** Community

Cataumet didn't get a station until eighteen years after the line to Woods Hole opened. The first depot, a Victorian-style frame structure, was destroyed by fire in 1925. This Spanish-style station was built in 1926 to replace the original. It is the smallest of many Spanish-style stations erected by the New York, New Haven & Hartford RR. It is now home to the Cataumet Civic Association.

Chatham Depot   *153 Depot Rd.*

Built: 1887   **Current RR:** None   **Material:** Wood
RLSNE: 80D-7   **Current Use:** Museum

The charming Queen Anne depot at Chatham has a unique tower with a candle snuffer roof. Built in 1887 by the Chatham RR, it is nearly identical to the Crescent Beach Station, which was built in 1875 for the Boston, Revere Beach & Lynn narrow gauge RR. That station was demolished in the early 1940s.

After service to Chatham ended, the station was neglected for decades. In 1951 it was bought by a private party and turned over to the town for a museum. The station was restored in 1960 and opened to the public as the Chatham Railroad Museum. The museum is open Tuesdays through Saturdays from June to October. Admission is free but donations are welcome. Chatham's depot has been listed on the National Register of Historic Places since 1978.

Chatham Freight House   *347 Stage Harbor Rd.*

Built: 1887   **Current RR:** None   **Material:** Wood
RLSNE: 80D-7   **Current Use:** Historical Society/Museum

The Chatham Freight House was built in 1887 by the Chatham RR and was located about thirty feet west of the station, on the same side of the tracks. The plain gable-roofed structure once sported a decorative cupola. Passenger service on the branch ended in 1931, with the final suspension of all service in 1937. Unused for years, the freight house was finally purchased at auction and moved to the home of artist Alice Stallknecht Wight during the Second World War. The artist's murals and the freight house were moved to the Chatham Historical Society's Old Atwood House Museum in 1977. The museum is open to the public from June through September.

Cheshire Depot   *Railroad St.*

Built: Ca. 1845-46   **Current RR:** None   **Material:** Wood
RLSNE: 30-8   **Current Use:** Commercial

Built around 1845-46, this former Western RR station is similar to surviving combination depots at Hinsdale and Chester. Today it is home to Chic's Auto and Repair. The Ashuwillticook Rail Trail runs within a few feet of the old depot, this section having been completed and opened in the fall of 2003.

Cheshire Freight House   *2 Railroad St.*

Built: Ca. 1845-46   **Current RR:** None   **Material:** Wood
RLSNE: 30-8   **Current Use:** Residential

This former Western RR freight house is similar to one surviving at Maple Grove. It has been modified for use as apartments.

Chester Combination Depot   *10 Prospect St.*

Built: 1841   **Current RR:** AMTK, CSXT   **Material:** Wood
RLSNE: 29-82, 29E-0   **Current Use:** Museum/Historical Society

This former Western RR combination depot was built in 1841. After passenger service ended in 1955, the station was used as a base for maintenance-of-way service. In 1987, when then owner Conrail announced its intention to raze the structure, the Chester Historical Commission and other concerned citizens rallied to preserve it. Two years later the Chester Foundation was formed and moved the building across the tracks and 100 feet south to its present location. The former street side faces the tracks. The depot has been beautifully restored and is now home to a railroad and local history museum, open weekends during the summer months. Since 1991 the foundation has sponsored annual Chester on Track, a day-long celebration of local railroad history held each May. A similar station survives nearby at Hinsdale.

Chestnut Street [North Attleboro] Depot   *197 Chestnut St.*

Built: Between 1815 & 1830   **Current RR:** None   **Material:** Wood
RLSNE: 27C-4   **Current Use:** Residential

In 1871 the Boston & Providence RR converted this residence into the Chestnut Street Station. Although not originally built as a railroad station, this structure is the only one of three intermediate stations on the five-mile Attleboro Branch that survives today. Railroad passenger service ended in 1903, but the line was converted to trolleys at that time. After the end of service, the residence-turned-station resumed service as a residence, the same purpose it continues to serve today.

Cliftondale Depot   *Eustis St.*

Built: 1853   **Current RR:** None   **Material:** Wood
RLSNE: 60-5.5   **Current Use:** Commercial

Just under ten miles long, the Saugus Branch once had fifteen stations. Today only two survive: Cliftondale and Saugus. This pre-Civil War era railroad structure was built by the Saugus Branch RR when the line opened in 1853. Although several different styles were used on the branch, Cliftondale, Saugus, East Saugus, and the recently demolished Maplewood were nearly identical. Each featured arched windows and a hip roof with ornate brackets.

Clinton Station 626 Main St.

Built: 1914-15   **Current RR:** CSXT, GRS   **Material:** Brick & Marble
RLSNE: 41-17, 65-23   **Current Use:** Commercial

RON KARR

In 1913 the New York, New Haven & Hartford RR started construction of a court-mandated elimination of four highway grade crossings and the railroad grade crossing of the Boston & Maine RR in Clinton. Construction of Union Station began in 1914, and the station was opened January 1, 1915. Built to serve the B&M and the NYNH&H, this L-shaped two-level structure served the B&M on the lower level, and via a grand staircase, it served the NYNH&H on the upper level. It is constructed of brick and marble with Spanish-style terra cotta tiles on its roof. The predecessor station, a single-level wooden structure, was demolished to make room for the new station.

The NYNH&H ended passenger service in 1931, followed three years later by the B&M; however, the B&M maintained a freight office here until about 1980. The station is currently occupied by Regonini A. Memorials in the former B&M baggage room and Clinton Speed Wash Laundry on the east end. The center section is being renovated for use by an interior design firm, but was previously occupied by Scooby Doo's Sports Bar.

Cohasset Station 107-119 Ripley Rd.

Built: Ca. 1885   **Current RR:** None   **Material:** Brick & Wood
RLSNE: 74-11   **Current Use:** Commercial/Community

The original Cohasset Station, which opened when the line was built in 1849, was destroyed by fire on Thanksgiving night in 1857. It was a very large two-story structure that included a train shed and the South Shore RR headquarters. It was replaced by a second station, which lasted until 1885, when the current Tudor-style station was built by the Old Colony RR to replace it. This station is similar to ones erected at North Attleboro, Middleboro, Southboro, Chelmsford, and Kingston, of which only the latter survives today.

Until the line was extended to South Duxbury in 1871, and three years later to Kingston, Cohasset was the terminus of the line. A freight house was located directly across the tracks from the station, and a four-stall engine house south of it.

Passenger service on this line ended in June 1959, but construction has recently begun to restore passenger service to Greenbush via Cohasset. Unfortunately, the station will be located off of Route 3A and not downtown. Today various commercial and retail tenants, including Bernard's restaurant and the South Shore Arts Center, occupy the enlarged station.

Concord Station   80-86 Thoreau St.

Built: Early 1890s   **Current RR:** GRS, MBTA   **Material:** Wood
RLSNE: 42-20   **Current Use:** Commercial

RON KARR

This large Queen Anne-style station was built in the early 1890s. It replaced the original wooden structure, which was built ca. 1844. The main building was rebuilt in 1895, when a fire severely damaged that section.

Like most large Fitchburg RR stations, this hip-roofed building included a square clock tower. What appears to be a large dormer on the trackside of the station is actually a former control tower. The windows have all been replaced with new styles.

Today this station is home to the Concord Depot Shops. The building's side wings have been completely rebuilt. The trackside doors and windows were closed off, and by 1985 a mural, which depicts a transition from country to city life, was completed. Until 1991 a freight house, similar to the one existing at Methuen, was located east of the station and across the tracks. The express office still survives just west of the station.

While some stations have retained their original appearance over many decades, others have been altered almost beyond recognition. This view shows Concord Station as it looked ca. 1890 prior to the adition of a trackside control tower and long before the additions, alterations, and boarding up of windows that resulted in today's Concord Depot Shops. (Courtesy of the Beverly Historical Society & Museum, Beverly, MA, Walker Transportation Collection)

Concord Express Office 68 Thoreau S

Built: Ca. 1907 **Current RR:** GRS, MBTA **Material:** Wood
RLSNE: 42-20 **Current Use:** Commercial

A baggage or express office was an integral part of most railroad stations, but in some cases business warranted a separate structure. To meet increasing demands, the Boston & Maine RR constructed this building ca. 1907 to house the Railway Express office. This Queen Anne-style structure, which sits just west of the station, is now home to Bedford Farms Ice Cream.

Conomo Depot
17 Southern Ave., Essex

Built: Ca. 1887   **Current RR:** None   **Material:** Wood
RLSNE: 58F-6   **Current Use:** Residential

The Conomo Depot was built by the Boston & Maine RR ca. 1887, when a half-mile extension from Essex was completed. Passenger service to Conomo began in September 1887. Today the simple station, which features a gabled-hip roof, is well cared for and serves as a private residence.

Dalton Station
450 Housatonic St.

Built: 1888   **Current RR:** AMTK, CSXT   **Material:** Granite & Brownstone
RLSNE: 29-101   **Current Use:** Commercial

The Boston & Albany RR commissioned Sheply, Rutan and Coolidge to design this station. It was built by the Norcross Brothers between April and December 1888 at a cost of $11,203. It replaced an earlier frame depot similar to the one surviving at Hinsdale. This attractive station, which features hooded end dormers, is now home to Ozzie's Steak & Seafood Restaurant.

Dalton Freight House
Housatonic St.

Built: 1840s   **Current RR:** AMTK, CSXT   **Material:** Brick
RLSNE: 29-101   **Current Use:** Commercial

In Dalton the railroad is located high on the side of the hill, while the industries are located below, near the Housatonic River. The river provided water power for the mills, but because of the topography, local industries were not directly served by rail, making the Dalton Freight House a busy place. The old freight station is one of only four extant standard Boston & Albany red brick freight houses; the other survivors are Warren, West Brookfield, and West Springfield. It is used by the Crane Paper Company, which has several mills in the Dalton and Pittsfield area. Crane manufactures the specialty paper used for our U.S. currency.

Danvers [Newburyport RR] Freight House   6 Hobart St.

Built: Between 1854 & 1875   **Current RR:** None   **Material:** Wood
RLSNE: 54-9.5   **Current Use:** Commercial

The Danvers Freight House is looking great, having recently been painted in its former Boston & Maine RR cream and maroon colors. Today the building is used for commercial purposes. The former Newburyport RR Danvers Station was located east of the freight house at the corner of Hobart and Maple Streets, between Hobart Street and the tracks.

Danvers East Depot   27 Cherry St.

Built: 1868   **Current RR:** None   **Material:** Wood
RLSNE: 57-5   **Current Use:** Commercial

In 1899 there were nine railroad stations located within the town limits of Danvers. Today there is only one remaining, the surviving Tapleyville Passenger Shelter having been moved to Maine (see Tapleyville Passenger Shelter). When erected by the Eastern RR in 1868, this depot was located 1000 feet from here at the junction of Elm and Essex Streets. It replaced an earlier wooden structure. The contractor was Charles Nathan Ingalls, who also built the Swampscott and Chelsea stations for the Eastern RR and the Danvers National Bank.

The depot was moved to its current location by the Boston & Maine RR in 1923 to serve the junction of the Essex and Newburyport lines. Passenger service ended ca. 1958, and the station was later sold to the Bursaw

Oil Company, who used it for a maintenance shed. In 2002 the Townsend Oil Company acquired the station. The new owner has agreed to donate the building to Danvers Preservation, Inc., provided that a viable plan for relocating and restoring the building can be developed. A similar station once existed in Peabody.

Dean Street [Taunton] Station   40 Dean St. (Rte. 44)

Built: 1876   **Current RR:** BCLR   **Material:** Brick
RLSNE: 76-22   **Current Use:** Commercial

Originally known as Taunton, the name of this station was changed to Dean Street in 1865, when the new Taunton Central Station opened. This decorative station was built by the Old Colony RR in 1876, replacing an earlier structure. The renovated Italianate station is currently occupied by a real estate agency. The structure was placed on the National Register of Historic Places in 1984. It has received a matching single-story brick addition on the south end.

Dover Combination Depot   14 Dedham St.

Built: Ca. 1861   **Current RR:** BCLR   **Material:** Wood
RLSNE: 66-13   **Current Use:** Commercial

The Boston & New York RR likely built the Dover Combination Depot in 1861, when it extended its line from Needham to Medway. The small station was enlarged after World War I with the addition of an ell. After serving for many years as the Dover Country Store, the old combination depot is now home to a realtor and an antique shop.

East Boxford Station   *129 Depot Rd.*

Built: 1853   **Current RR:** None   **Material:** Wood
RLSNE: 54-18   **Current Use:** Residential

This two-story station seems over-sized when one considers the tiny East Boxford community it served. When the Newburyport RR built this depot in 1853, it came complete with living quarters for the stationmaster and his family. Passenger service ended December 13, 1941. For a period of time the building housed the local post office. It has been moved back from the tracks and now serves as a private residence.

East Boxford Freight House   *Depot Rd. near Pond St.*

Built: Ca. 1850   **Current RR:** None   **Material:** Wood
RLSNE: 54-18   **Current Use:** Commercial

This former Boston & Maine RR freight house is currently used for storage by the Charles M. Rollins Company, a water well drilling contractor. The narrow gable-roofed structure was likely built by the Newburyport RR ca. 1850.

East Brewster Depot   *Garder Rd. (off Ellis Landing St.)*

Built: Ca. 1889   **Current RR:** N/A   **Material:** Wood
RLSNE: 80-58   **Current Use:** Residential

After passenger service ended in 1938, the New York, New Haven & Hartford RR sold this station to an individual who moved it to a location near Ellis Landing and converted it to a summer cottage. The station was formerly located about one-and-a-quarter miles east of here, on Main Street

(Route 6A). Although modifications to both structures make it difficult to tell, this station and the one surviving in East Sandwich were built to a common Old Colony RR design. The depot, which is difficult to find, is located on a narrow dirt lane off Ellis Landing Road, on the left just before the sign for the Ellis Landing Cottages.

East Brookfield Station
Depot Sq.

Built: 1893-94   **Current RR:** AMTK, CSXT   **Material:** Granite & Brownstone
RLSNE: 29-20, 29D-0   **Current Use:** Railroad

The Norcross Brothers started construction of this station in 1893 and finished it in May 1894 at a cost of $9,778. It was one of many H. H. Richardson-inspired Romanesque-style depots designed by Shepley, Rutan and Coolidge for the Boston & Albany RR. A standard B&A freight house once stood directly across the tracks from the station. The depot now serves as a base for the CSX Transportation signal department. East Brookfield was once the junction of the North Brookfield Branch. This four-mile branch only had two stations, both of which survive today.

East Holliston Depot
100 Washington St.

Built: Between 1848 & 1879   **Current RR:** None   **Material:** Wood
RLSNE: 64E-4   **Current Use:** Residential

RON KARR

This former Boston & Albany RR depot was likely the original station to serve East Holliston. The depot, which served as the local post office as late as 1952, has been turned forty-five degrees and is now a private residence. Passenger service here ended in 1959. Plans are well underway to build the 27-mile Upper Charles Trail, a proposed rail-trail through Framingham, Sherborn, Holliston, Milford, Hopkinton, and Ashland, part of which will go right past this depot.

East Longmeadow Combination Depot   *64 Maple St.*

Built: Ca. 1876   **Current RR:** None   **Material:** Wood
RLSNE: 18-22   **Current Use:** Commercial

This ca. 1876 combination depot is the last surviving station on the Connecticut Central RR between East Hartford and Springfield. Similar stations existed at East Windsor, East Windsor Hill, Melrose, and Hazardville. Closed in 1950, the depot was sold to A. T. Rintoul, the owner of Community Feed Stores. Although the rails have been removed, the well-preserved depot continues to be used for storage by the same feed store.

East Lynn Station   *3 Depot Rd., Durham, NH*

Built: 1896   **Current RR:** AMTK, GRS   **Material:** Brick & Stone
RLSNE: 58-12   **Current Use:** Railroad/Commercial

MATT COSGRO

This Victorian-style station was built in 1896 by the Boston & Maine RR. It was originally located at Chatham Street in East Lynn, MA. In preparation for a grade crossing elimination in Lynn, the former East Lynn, MA, station was dismantled brick by brick and moved to Durham, NH, in 1912. It was reassembled on a stone base and enlarged. The replacement station in East Lynn was a small wooden gable-roofed structure with a passenger awning.

In 1911 the B&M relocated and double tracked several miles of right of way to the west of the present University of New Hampshire campus in Durham. This was done to ease a single-track bottleneck. The B&M—smartly—reused the East Lynn Station to replace the original Durham Station, which was located on Main Street near the junction of Edgewood Road. That depot was a simple wooden structure with a large overhanging gable roof.

The station was purchased in 1964 by the university and became the home of UNH's Dairy Bar, a training facility for restaurant management students. The B&M had discontinued passenger service at Durham by

1967, but Amtrak restored it in December 2001. While still used by UNH, the station underwent a complete restoration, including rebuilt canopies and a new mini-high platform for Amtrak's *Downeaster* service. Passenger service at East Lynn continued for many years, but the replacement station no longer exists, and today the MBTA does not stop there.

East Sandwich Depot   *Main St. (Rte. 6A)*

Built: 1889   **Current RR:** BCLR, CCCR   **Material:** Wood
RLSNE: 80-31   **Current Use:** Residential

This former Old Colony RR station was the second to serve East Sandwich. Built in 1889, it replaced the original station, which was moved some 300 feet west and converted to a freight house. After the second station was closed, a railroad employee purchased it, moved it across the tracks, and turned it 90 degrees. It now resides just east of the railroad crossing between the tracks and Main Street (Route 6A). Although several large ells were added, the distinctive eight-panel window still remains. Similar stations were built at East Brewster and Crystal Springs, MA (see East Brewster).

East Walpole Freight House   *3 East St.*

Built: Between 1890 & 1898   **Current RR:** None   **Material:** Wood
RLSNE: 69-2   **Current Use:** Commercial

In addition to being called East Walpole, this station was also named Bird Mills after the former cotton mill and later paper mill that operated here. The mill's owner, Frank W. Bird, who despised the waste of taxpayers' money, was instrumental in controlling the cost of completing the state-owned Hoosac Tunnel. The interesting wooden tower located across the street from the freight house is all that remains of the ca. 1884 Bird Hall (tower added 1894), a company-sponsored recreation hall. Even the mill itself, which comprised some twenty-two buildings and was located south of the freight house, has been replaced by a new condominium complex. The station, located in the triangle formed by Washington, Union, and Chestnut Streets, where the Sharon Credit Union is now, was a large hip-roofed structure. Today this former New York, New Haven & Hartford RR freight house is home to Impact Engineering, an auto body shop.

Easthampton Station — *1 Railroad St.*

Built: 1914   **Current RR:** None   **Material:** Brick
RLSNE: 7-72, 33B-3   **Current Use:** Community

The Hampden RR reached Easthampton first in 1856 as part of a through route from New Haven, CT, to Northampton, MA. In 1872, the Mount Tom & Easthampton RR opened a short three-mile line from a connection with the Connecticut River RR at Mount Tom. Each railroad maintained its own station until 1914, when the present union station was built on the site of the former New Haven & Northampton RR station. The original NH&N freight house was located south of the station on Railroad Avenue. The former Mount Tom RR station and freight house were located north of Union Street between Liberty Street and the right of way. A large union freight house, similar to others built by the New York, New Haven & Hartford RR at Franklin Junction and Lee, was also erected on the site of the Mount Tom station and freight house. That freight house survived at least into the late 1960s, but is no longer extant.

Today the Easthampton Station is owned by the Williston Northampton School and serves as an artist studio/gallery. The rails have been pulled up, and since June 2004 the right of way from Easthampton to Mount Tom serves the public as the Manhan Rail Trail.

Erving Depot
3 East Main St. (Rte. 2)

Built: 1898 **Current RR:** GRS **Material:** Wood
RLSNE: 31-41 **Current Use:** Commercial

RON KARR

This former Boston & Maine RR depot was last used for passenger service in 1959. The Fitchburg RR built it in 1898 to replace an earlier wooden station. The depot had long been the home of the Whistle Stop restaurant, but it is currently occupied by the Box Car Restaurant.

Erving Freight House
11 East Main St. (Rte. 2)

Built: Between 1851 & 1875 **Current RR:** GRS **Material:** Wood
RLSNE: 31-41 **Current Use:** Commercial

RON KARR

Dominating this small mill town, the Erving Paper Mill was established in 1909 and is one of the world's largest producers of printed paper napkins. Located just east of the depot, this former Boston & Maine RR freight house is now occupied by Freight House Antiques. From the size of the buildings, it is obvious that the B&M made more money on mill-related freight than on passengers in this town.

Essex Freight House   *Island Rd.*

Built: 1872   **Current RR:** N/A   **Material:** Wood
RLSNE: 58F-5.5   **Current Use:** Commercial

The Essex Freight House was moved from the Essex yard area one and one-half miles north to Island Road, where it is used for storage by Hardy's Hatchery, a chicken farm. The freight house is located about one-half mile down Island Road on the left hand side. It is behind one of the chicken houses, but can be seen from the road.

Falmouth Station   *59 Depot St.*

Built: 1912-13   **Current RR:** None   **Material:** Brick
RLSNE: 80B-14   **Current Use:** Transit

This brick station was completed in 1913 by the New York, New Haven & Hartford RR to replace the original 1872 depot. That old wooden depot, which featured an oversized hip roof, was similar to others built by the Cape Cod RR. It was sold and moved across the tracks in 1912, but today it no longer exists.

The New Haven ended passenger service to Falmouth in 1963; however, the Cape Cod & Hyannis RR temporarily restored summer weekend-only service from 1982-88. The station was renovated in 1989 at a cost of a million dollars, and today it serves the traveling public as a bus station. The very popular Shining Sea Bikeway begins here and ends at the site of the former Woods Hole Depot, which was torn down in 1969. The tracks between here and North Falmouth are out of service.

Farm Hill Depot   *152 Central St., Stoneham*

Built: 1881   **Current RR:** N/A   **Material:** Wood
RLSNE: 51B-1.5   **Current Use:** Residential

The railroad reached the Farm Hill section of Stoneham in 1861. The original depot burned in 1880, and the Boston & Lowell RR built this one the following year. Although largely unchanged, it looks more like a home than a train station, with its New England gambrel roof. The station, originally located where the railroad crossed Central Street, was moved two-tenths of a mile in May 1948 to its present location, where it now serves as a private residence.

Fitchburg Modern Station   *100 Main St.*

Built: 2000   **Current RR:** GRS, MBTA   **Material:** Brick
RLSNE: 31-0, 40-0   **Current Use:** Railroad/Commercial/Transit

Fitchburg's new $1.5 million Montachusett Regional Transit Authority (MART) Intermodal Center was opened on May 15, 2000. Perhaps as a tribute to the Fitchburg Union Station, which was torn down in the fall of 1962, the new terminal came complete with a clock tower. This is at least the fourth station to serve Fitchburg. The nineteenth-century brick union station was replaced by a concrete block structure similar to ones that existed at Dover and Concord, NH, and Lowell and Lynn, MA. The third structure was a typical MBTA three-sided glass passenger

Located on Water Street, Fitchburg's Union Station was an ornate late nineteenth-century building with a five-story clock tower that rose above the downtown neighborhood. It was largely unchanged prior to its demolition in 1962 for highway construction on nearby Main Street. (Courtesy of the Beverly Historical Society & Museum, Beverly, MA, Walker Transportation Collection)

shelter that was demolished when the MART Intermodal Center was completed.

Forest Hills Modern Station   *Washington St. near Hyde Park Ave.*

Built: 1987   **Current RR:** AMTK, CSXT, MBTA   **Material:** Steel & Concrete
RLSNE: 27-5, 27A-0   **Current Use:** Railroad/Transit/Commercial

RON KARR

This station was built in 1987 by the MBTA as part of the Southwest Corridor Project, a 4.7-mile mass transit corridor with a linear park built above it. Cambridge Associates-Robert L. Wilson Associates designed the station, dedicated in May 1987 by then Governor Michael S. Dukakis. The project included the combining of the elevated railway and the former Boston & Providence RR main line in a large concrete channel below street level. During construction, the el continued to serve local commuters, but all local and long distance rail service between South Station and Readville was rerouted via the Dorchester Branch, the tracks having been removed during construction.

This station replaced a pair of large hip-roofed structures built by the New York, New Haven & Hartford as part of their 1896-97 grade-separation project, which raised the entire right of way between here and Boston on a high embankment, which was demolished as part of the Southwest Corridor project. These stations were similar to one that exists at Norwood Central. The old elevated railway terminal was also demolished shortly after the station was opened. Although commuter service was suspended for a period of 33 years from 1940 to 1973, today Forest Hills is served by the Orange Line subway, which terminates here, and by Needham Branch commuter trains and connecting MBTA buses.

Forge Park Modern Station   *1000 West Central St. (Rte. 140), Franklin*

Built: 1989-90   **Current RR:** CSXT, MBTA   **Material:** Brick
RLSNE: 71-2.5   **Current Use:** Railroad/Commercial

This attractive modern brick station is now the terminus of the MBTA's Franklin commuter line. Built in 1989-90 by the MBTA, this station is strategically located to provide easy access from Interstate 495, and it includes much needed parking for commuters. The depot is currently occupied by the Choo-Choo Stop, a coffee shop that sells train tickets and caters to commuters.

Framingham Station   *417 Waverly St.*

Built: 1884-85   **Current RR:** AMTK, CSXT, MBTA   **Material:** Granite & Brownstone   **RLSNE:** 64-21, 64E-0, 65-0, 72-0   **Current Use:** Commercial

RON KARR

Henry Hobson Richardson designed nine stations for the Boston & Albany RR, this being the largest and most expensive at $62,718. It was called South Framingham when Richardson's master builders, Norcross Brothers, built it in 1884-85. It featured a separate baggage room, which survives just east of the station. The pink granite used in the building was quarried nearby, in Milford, MA. Although commonly thought of as only a B&A station, the Old Colony RR also used it.

The predecessor station, which was a large Dutch Colonial-style wooden structure with a steeply-sloped gable roof with flared eaves, was located just west of this station, where the new commuter platform and parking lot are now. That structure, built in 1848, was moved west several feet on rollers and converted to a freight house. It survived at least until the mid 1960s before being torn down.

Although the station was added to the National Register of Historic Places in 1975, the unused and abandoned structure had fallen into severe disrepair, including a partial roof collapse in 1978. Fortunately, the station was restored in 1985 and has served as home for several restaurants over the last two decades. An Indian restaurant currently occupies it.

Framingham Baggage Office/Room   *417 Waverly St.*

Built: 1884-85   **Current RR:** AMTK, CSXT, MBTA   **Material:** Granite & Brownstone   **RLSNE:** 64-21, 64E-0, 65-0, 72-0   **Current Use:** Commercial

RON KARR

Designed by H. H. Richardson, this former baggage room was built of pink granite to match the Framingham Station. Located at the east end of the platform, it now serves as a bank ATM.

Franklin Station   *Depot St.*

Built: 1912   **Current RR:** CSXT, MBTA   **Material:** Stucco & Brick
RLSNE: 67-16   **Current Use:** Railroad/Commercial

RON KARR

Similar to the one at Needham Junction and one that no longer exists at Hanover, this station was built by the New York, New Haven & Hartford RR in 1912. It succeeded a gable-roofed wooden structure built on the same site. A freight house once stood east of the station. When the New York & New England RR completed its connection between Waterbury and Hopewell in 1881, the line was double tracked to Franklin, which, at the time, was the terminus of local passenger service to Boston. Although trains still stop here, and the MBTA has a train layover facility located just east of here, most trains on this line originate or terminate at the Forge Park Station, which is three miles west. The depot is currently occupied by the Choo-Choo Stop, a coffee shop that sells train tickets and caters to commuters.

Franklin Junction Freight House
Union St., Franklin

Built: Ca. 1905-12   **Current RR:** CSXT, MBTA   **Material:** Wood
RLSNE: 67-16.5, 71-0   **Current Use:** Commercial

This former New York, New Haven & Hartford RR freight house was built around the same time as those surviving in Lee, MA, and Seymour, CT. With its seven freight doors, it is the largest of the three. A CSX Transportation maintenance-of-way office is located in a trailer between the freight house and the tracks. The freight house appears to be used for storage.

Gilbertville [B&A] Depot
248 Main St. (Rte. 32)

Built: Ca. 1870   **Current RR:** MCER   **Material:** Brick
RLSNE: 36-16   **Current Use:** Commercial

The Ware River RR built this depot ca. 1870. Gilbertville was the terminus of the line for three years, until the line was opened to Winchendon. Although the WR was leased to the New London Northern in 1870, the Boston & Albany RR wrestled it away from the Vermont Central RR (successor to the NLN) by 1873. Similar but larger brick structures (combination depots) were also built at Old Furnace, Templeton, Barre Plains, and Williamsville. The B&A's influence can be seen through careful comparison of the WR's stations with those on the B&A that existed at North Wilbraham, Mittineague (West Springfield), and Russell. The attractive depot has been home to the Whistle Stop restaurant since 1965.

Gilbertville [B&M] Depot   *76 Main St. (Rte. 32)*

Built: 1887   **Current RR:** None   **Material:** Wood
RLSNE: 34-66   **Current Use:** Commercial

This depot was a built to a standard Central Massachusetts RR hip-roofed design (see Amherst [B&M] Depot). Although both the Boston & Maine and Boston & Albany RRs served Gilbertville, they were located on opposite sides of the Ware River, and each had its own facilities. The B&M freight house was located on the opposite side of the tracks and about thirty feet east of the depot. Today the former B&M depot is home to the Hardwick House of Pizza.

Gilbertville [B&A] Freight House   *248 Main St. (Rte. 32)*

Built: Ca. 1870-74   **Current RR:** MCER   **Material:** Brick
RLSNE: 36-16   **Current Use:** Commercial

This is the original Gilbertville Freight House, which was built by the Ware River RR ca. 1870-74. The fancy white dentils are still very much evident on this well-cared-for red brick structure. Today it serves as a warehouse for the Whistle Stop restaurant, located next door in the old Boston & Albany RR station.

Gray Gables Depot

24 Aptucxet Rd., Bourne

Built: 1892   **Current RR:** N/A   **Material:** Wood
RLSNE: 80B-1   **Current Use:** Museum

This small station was built in 1892 to serve President Grover Cleveland, whose summer home, Gray Gables, was located nearby. It was originally located at Presidents Road and Monument Beach Road. In 1940 it was moved to a location on Shore Road and used as a cottage. The station was later bought by the Bourne Historical Society and moved to the Aptucxet Trading Post Museum in 1976.

Great Barrington Station

Castle St. near Taconic Rd.

Built: 1901   **Current RR:** HRR   **Material:** Stone & Brick
RLSNE: 3-85   **Current Use:** Commercial

The Great Barrington Station was built in 1901 by the New York, New Haven & Hartford RR as part of a grade crossing elimination project. It is similar to another Tudor Revival station still surviving in Lenox. Its predecessor was a wooden structure similar to the one surviving at Housatonic; it was located north of this station and on the east side of the tracks. Great Barrington was also home to a one-stall engine house located north of the station on the west side of the tracks. The restored station has received a new, more modern roof, but it is still very attractive. Today it is home to an art gallery.

Groton Freight House

40 Station Ave.

Built: Between 1848 & 1875   **Current RR:** None   **Material:** Wood
RLSNE: 41-32   **Current Use:** Commercial

Originally called Groton Centre by the Worcester & Nashua RR, the station here was renamed Groton in 1886. The original depot and freight house were erected ca. 1848 when the line was built. That depot was a small wooden gable-roofed structure located south of the freight house. The small depot was replaced ca. 1907 by a larger wooden structure with a carriage porch, but that station was destroyed by fire on December 29, 1932. Today the old freight house is the home of the Buckingham Bus Company. The Nashua River Rail Trail, which officially opened on October 25, 2002, passes behind the freight house.

Hadley Freight House

12 Railroad St.

Built: Ca. 1887   **Current RR:** None   **Material:** Wood
RLSNE: 34-97   **Current Use:** Commercial

RON KARR

This former Boston & Maine RR freight house was likely built in 1887, when the railroad finished building the line started by the Massachusetts Central RR some sixteen years earlier. Another building formerly served by the rail line abuts the east end of this tiny freight house. The Norwottuck Rail Trail passes within a few feet of the old freight house.

Haverhill Freight House (1 of 3)

Built: Between 1840 & 1870   **Current RR:** N/A   **Material:** Brick
RLSNE: 52-33   **Current Use:** Commercial

This building is one half of an early Boston & Maine RR freight house that was originally located on Essex Street, where the railroad underpass is now. By the 1870s the railroad had outgrown this old freight house and built a much larger one on Hale Street (still surviving). In 1905 the former freight house, then occupied by Campbell Coal and others, was cut in half and moved west along Essex Street as part of the 1905-06 grade crossing elimination project in Haverhill. Although the two halves were not rejoined, they were placed side by side, and both survive today. Merrimac Spool & Reel Company currently occupies this portion of the old freight house.

Haverhill Freight House (2 of 3)

Built: Between 1840 & 1870   **Current RR:** N/A   **Material:** Brick
RLSNE: 52-33   **Current Use:** Commercial

This building and the one adjacent to it were once a single structure. This is the second half of the former Boston & Maine RR's Essex Street Freight House. It is also used for commercial purposes.

Haverhill Freight House (3 of 3) 20 Hale St.

Built: Ca. 1870   **Current RR:** AMTK, GRS, MBTA
Material: Brick   **RLSNE:** 52-33   **Current Use:** Commercial

RON KARR

This large Boston & Maine RR freight house was likely built in the 1870s to meet the increasing demands of a growing city. It replaced an early brick freight house, which is still extant, although divided into two buildings. Originally this building extended all the way to Winter Street, but a fire within the last thirty years destroyed the south end of the building, including the two-story office section. The station was originally located at grade, but a 1905-06 grade crossing elimination project raised the main line above the freight house. The building's roof is still covered with slate, although a portion on the northern half was damaged in a fire on March 6, 2006. Despite the fire, the freight house continues to serve as a commercial warehouse.

Hingham Station (1 of 2) 142 North St.

Built: Ca. 1949-50   **Current RR:** None   **Material:** Brick
RLSNE: 74-7   **Current Use:** Commercial

The original Hingham Station was built by the South Shore RR in 1849. It was a two-story stucco structure with a hip roof. After one hundred years of service, that station was torn down and passengers used a temporary shack while this structure was built.

Primarily used for retail, this new station provided no passenger facilities beyond an awning. The New Haven RR did something similar in Plymouth, where the station was demolished and passengers had to wait for trains under an awning at the back of an A&P grocery store. This arrangement in Hingham didn't last long, as a new station was built east of here ca. 1952-54 (see Hingham Station 2 of 2). Today this building, which is located in the heart of Hingham Square, is home to several retail stores.

Hingham Station (2 of 2)   *27-41 Station St.*

Built: Ca. 1952-54   **Current RR:** None   **Material:** Stucco
RLSNE: 74-7   **Current Use:** Commercial

This station was built in the early to mid 1950s to replace the limited facilities provided at Hingham Square. Its location a quarter mile east of the old station provided much-improved parking and eliminated the blocked grade crossings caused by trains stopping at the old station. Like its predecessor, this station was built with storefronts on the street side, which the railroad rented out to enhance revenue. Ironically, the station still serves one of its original purposes: retail.

Hinsdale Combination Depot   *39 Main St.*

Built: Late 1830s   **Current RR:** N/A   **Material:** Wood
RLSNE: 29-98   **Current Use:** Residential

This wooden combination depot was the predecessor to the granite Sheply, Rutan and Coolidge station erected in 1892. Originally located east of the former Maple Street grade crossing, it was moved to make room for the new station. Today it is located nearby, on Main Street, where it serves as a private residence. Similar stations still exist at Chester and Cheshire. The 1892 replacement station and a separate freight house, which was located across the tracks from the station, have both been demolished.

Holden Depot
Pleasant St.

Built: 1871-72   **Current RR:** PW   **Material:** Wood
RLSNE: 37-8   **Current Use:** Commercial

Used for many years by the Raymond Concrete Construction Company, this former Boston, Barre & Gardner RR depot is now home to a machine shop. The station, completed by February 7, 1872, has been modified, with a garage door added to the north end and an addition on the south end. However, the structure still retains its order boards, which were added by the railroad to improve train operations. Passenger service here ended in March 1953.

Holden Freight House
Pleasant St. near Sunnyside Ave.

Built: Ca. 1871-76   **Current RR:** PW   **Material:** Wood
RLSNE: 37-8   **Current Use:** Commercial

RON KARR

This former Boston, Barre & Gardner RR freight house has been remodeled for commercial use. The building has been placed on a concrete foundation, its freight doors removed, and a garage door added to the north end. E. H. Fairbanks, master carpenter for the BB&G, built all the original freight houses on this line, including this one.

Holliston Depot   *81-83 Railroad St.*

Built: Between 1847 & 1880   **Current RR:** None   **Material:** Wood
RLSNE: 64E-5   **Current Use:** Commercial

RON KARR

Passenger service to Holliston came in with a bang on the Fourth of July, 1847. The citizens of Milford had to wait until July the following year before the Boston & Worcester RR completed their Milford Branch, which served this depot. Passenger service on this line ended in 1959. The freight house was located across the tracks from the station. Today this simple gable-roofed station is home to Casey's Crossing Tavern. Plans are well underway to build the 27-mile Upper Charles Trail, a proposed rail-trail which will go right past this depot.

Holyoke [B&M] Station   *Bowers St.*

Built: 1884-85   **Current RR:** GRS   **Material:** Granite & Brownstone
RLSNE: 33-8   **Current Use:** Commercial

RON KARR

The Connecticut River RR commissioned H. H. Richardson to design the Holyoke Station in 1883. James Rumrill, a director for both the CR and the Boston & Albany RR was friends with Richardson. As for most other Richardson stations, the contractor was Norcross Brothers of Worcester. Construction began in 1884 and was completed the following year. The Boston & Albany RR station at Chatham, NY, although designed by Richardson's successor, the firm of Sheply, Rutan and Coolidge, is very similar. This station replaced a wooden Gothic Revival gable-roofed structure located off Main Street at Dwight Street.

The Boston & Maine RR discontinued passenger service to Holyoke in 1967. The building's windows have been blocked up, presumably to better serve its various commercial occupants over the years. A separate express office survives nearby.

Holyoke [B&M] Express Office
Lyman St. near Bowers St.

Built: Between 1900 & 1920   **Current RR:** GRS   **Material:** Brick
RLSNE: 33-8   **Current Use:** Commercial

RON KARR

Located adjacent to the station, this former Boston & Maine RR express building provided much-needed additional space for the booming package business that many railroads experienced around the turn of the last century. Currently used by the Holyoke Screw Machine Company, this hip-roofed building's brick exterior has been painted brown. As on the station, its windows have been blocked up. Over the years it was enlarged with a wood extension on the trackside and a concrete block addition on the front.

Holyoke [B&M] Freight House (1 of 2)
East of 170 Main St.

Built: Between 1845 & 1877   **Current RR:** GRS   **Material:** Brick
RLSNE: 33-8   **Current Use:** Commercial

The Connecticut River RR, later part of the Boston & Maine RR, built this brick freight house in the mid nineteenth century. Occupied by Hampshire Towing, today it is only half its original size, the western portion no longer extant. The original depot was located just east of here.

Holyoke [B&M] Freight House (2 of 2)

Built: Between 1877 & 1895   **Current RR:** GRS   **Material:** Brick
RLSNE: 33-8   **Current Use:** Commercial

This former Boston & Maine RR freight house was built to increase capacity at Holyoke, a bustling mill city with an abundance of waterpower. It is located just west of the remaining portion of the earlier Connecticut River RR freight house. Today Hampshire Towing occupies the building.

Hopedale Combination Depot

Depot St.

Built: Ca. 1890   **Current RR:** GU   **Material:** Wood
RLSNE: 70-11   **Current Use:** Commercial

This combination depot was built by the Grafton & Upton RR ca. 1890. Eleven years later trolley wires were strung over the G&U tracks, and passenger operations were leased to the Milford & Uxbridge Street RY. All passenger service on the G&U ended in 1928 when the M&U converted to buses. The remains of the Draper Company, a former textile machinery manufacturer, are located across the tracks from the station.

Hopkinton Depot
West Main St. (Rte. 135)

Built: 1872   **Current RR:** N/A   **Material:** Wood
RLSNE: 71-15   **Current Use:** Municipal

RON KARR

This two-room station was built when the line to Hopkinton was opened in 1872 by the Hopkinton RR. The station originally stood near the intersection of Main and Meserve Streets. In the 1940s it was moved behind the Pond Street home of J. Howard Leman, where it stood in obscurity until 2002. The small gable-roofed depot was carefully disassembled and moved to Weston Nurseries on Route 135 in Hopkinton. As of April 2006 the local Historical Commission had rebuilt the depot near Ice House Pond and was restoring it for use as a tourist information center and shelter for ice skaters.

Housatonic Depot
168 Front St. (Rte. 183)

Built: Ca. 1850   **Current RR:** HRR   **Material:** Wood
RLSNE: 3-90   **Current Use:** Commercial

This station was built by the Stockbridge & Pittsfield RR ca. 1850 and is very similar to the original depot at Lenox. Regular passenger service on this line ended on April 30, 1971, with the formation of Amtrak. With the exception of a modern asphalt shingle roof and two small skylights, the station remains very true to its original appearance, including the decorative braces and board-and-batten siding. Today Soultube Music occupies the station.

Housatonic Freight House   *174 Front St. (Rte. 183) Building #3*

Built: Ca. 1850   **Current RR:** HRR   **Material:** Wood
RLSNE: 3-90   **Current Use:** Commercial

The Housatonic RR erected this freight house around 1850, when the line opened. Built to a standard design, it is similar to combination depots surviving at Kent, West Cornwall, and Falls Village, as well as the original New Milford and Lime Rock depots, which are no longer extant. One only needs to look around at all the old mill buildings to see why the freight house is larger than the station. Today it is occupied by R. H. Pace, Pallets & Skids.

Hudson [CM] Station   *34 Pope St.*

Built: Early 1930s   **Current RR:** None   **Material:** Brick & Wood
RLSNE: 34-23   **Current Use:** Commercial

Hudson was served by two railroads, the Central Massachusetts and a branch of the Fitchburg. Each had its own facilities, located about a quarter of a mile from each other. The current station was built by the Boston & Maine RR in the 1930s. It replaced the original CM depot, a large standard-designed structure with a gabled-hip roof. The station has received additions on both ends and is now used for commercial office space.

Hyannis Station   *252 Main St.*

Built: Between 1900 & 1930   **Current RR:** BCLR, CCCR   **Material:** Wood
RLSNE: 80C-3   **Current Use:** Railroad/Commercial

The Cape Cod Branch RR built the original Hyannis station in 1853. It was a two-story hip-roofed structure with an awning around all four sides. That structure was replaced in the early 1900s by the New York, New Haven & Hartford RR with an almost identical building. The new station had trackside bay windows on both floors, while the old one only had a bay window on the first floor; there were also subtle differences in window placements, and the new station had only one chimney versus the two on the old one. In 1953 the New Haven opened a new combination depot (see Hyannis Combination Depot), moving its service about a mile and a half north of here, away from the downtown area. The older station was torn down. This building, which was once occupied by a service station, was likely built between 1900 and 1930. It was modified and has been used by the Cape Cod & Hyannis RR, Amtrak, the Cape Cod Scenic RR, and now by the Cape Cod Central RR. The CCC, a tourist railroad, was expected to move into the then new Hyannis Transportation Center (see Hyannis Modern Station, Appendix A), but as of this writing it has not done so yet.

Hyannis Combination Depot   *477 Yarmouth Rd.*

Built: Ca. 1952-53   **Current RR:** BCLR, CCCR   **Material:** Wood
RLSNE: 80C-3   **Current Use:** Commercial

This combination depot, with its unusual clock tower, was built in 1952-53 by the New Haven RR. It was part of a station relocation project that brought an end to downtown Hyannis's passenger service. This rather large station was erected surprisingly late into the New Haven era, at a time when the railroad was struggling to maintain solvency. It served passengers for only eleven years before closing. Since the 1970s it has served a variety of commercial purposes and is currently occupied by the Mallory Dock Restaurant.

Ipswich Freight House   *13 Essex Rd.*

Built: Between 1838 & 1875   **Current RR:** N/A   **Material:** Wood
RLSNE: 58-28   **Current Use:** Private

This former Boston & Maine RR freight house has been moved approximately a mile and a half from its original location. Today a private party uses it for storage.

Jefferson [Fitchburg RR] Depot   *176 Reservoir St. (Rte. 31), Holden*

Built: Ca. 1870-71   **Current RR:** N/A   **Material:** Wood
RLSNE: 37-10   **Current Use:** Commercial

This is probably the original Boston, Barre & Gardiner RR's Jefferson Depot, which passed to the Fitchburg RR along with the BB&G in 1885. When built it was located on the south side of Quinapoxet Street, west of the railroad tracks. It was moved in the 1970s to nearby Holden. It currently resides on the grounds of the Wong Dynasty Restaurant, where it is used for storage.

Kendal Green Depot   *200 Church St., Weston*

Built: 1896   **Current RR:** GRS, MBTA   **Material:** Wood
RLSNE: 42-13   **Current Use:** Residential/Railroad

The Fitchburg RR built their first station in Weston ca. 1843; it was a two-story wooden building with the station on the first floor and a station master's apartment on the second floor. A freight house was built next to the station in 1875 but no longer exists. Following the lead of the town and post office, the railroad renamed this station Kendal Green around 1883. This likely helped alleviate confusion that arose when the Massachusetts Central RR opened its Weston Station in 1881 (see Weston Combination Depot). The MC station was much closer to the town center.

The Fitchburg RR built the present station in 1896 to replace the original, which was torn down. The depot is now a private residence, but the MBTA owns the land, and outbound commuters still disembark from their trains here. The trackside windows and doors, including the corner bay windows, have been closed off to provide some privacy for the occupants.

Kingston Station   *63 Summer St. (Rte. 3A)*

Built: 1889   **Current RR:** MBTA   **Material:** Brick & Wood
RLSNE: 73-33, 74-32   **Current Use:** Commercial

Similar to other Old Colony RR stations that existed in North Attleboro, Middleboro, Southboro, Chelmsford, and Cohasset (only the later survives today), this Tudor-style station was built in 1889. It replaced an earlier depot erected between 1845 and 1849. That station, a one-and-a-half-story hip-roofed structure with large arched windows, was located on the opposite side of Summer Street, where Pottle Street is now. No longer needed, it was sold and moved north several hundred feet along the west side of Summer Street to where the post office is now. For many years it served Kingston Steam Laundry, but it was torn down ca. 1953.

Since the abandonment of passenger service by the New Haven RR in 1959, the current station has served a variety of commercial enterprises. Although passenger service to Plymouth was restored in 1997, the Kingston Station was not used. It was renovated and began a new life in September 2003 as the Solstice restaurant.

Kingston Freight House   *Pottle St.*

Built: Between 1845 & 1889   **Current RR:** MBTA   **Material:** Wood
RLSNE: 73-33, 74-32   **Current Use:** Commercial

This is only a portion of the original Kingston Freight House. It was formerly located along the tracks, the original station having been between it and Summer Street. Although in poor shape, the building is still used for storage.

Lakeville Station   *162 Bedford St. (Rte. 18)*

Built: Between 1854 & 1875   **Current RR:** None   **Material:** Wood
RLSNE: 78-25   **Current Use:** Residential

This former Old Colony RR station likely replaced the original station, which was a small wooden depot valued at $200 in 1854. Originally called Haskins, by 1854 the station had been renamed Lakeville. Later, in 1893, when the Old Colony was consolidated with the New, York, New Haven & Hartford RR, the name was changed from Lakeville to Montwait, then back to Lakeville.

Passenger service from this station ended in 1931. Today the building is privately owned. Although it is leaning slightly to one side, it appears to be in otherwise good shape.

Lancaster Freight House   *Central Bridge Rd.*

Built: Between 1848 & 1875   **Current RR:** GRS   **Material:** Wood
RLSNE: 41-19   **Current Use:** Commercial

Left open to the elements for years, this fire-damaged post-and-beam structure has soldiered on. A new aluminum roof and exterior siding have been placed over the damaged parts, and the building is now being used again. The agency at Lancaster was closed in 1951.

The station here, formerly located across the tracks from the freight house, was a simple wooden gable-roofed building that was similar to, but narrower than, the one surviving at Thayer.

Lawrence Station   *65 Merrimack St.*

Built: 1931   **Current RR:** AMTK, GRS, MBTA   **Material:** Brick & Marble
RLSNE: 51D-10.5, 52-26, 53-0   **Current Use:** Commercial

The area now occupied by the city of Lawrence was a remote section of Andover until 1845, when construction of the Great Stone Dam on the Merrimack River began. In 1848 the Boston & Maine RR relocated seven miles of its main line between what is now North Andover and Lowell Junction to loop through the new city. That same year the Lowell & Lawrence RR arrived from the west. One year later the Essex RR, via trackage rights on the B&M, arrived from the east, and the Manchester & Lawrence arrived from the north.

The first depot in Lawrence was located in South Lawrence; it was a frame building at the corner of Market and Merrimac Streets (these streets no longer meet). Erected ca. 1848, it was enlarged only two years later.

The first North Lawrence Depot was a temporary wooden structure built in 1848 or 1849. A permanent depot, similar to Andover's, was erected in 1851 on the M&L line at the corner of Broadway and Essex Streets. This station was converted to a freight house when the third station, a Victorian Gothic structure made of brick and trimmed with freestone, was opened on March 17, 1879. Designed by N. P. Bradlee of Boston, this large station included a seventy-foot clock tower and a three-track train shed on the north end. The name of the North Lawrence Station was changed to Lawrence in 1927.

The second South Lawrence Station, built by the B&M, opened on June 3, 1872. This was a large one-story brick structure with a separate baggage house and American Express office.

The Boston & Lowell RR, having taken control of the L&L, built an extension across the Merrimack River to more directly serve the North Lawrence area. Their new station, called Lawrence, was completed in 1880. It was located between Lawrence and Amesbury Streets on Canal Street. It was a large brick terminal with a train shed. After the B&M absorbed the B&L, this station became redundant and was eventually abandoned in 1918.

Finally, in 1931, the B&M consolidated all Lawrence service into one station located within the wye between the former North Lawrence and South Lawrence Stations. Although smaller than its predecessors, the new Lawrence Station provided commuters and long distance travelers the amenities one would expect in a large city. The station once proclaimed its builder's name, "Boston and Maine Railroad," in large brass letters over the main entry, where it now says "Olde Station Square."

By 1976 Andover, Haverhill, and Lawrence had terminated local commuter subsidies, and the MBTA dropped service to Lawrence. For three years Lawrence did without rail passenger service. Fortunately, in 1979 the Merrimack Valley Regional Transit Authority restored service to many of the area's communities, including Lawrence.

The station is currently used for commercial office space and retail purposes. The MBTA has built a new station at the corner of South Union and Merrimack Streets.

Lawrence Modern Station · *Merrimack St. near South Union St.*

Built: 2004-05   **Current RR:** AMTK, GRS, MBTA   **Material:** Brick & Concrete
RLSNE: 51D-10.5, 52-26, 53-0   **Current Use:** Railroad/Transit

The Senator Patricia McGovern Transportation Center was designed for the Merrimack Valley Regional Transit Authority by the firm of DMJM Harris of Boston. Macomber Builders, also of Boston, began construction of the $23.6-million station in the summer of 2004. The station was opened on December 5, 2005, with the official dedication taking place the next day. Like many modern commuter stations, it offers only a small no-frills waiting area for passengers but includes a large four-story parking garage. Since the previous facilities comprised the old station's passenger awnings and a dirt parking lot, MBTA passengers likely consider this an improvement.

Lee Depot · *Railroad St. near Elm St.*

Built: 1893   **Current RR:** BSRM, HRR   **Material:** Wood
RLSNE: 3-100   **Current Use:** Commercial

Lee had once been served by a two-story gable-roofed station, but in the 1890s it was served only by a tiny wooden structure located across the tracks from the current station. Lee merchant and contractor Thomas Heaphy convinced the local paper mill owner, Wellington Smith, to represent the town in meetings with the railroad to petition for a new station. Smith was successful, and the New York, New Haven & Hartford RR contracted Heaphy to build a typical New England saltbox-style depot. Heaphy purchased the first ticket from the new station when it opened on November 4, 1893.

Lee Station served passengers until 1971, when service was abandoned. It continued to be used for a freight office for the Penn Central RR until purchased by its current owners in 1975. Occupied by Barritt Oil Company, and later by Iron Horse Realty, it was restored in 1981 and has since been home to the Sullivan Station Restaurant. The depot originally had a trackside canopy that balanced the structure. Similar stations existed throughout the NYNH&H system; nearby West Stockbridge is a good example.

Lee Freight House   *60 Railroad St.*

Built: Ca. 1908   **Current RR:** BSRM, HRR   **Material:** Wood
RLSNE: 3-100   **Current Use:** Commercial

The Dresser-Hull Lumber Company now owns this former New York, New Haven & Hartford RR freight house. Built ca. 1908, this flat-roofed design was not unique; similar structures existed elsewhere on the New Haven (see Seymour, CT, and Franklin Junction, MA, Freight Houses).

Lenox Station   *10 Willow Creek Rd.*

Built: 1902-03   **Current RR:** BSRM, HRR   **Material:** Stucco
RLSNE: 3-103   **Current Use:** Railroad/Museum

On January 24, 1902, the first Lenox Station burned to the ground. It had been built by the Stockbridge & Pittsfield RR around 1850 and was very similar to the depot at Housatonic. The new Lenox Station was built by the New York, New Haven & Hartford RR in 1902-03. This Tudor Revival-style building was designed by NYNH&H architects and built by James Clifford & Sons. It is similar to the one surviving at Great Barrington.

Passenger service to Lenox was discontinued in the late 1950s. The station was then used for commercial purposes until the mid 1980s, when it was donated to the Berkshire Scenic Railway Museum, which completed its restoration in 1998. The museum is open weekends from May to October, offering scenic train rides from Lenox to Stockbridge. Passengers pass four depots and one freight house on the 18-mile round trip (Lenox,

Lee Depot and Freight House, South Lee, and Stockbridge). The station has been listed on the National Register of Historic Places since 1989.

Leominster Station   *24 Columbia St.*

Built: 1878   **Current RR:** None   **Material:** Brick & Granite
RLSNE: 40-5   **Current Use:** Commercial/Community

The Fitchburg & Worcester built the first Leominster Center (later changed to Leominster) Depot in 1849. It was a temporary structure intended to support commencement of passenger service, which occurred the following February. That depot, a small wooden gable-roofed structure, was located just south of the current station. It was the source of much controversy; the townspeople felt it was grossly inadequate, and in 1873 they petitioned the F&W for a much-needed replacement. Five years later the railroad, then under the control of the Boston, Clinton & Fitchburg RR, capitulated and replaced it. The old depot was sold and moved across Water Street, where for many years it was used for commercial purposes until demolished ca. 1930.

Construction of the current Gothic Revival-style station began on June 12, 1878, and was completed on December 3 that same year. It is made of brick and trimmed with Leominster granite. The attractive station features a hip roof with decorative brackets, matching gables, and a narrow 75-foot clock tower. The New York, New Haven & Hartford RR operated the last regular passenger train to Leominster on March 6, 1928. Today the depot is used for commercial purposes, including a liquor store, hobby shop, and social club. It has received an addition on the north end, and the clock has been removed from its tower. The tracks have been pulled up between the station and Fitchburg in preperation for construction of the Fitchburg-Leominster Rail Trail. The station is listed on the National Register of Historic Places.

Lexington Station

Built: 1846   **Current RR:** None   **Material:** Wood
RLSNE: 50-8   **Current Use:** Historical Society

Built by the Lexington & West Cambridge RR and opened on October 14, 1846, this Italianate station has the distinction of being the only railroad station in New England that still has its train shed. The station was damaged by fire in 1919 but was rebuilt by the Boston & Maine RR in 1921. The new version featured a cupola and colonnade designed by William Rodger Greeley. In the 1970s the building was converted to a bank. Finally, in the fall of 1999, the historic structure was purchased by the Lexington Historical Society from Citizens Bank for $700,000. The group has renovated the old station for use as its headquarters. Today's passersby on the Minuteman Bikeway can only imagine the fire-breathing steam engines that passed though the station's train shed.

Littleton Station

Built: 1879   **Current RR:** GRS, MBTA   **Material:** Wood
RLSNE: 42-31.5   **Current Use:** Commercial

The Fitchburg RR built this Victorian-style station in 1879. It replaced their original station, a large two-story frame structure with two chimneys, built ca. 1844. That station, formerly located between the Victorian station and King Street, was moved and converted into a two-family home, but today it no longer exists. The freight house, no longer extant, was located east of the depot. The restored Victorian station has been home to Erikson Antique Stoves since 1977. Located next to the station is a replica of the original King Street crossing tender's shanty, which was built using parts from the original.

Lowell [B&L] Modern Station   *101 Thorndike St.*

Built: Ca. 1983   **Current RR:** GRS, MBTA   **Material:** Brick & Concrete
RLSNE: 47-27, 48-0, 51-26   **Current Use:** Railroad/Commercial/Government/Transit

Lowell's first station, built by the Boston & Lowell RR in 1835, was located where the National Park Service trolley crosses Merrimack Street. That terminal location proved to be troublesome just three years later when the Nashua & Lowell RR built their line. Through trains were then required to back in or out of the short stub of track from Middlesex to Merrimack Streets. This problem was alleviated in 1848 when a new Union Station was built at Middlesex Street. The original Merrimack Street station was replaced in 1852 by a combination town hall/station. Trains that terminated in Lowell continued to serve Merrimack Street until 1905.

The N&L and the Lowell & Lawrence RRs built the 1848 Union Station. The Colonial-style brick structure was located on Middlesex Street, which was still at grade. The street entrance was two stories high, with a large four-sided clock tower directly above the entrance. The rear of the building, located within the junction, was one-story high with a unique two-story domed round tower.

After the demise of the Colonial-style brick station, the Boston & Maine RR built a Romanesque-style station at the same location. Designed by Bradford Lee Gilbert in 1893, it was a striking two-story granite and brownstone building with a pyramid-roofed clock tower. The station opened on April 28, 1894.

In the early 1950s, the Gilbert-designed station was demolished to make room for highway improvements. It was replaced by a small flat-roofed cinder block structure located south of Chelmsford Street. This structure was similar to other B&M structures built around the same time in Dover, Concord, Lowell, Lynn, and Fitchburg, none of which survive. It was torn down, and operations were conducted from a trailer while the current station was being built. Today's station, the Charles Gallagher Transportation Center, was designed by Meyer and Meyer Architecture and Interiors for the MBTA and built ca. 1983. That firm also designed the station at Anderson RTC. Today the station is an intermodal transportation center providing bus and commuter rail services, and it is home to the North Middlesex Council of Governments.

Lowell [B&M] Station   *238-254 Central St.*

Built: 1876   **Current RR:** None   **Material:** Brick
RLSNE: 52C-9   **Current Use:** Vacant

This Renaissance Revival-style station was built by the Boston & Maine RR in 1876. When originally built it had two asymmetrical towers, one on each end of the Central Street entrance. The tower on the Green Street side was four stories tall, while the one on Williams Street was only three stories tall. The location of the station, while convenient for both passengers and freight, did not afford any connections with other railroads, and therefore it was built as a terminal.

By 1887 the B&M had taken control of the Boston & Lowell RR, and just eight years later it built a connection to allow Lowell Branch trains to reach the new Bradford Lee Gilbert-designed station at Middlesex Street. Finally, all trains serving Lowell were united within one station. After serving just eighteen years, the station at Central Street was abandoned. It has since served a variety of commercial enterprises, including the classic Rialto Theatre in 1923; in the 1980s it was home to a bowling alley. The building was purchased by the National Park Service and the Lowell Historic Preservation Commission in 1989 to prevent its demolition. The station has received a multi-million-dollar renovation including roof repairs, new floors, and replication of the two historic towers, which were previously removed. Once the doors and windows have been replaced, the National Park Service plans to lease the building to a long-term private tenant who will then be expected to finish the renovations.

Lynn Modern Station   *Monroe St. near Market St.*

Built: Ca. 1988-1992   **Current RR:** GRS, MBTA   **Material:** Concrete & Steel
RLSNE: 58-11.5, 61-8.5   **Current Use:** Railroad/Transit/Commercial

RON KARR

The first Lynn Depot was erected by the Eastern RR near Central Square in 1838. It was a small wooden structure with a cupola. Around 1848 that station was replaced with larger brick affair with a two-track train shed at the junction of Union and Willow Streets.

By the spring of 1865, "the Great Lynn Depot War" had begun over the location of the much needed replacement station. Two factions each supported separate locations: Market Street, near the city center, and Central Square, near the factories and trade center of the city. Local pressure persuaded the Eastern to consider the new Market Street location, but a recently enacted state law would not allow the Eastern to abandon the old Central Square location. By 1871 the case eventually reached the United States Supreme Court, where it was decided that there would be two stations in Lynn. The following year two costly and attractive Victorian-style stations were built, one at Market Street along State Street and the other in Central Square. When the political climate cooled in 1873, the railroad quietly petitioned the state legislature to abandon the Market Street Station. The station, which had cost $55,000, was demolished just months after being completed!

The Central Square Station was severely damaged in a large fire in 1889, which destroyed many buildings in the downtown area. What remained of the station was removed, and the Boston & Maine RR erected a temporary structure to serve until March 1895, when a new station was opened. That structure, which was designed by Architect Henry W. Rodgers, was constructed of stone, with a seventy-five-foot tall, four-sided pyramidal clock tower. It was later modified—and not for the better—in 1913, when the tracks were raised to eliminate grade crossings throughout town.

The next Lynn Station was a modern streamlined structure built by the B&M and opened on March 31, 1952. Designed by railroad employees Howard L. Rich and John P. Cronin, it replaced the fifty-seven-year-old Rodgers-designed station, which was demolished shortly after that to make room for a parking lot. Located at the junction of Mt. Vernon and

Interior, Lynn Modern Station (Ron Karr)

Exchange Streets, the flat-roofed single-story brick building proudly proclaimed "BOSTON AND MAINE" in three-dimensional letters above the roof. The station was the first on the B&M to feature radiant heat. The interior included a ticket office, restaurant, and newsstand. It served for forty-plus years before being replaced and subsequently demolished, like its predecessor.

The MBTA began construction of the current station in 1988, and after four long years it opened in January 1992. The station consists of a unique sprawling multi-story glass, steel, and concrete atrium which links the two streets on either side of the tracks and joins the north and south halves of a 965-space, five-story parking garage. The arched atrium houses ticket windows, office and retail space, stairwells to the elevated tracks, and pedestrian bridges that connect the parking lots at each level. The station was built with excess capacity to support a yet-to-be-realized Blue Line extension. Despite free parking, more than half the spaces go unused, and the area is subject to vandalism and theft.

Lynnfield Centre Depot — 49 Tuttle St., Wakefield

Built: Early 1950s   **Current RR:** N/A   **Material:** Wood
RLSNE: 54-3   **Current Use:** Commercial

The Boston & Maine RR built this small depot in the early 1950s. It is similar to one still surviving in South Sudbury. Today an ATM of the Savings Bank occupies the depot. Formerly located at Summer Street in Lynnfield, it was moved to Wakefield in 1959 after regular passenger service to Lynnfield was suspended. Its predecessor station was a small hip-roofed wooden structure.

Malden Station   *53 Summer St.*

Built: 1892   **Current RR:** GRS, MBTA   **Material:** Brick & Granite
RLSNE: 52-4.5   **Current Use:** Commercial

RON KARR

Malden's first station, a large two-story wooden structure built in 1845, was located on the east side of the right of way. That station was replaced by a second smaller frame structure in 1871, which was constructed in conjunction with a project that rearranged some local roads. In 1892 the Boston & Maine RR built what would be their final Malden Station as part of a grade separation project. The station, still bearing the B&M initials above its entrance, is now home to the Pearl Street Station restaurant. Today's MBTA passengers board their trains at the modern MBTA station located south of here on Pleasant Street.

Malden Modern Station   *Pleasant St. near Commercial St.*

Built: 1975   **Current RR:** GRS, MBTA   **Material:** Concrete & Brick
RLSNE: 52-4.5   **Current Use:** Railroad/Transit/Commercial

RON KARR

This station, now called Malden Center, was built in 1975 by the MBTA. It was the first Boston commuter rail station to have high-level platforms. In March 2003 the MBTA started a $4.7-million renovation of the structure to bring it into compliance with the Americans with Disabilities Act (ADA), giving the station a complete makeover in the process. This intermodal station is served by commuter rail, the Orange Line subway, and local buses.

Manchester Freight House   *Summer St.*

Built: Between 1847 & 1875   **Current RR:** GRS, MBTA   **Material:** Wood
RLSNE: 59-7   **Current Use:** Community

This freight house has been modified and now serves the Manchester Community Center. It was built by the Eastern RR and is likely the original freight house. It has survived two passenger stations, the original and a second built in 1895.

Mansfield Modern Station   *Crocker St.*

Built: 2002-04   **Current RR:** AMTK, CSXT, MBTA   **Material:** Brick & Granite
RLSNE: 72-21, 77-0   **Current Use:** Railroad

The town of Mansfield and the regional transportation agencies built this attractive brick and granite station as part of a $1.5-million improvement project for Mansfield commuters. The general contractor, Colantoni, began preliminary construction in summer 2002, and the station was completed by January 2004. An antique clock, formerly located in Mansfield Town Hall, has been incorporated into the station's cupola. Included in the new station is a meeting room that town officials use for community functions.

The temporary single-story wooden station, built in 1954 by the New Haven RR as part of a grade separation project, was swiftly demolished when the new station opened. That station had replaced a two-story Italianate structure that was located between the two sets of tracks. The old station and the rail line to Taunton were both removed as part of the grade separation project.

Maple Grove Freight House   *15 Commercial St. (Rte. 8)*

Built: Ca. 1845-46   **Current RR:** None   **Material:** Wood
RLSNE: 30-12   **Current Use:** Commercial

The former Maple Grove Freight House is now the home of a satellite office of the Pierce Machine Company, a full-service machine shop headquartered in Dalton, MA. This former Western RR freight house was moved when the 1949 flood washed away the Commercial Street Bridge. The new bridge was relocated and angled to eliminate sharp curves at both approaches. This structure is now located off Commercial Street on a dirt access road located south of 9 Commercial. The Ashuwillticook Rail Trail runs directly behind the building.

Marion Combination Depot   *381 Front St.*

Built: 1854   **Current RR:** None   **Material:** Wood
RLSNE: 80A-5   **Current Use:** Commercial

This station was built by the Fairhaven Branch RR in 1854 when the line was opened. A similar one was built at Mattapoisett, the only other intermediate station on the line. In 1904 the New Haven RR built a new station, and this building was moved across the street and used as a combination express office and trolley station. The station is now home to the Children's Depot, a day care center.

Marlboro [B&M] Combination Depot   *305 Lincoln St.*

Built: Ca. 1854-55   **Current RR:** None   **Material:** Wood
RLSNE: 42B-13   **Current Use:** Commercial

The Fitchburg RR built this combination depot ca. 1854-55 when they completed the branch to Marlboro. When a new station was opened in 1893, it was relegated to freight service only. The demoted depot and the entire branch were acquired by the Boston & Maine RR just seven years later.

The 1893 Fitchburg station, a Stick-style wooden depot with Eastlake ornamentation, was located three hundred feet west on the corner of Lincoln and Mechanic Streets. It comprised a station building and a separate baggage/express building. The main building had a large clock tower with a weathervane on top. Despite local efforts to preserve the building, it was demolished on June 9, 1987. Having outlasted its replacement and the railroad itself, the original combination depot is now occupied by Middlesex Cooling. The rapidly expanding Assabet River Rail Trail is open from here to Hudson, with plans to go all the way to South Acton.

Mattapan Depot   *1672 River St.*

Built: Between 1895 & 1900   **Current RR:** None   **Material:** Stone
RLSNE: 73B-3   **Current Use:** Vacant

The original wooden station at Mattapan was built by the Dorchester & Milton Branch RR in 1847 and was immediately leased to the Old Colony RR. This is the second station to serve Mattapan. It is the only former railroad station that survives on the MBTA's converted high-speed line, most having been removed in 1927 when the line was double tracked and electrified. The depot was sold after the Boston Elevated RY took over the line, and it has served numerous businesses since. Most recently it was home to Nick's Seafood, Pizza & Subs, but currently it is vacant.

Methuen Station   *55 Union St.*

Built: 1908 **Current RR:** None **Material:** Brick
RLSNE: 53-2 **Current Use:** Community

The first depot in Methuen was built in 1851 by the Concord RR. It was replaced just eleven years later with a second frame structure. By the 1890s the local townspeople had become displeased with the accommodations and petitioned the railroad for a better station. After many years of waiting, Edward F. Searles, a major stockholder of the Boston & Maine RR, finally donated the land and paid for the construction of a new station. Designed by H. B. Fletcher and opened on July 13, 1908, this would be the third and final station to serve Methuen.

Passenger service here ended June 1953, and since then the building has been used for commercial purposes. Although it was renovated in the 1980s, the handsome brick depot no longer sports its covered stairs and carriageway, formerly located on the east side of the structure. The station at Shawsheen is very similar. Today the station is occupied by Local #175 of the Laborers International Union of North America. The track in front of the station has been ballasted, and a granite marker, flag pole, and flower bed have been added.

Methuen Freight House   *Railroad St. near Union St.*

Built: Ca. 1849-50 **Current RR:** None **Material:** Wood
RLSNE: 53-2 **Current Use:** Vacant

This freight house was built by the Manchester & Lawrence RR ca. 1849-50, when they built this line. It is located almost directly across the tracks from the station.

RON KARR

Middleboro Freight House   *Station St.*

Built: Between 1890 & 1918   **Current RR:** BCLR, CSXT, MBTA   **Material:** Wood
RLSNE: 77B-8, 78-23, 79-0, 80-0   **Current Use:** Vacant

Middleboro was once an important freight yard for the New Haven RR and included locomotive service facilities and a large wooden water tower. Today CSX Transportation and the Bay Colony RR interchange freight here. The 1887 passenger station, located south of the freight house at least until 1979, was similar to the one surviving at Kingston, MA. The former freight house was home to a plumbing supply dealer, but is now vacant.

Middleton Depot   *38 Central St.*

Built: Between 1848 & 1874   **Current RR:** N/A   **Material:** Wood
RLSNE: 57-10   **Current Use:** Residential

This former Eastern RR depot was likely the original station to serve Middleton. The depot, now a private residence, has been moved one lot up Central Street toward the village center, but is still within sight of its original location. The station was last used for passenger service in 1926.

Milford [B&A] Station   *170 Central St.*

Built: 1909   **Current RR:** None   **Material:** Granite & Brownstone
RLSNE: 64E-12, 70-12   **Current Use:** Commercial

RON KARR

The Boston & Albany RR con-structed this Milford Station in 1909, made from local granite at a cost of $20,000. It replaced the original 1848 wooden de-pot built by the Boston & Worcester RR. Milford was a busy place, with the B&A freight house just south of the station and the New York, New Haven & Hartford RR depot 150 feet west and across the street. The last train to Boston pulled out of the station on March 27, 1959. The building has served various commer-cial purposes over the years and is now home to Countryside Discount Li-quors & General Store.

Millbury [B&A] Freight House   *Canal St. near Howe Ave.*

Built: Between 1837 & 1875   **Current RR:** None   **Material:** Wood
RLSNE: 64F-3   **Current Use:** Vacant

Vacant and forlorn, this former Boston & Albany RR freight house has not received any re-cent maintenance. The 1892 Sheply, Rutan and Coolidge sta-tion, made of granite and brownstone with a hip roof with flared eaves, once stood just north of the freight house. The Providence & Worcester RR also served Millbury, but there was never a connection between the two lines, and the P&W station no longer exists. See Millbury [P&W] Station in Appendix A for more information.

Millis Station   64 Exchange St.

Built: 1885   **Current RR:** BCLR   **Material:** Stone & Wood
RLSNE: 66-20   **Current Use:** Municipal

This station was built in 1885 by the heirs of Henry Lansing Millis, a prominent local citizen, for joint use of the town and the New York & New England RR. The lower level was used by the railroad, while the upper level was occupied by town offices and a library. The station is made of rough field stone with brownstone trim and features a three-story tower with a conical roof. It was originally called East Medway, Millis having been part of Medway at the time. Passenger service ended in April 1967. Today the station, now known as the Lansing Millis Memorial Building, still serves the town as their office building.

Monument Beach Station   440 Shore Rd. near Worcester Ave.

Built: Ca. 1906-07   **Current RR:** BCLR   **Material:** Brick
RLSNE: 80B-2   **Current Use:** Residential

Constructed by the New York, New Haven & Hartford RR ca. 1906-07, this station was the third to serve Monument Beach. The original station (then called Monument) was located in a general store, which was built in 1875 by O. R. Swift, the proprietor. It wasn't until 1883 that the Old Colony RR built its own depot. That small Victorian-style frame building was moved the following year to the site of the current station. The second depot, as well as half the village, was destroyed in 1906 by a spectacular fire. The present station received a second floor apartment ca. 1981, and today it serves as a private residence.

Nantasket Station
205 Nantasket Ave.

Built: Between 1900 & 1915 **Current RR:** None **Material:** Brick & Stucco
RLSNE: 74A-2 **Current Use:** Commercial/Historical Society

Nantasket was the home of Paragon Park, an ocean-front amusement park, from 1905-84. In the late 1980s the closed park was demolished and a new condominium complex put up in its place. The 1928 Paragon Park Carousel was saved and relocated adjacent to the station in 1986. The preserved carousel is open to the public seasonally. The Spanish-style station is now owned by the Friends of the Paragon Carousel, and they lease space to Noah's Ice Cream Shop. The group is currently raising money to repair the clock and restore the three-story clock tower.

Needham Station
1025-1027 Great Plain Ave.

Built: Ca. 1887 **Current RR:** BCLR, MBTA **Material:** Brick
RLSNE: 66-9 **Current Use:** Railroad/Commercial

The Charles River RR came to Needham in June 1853. Denied permission to pass through the town center, the railroad diverted the tracks southeastward toward Great Plain Village. With the coming of the railroad, Great Plain Village became the de facto center of Needham, and in 1879 it became the official center.

The original Needham Station, a simple wooden gable-roofed building, burned down in 1887. The New York & New England RR replaced it with this stone structure, which had a turreted roof. Today only a portion of this building still stands as the Fava Restaurant, the rest having been torn down.

Needham Junction Depot   *Junction St.*

Built: 1906   **Current RR:** BCLR, MBTA   **Material:** Brick
RLSNE: 66A-0   **Current Use:** Railroad/Commercial

Needham Junction Depot, originally called West Street, was
built by the New York, New Haven & Hartford RR in 1906 as
part of a four-mile connection
to West Roxbury. The connection was built to allow Charles
River line trains access to
Boston without using the
Boston & Albany tracks. Today
the station is home to Needham Junction Ice Cream, where Massachusetts Bay Transit Authority patrons can purchase their tickets and wait
for their trains.

New Lenox General Store/Station   *255 New Lenox Rd.*

Built: Before 1850   **Current RR:** HRR   **Material:** Wood
RLSNE: 3-106   **Current Use:** Residential

The New Lenox Station, also
known as Deweys and Yukon,
sits at the intersection of the railroad and New Lenox Road. This
building was erected before the
railroad arrived and was never
owned by the railroad. It was
built by C. E. Dewey to serve as a
general store, with a separate living area for Dewey and his fam-
ily; it also housed the local post office for many years. By 1934, when the
general store and post office closed, the railroad was no longer stopping
here. The building went unused and fell into disrepair until 1953. It was
then restored and converted to an apartment house, the same purpose it
continues to serve today.

New Salem Combination Depot   *423 Daniel Shays Hwy.*

Built: Ca. 1871   **Current RR:** N/A   **Material:** Wood
RLSNE: 35-37   **Current Use:** Commercial

RON KARR

The Athol & Enfield RR built this combination depot ca. 1871, when it opened the line from Athol to Barretts Junction. It was similar to other combination depots located at North Dana, Collins, and South Athol (see South Athol). The line was abandoned between Athol and Bondsville in 1935 to make way for the Quabbin Reservoir. The combination depot was moved to its current location from a section of the right of way that now lies on the shore of the reservoir. Now called Millington Crossing, it is occupied by two businesses, Whitier Plumbing and Anne Clukay-Whitter, Attorney at Law.

Newburyport Modern Station   *Boston Way near Parker St.*

Built: 1998   **Current RR:** MBTA   **Material:** Brick
RLSNE: 54-30, 58-37, 58H-0   **Current Use:** Railroad/Commercial

After a twenty-two-year hiatus, passenger service returned to Newburyport on October 26, 1998. The current station was built as part of the MBTA's $2.1-million nine-mile service extension from Ipswich to Newburyport. Although station construction was largely completed in the summer of 1998, the interior of the building did not open to the public until February 11, 2002. Today it is the home of the Digital Café, a sandwich and coffee shop. The building incorporates two granite arches from the former Newburyport YMCA, which burned down in 1987.

The original 1840 Eastern RR depot was a single-story wooden structure with a train shed. It was replaced by an imposing brick structure with a round turret with a conical roof, but neither of these stations survives today.

Newton Center Station   *70 Union St.*

Built: 1890-91   **Current RR:** None   **Material:** Granite & Brownstone
RLSNE: 66-4   **Current Use:** Commercial/Transit

The Boston & Albany RR commissioned the prestigious Boston firm of Sheply, Rutan and Coolidge to design this station in 1890. Constructed of granite and brownstone, this Romanesque-style structure was built by the Norcross Brothers of Worcester between October 1890 and May 1891. It replaced an earlier Newton Centre (later changed to Newton Center) depot located across the tracks. That structure, made of wood, was likely the original 1852 station.

As part of a ca. 1907 grade crossing elimination project, the rails were lowered and the station was remodeled to reach the new grade. A portion of the original roofline survives, having been reused for the three new dormers. The two heavily hooded dormers located above are original.

Today the station is home to a Starbucks Coffee franchise. The interior is beautifully restored and is worthy of a visit. The building was placed on the National Register of Historic Places in 1976.

Newton Center Express Office   *50 Union St.*

Built: 1891   **Current RR:** None   **Material:** Stone
RLSNE: 66-4   **Current Use:** Commercial

RON KARR

This former express office, like the adjacent station, was designed by Sheply, Rutan and Coolidge and built for the Boston & Albany RR in 1890-91. A grade crossing elimination project done around 1907 lowered the rails, and this small express office was disassembled, moved, and reassembled nearby, where it has been integrated into a much larger commercial building. Today the combined structure is home to Holden's Taxi Cab Company and the Newton Center Medical Associates.

Newton Highlands Station   *18 Station St.*

Built: 1886-87   **Current RR:** None   **Material:** Granite & Brownstone
RLSNE: 64B-3.5, 66-5   **Current Use:** Transit

This commission was the first of twenty-three Boston & Albany RR stations to be designed by Sheply, Rutan and Coolidge. The Norcross Bothers began construction of the station in September 1886 and completed it by March the following year. It replaced an earlier wooden depot that featured a corner bay window.

A ca. 1907 grade elimination project resulted in the depression of tracks, which required modifications to the rear of the station to provide a new platform and canopy at the former basement level of the building. Passengers on light rail vehicles of the MBTA's Riverside Line still board and disembark from the platforms here. The station was home to Highland Auto Parts for many years, but the MBTA, in an effort to dispose of

The renowned architectural firm of Sheply, Rutan and Coolidge, successors to H. H. Richardson's firm, designed at least thirty stations in New England and New York State between 1886 and 1918, twenty-three of them commissioned by the Boston & Albany RR. Of these, a third have been lost. As for Richardson's stations and those of their contemporary, Bradford Lee Gilbert, these stations were typically substantial structures built of brownstone and/or granite, and featuring large overhanging roofs, stone-trimmed windows, and distinctive dormers of matching stone.

surplus property, is currently negotiating its sale to a private party. It was placed on the National Register of Historic Places in 1976.

Newton Upper Falls Depot   *1225 Chestnut St.*

Built: 1852   **Current RR:** BCLR   **Material:** Wood
RLSNE: 66-6.5   **Current Use:** Commercial

The Charles River RR built this depot when the line was opened from Brookline to Newton Upper Falls in 1852. It was originally called Upper Falls, but the name was later changed to Newton Upper Falls. A separate loading dock with a lean-to type awning was located just north of the depot until it was torn down in 1948. This depot is the only surviving Charles River station. With the exception of the baggage room, which was abbreviated in the 1960s, the well-cared-for station looks much the same as it did when built. Today it is home to the Depot Cafe.

North Abington Station   *101 Railroad St.*

Built: 1893-94   **Current RR:** MBTA, CSXT   **Material:** Granite & Brownstone
RLSNE: 73-18, 73D-0   **Current Use:** Commercial

The famous New York City architect Bradford Lee Gilbert designed this Romanesque-style station. Gilbert, best known for his work on the old Grand Central Terminal, also designed Canton Junction and Bridgewater Stations. The North Abington Station was built by the New York, New Haven & Hartford RR in 1893-94 as a peace offering to the town after the August 16, 1893, North Abington Riot, a dispute brought about by the NYNH&H's unwillingness to allow the Abington & Rockland Streetcar Company to cross its tracks at grade. The granite station replaced a small hip-roofed wooden structure, which was located on the south side of the North Avenue crossing in the fork of the junction between the main line and the Hanover Branch.

The New Haven RR dropped passenger service on this line in 1959, when they abandoned all Old Colony Service. The station continued to be used as a freight office into the Penn Central era. Even though commuter service was restored in 1997, trains do not stop here; commuters board their MBTA trains at a high-level platform in Abington. The station, which was added to the National Register of Historic Places in 1976, is now home to the Abington Depot restaurant.

North Adams Freight House   *115 State St., Building #4*

Built: 1894   **Current RR:** GRS   **Material:** Wood
RLSNE: 30-18, 31-93   **Current Use:** Museum

The Fitchburg RR built this large freight house in 1894. Although the station was shared by the Boston & Albany RR, each railroad had separate freight facilities. The B&A's facilities are no longer extant. Today the North Adams Freight House is occupied by the Western Gateway Heritage State Park. Restoration began in 1981, and the park was opened to the public in October 1985. The building was placed on the National Register of Historic Places in 1972.

North Andover Depot   *109 Sutton St.*

Built: Ca. 1875   **Current RR:** AMTK, GRS, MBTA   **Material:** Wood
RLSNE: 52-27, 57-19.5   **Current Use:** Commercial

This station was built by the Boston & Maine RR ca. 1875. It replaced the original North Andover Depot built ca. 1851, after the main line was rerouted through Lawrence. The bi-level station was located at the junction of the B&M main line and the Eastern RR's Lawrence Branch. The station was closed on April 6, 1955. It has undergone extensive remodeling and, with the exception of the original roofline, is barely recognizable. Today it is home to the Pridecraft Furniture Shop.

North Andover Freight House   *10 Main St.*

Built: 1840   **Current RR:** None   **Material:** Fieldstone
RLSNE: 52-27, 57-19.5   **Current Use:** Commercial

The Andover & Wilmington RR built this unique two-story fieldstone freight house in 1840. The building, which is one of New England's oldest railroad structures and is still in great shape, looks more like an old stone mill than a freight house. It was located on the original main line, which was relocated west of here just eight years after opening in order to reach Lawrence. Remnants of the original right of way can still be seen by looking north while standing behind the building, which is now occupied by Mel B's Gifts.

North Billerica Depot   *11 Station St.*

Built: Ca. 1867   **Current RR:** GRS, MBTA   **Material:** Wood
RLSNE: 49-8.5, 49A-9, 51-22   **Current Use:** Railroad

When the Boston & Lowell RR opened in June 1835, there were only two stations: Boston and Lowell. The towns along the route later petitioned the railroad for their own stations. Finally, in 1867, the B&L constructed the North Billerica Depot. A similar station was built at East Billerica, but it no longer exists.

The town-owned station was in poor shape when it was leased to the Lowell Regional Transit Authority in 1996. The LRTA restored the station in 1998 and uses it to provide connecting bus service to the MBTA's commuter rail service. The main station is the southern portion of the building, the center section is the old baggage room, and the northern section was added in 1998. Iron Horse Park in North Billerica is the headquarters of Guilford Rail System, the modern-day successor of the B&L.

North Billerica Freight House
15 Letchworth Ave.

Built: Between 1867 & 1875   **Current RR:** GRS, MBTA   **Material:** Wood
RLSNE: 49-8.5, 49A-9, 51-22   **Current Use:** Commercial

Hughes Lumber currently uses this former Boston & Maine RR freight house for storage. The restored station and the new MBTA high-level platforms are located adjacent to it.

North Brookfield Combination Depot
School St. near Elm St.

Built: 1875   **Current RR:** None   **Material:** Brick
RLSNE: 29D-4   **Current Use:** Commercial

This station was erected in 1875 when the North Brookfield RR built its four-mile branch to connect with the Boston & Albany RR at East Brookfield. The primary reason for the branch was to serve the Batcheller Shoe Factory, which at the time employed nearly one-quarter of the town's residents. The two-story structure had a gathering hall on the second floor, which was used by local civic groups. Passengers last used the station in 1935. The town owns the building and has leased it out.

North Easton Station

80 Mechanic St.

Built: 1881-82   **Current RR:** None   **Material:** Granite & Brownstone
RLSNE: 76-10   **Current Use:** Historical Society

North Easton is one of eight stations Henry Hobson Richardson designed in Massachusetts and Connecticut in the 1880s, seven of which are still extant. The arched stone entrances, two-tone granite and brownstone exterior, and large contoured overhanging roof are all notable examples of features he incorporated into these stations and which his successors, Sheply, Rutan and Coolidge, adapted in the many stations they designed in succeeding decades. Other examples of Richardson's work can be seen in Framingham, Holyoke, Palmer, Wellesley Hills, and Woodland, MA, and in New London, CT.

The Easton Branch RR brought the rails to North Easton on May 16, 1855. North Easton Station was built by F. L. Ames, owner of the world's largest shovel factory and a director of the Old Colony RR. Upon its completion in 1882, Ames conveyed it as a gift to the railroad. It is one of several structures in North Easton designed for Ames by H. H. Richardson. The landscaping was completed later, in 1884, by Frederick Law Olmsted. The last passenger train to serve this station departed on September 5, 1958. In 1969 the Ames family bought the station from the railroad and gave it to the Easton Historical Society, which uses it to display its historical collection. Three years later the Romanesque-style building was added to the National Register of Historic Places.

North Grafton Freight House 50 Westboro Rd.

Built: Between 1930 & 1957   **Current RR:** AMTK, CSXT, GU, MBTA
Material: Wood   **RLSNE:** 64-38, 70-0   **Current Use:** Railroad

This freight house was built by the Grafton & Upton RR. It has been recently improved with new siding and a concrete loading dock. Today North Grafton is the base of the G&U operations.

North Hatfield Depot 166 Depot Rd.

Built: Between 1846 & 1880   **Current RR:** GRS   **Material:** Wood
RLSNE: 33-24   **Current Use:** Residential

This depot, now a private residence, has been moved away from the tracks. It was likely built by the Connecticut River RR when they opened the portion of their line from Northampton to South Deerfield in 1846. The station also served for many years as the local post office.

North Hatfield Freight House
164 Depot Rd.

Built: Between 1846 & 1880   **Current RR:** GRS   **Material:** Wood
RLSNE: 33-24   **Current Use:** Commercial

This former Boston & Maine RR freight house is now occupied by Pomeroy Lumber. It was likely built by the Connecticut River RR at the same time as the depot, which has been moved and is currently east of the tracks.

North Reading Depot
112 Haverhill St. (Rte. 97)

Built: Between 1850 & 1875   **Current RR:** N/A   **Material:** Wood
RLSNE: 56-9   **Current Use:** Commercial

All passenger service on the Salem & Lowell Branch ended in 1932, and the entire line was abandoned by 1987. This former Boston & Maine RR depot is the only remaining station on this line still in its original location. It has received several additions and is now occupied by Wolsey Associates.

North Scituate Station
371 Gannett St.

Built: Ca. 1908-09   **Current RR:** None   **Material:** Stucco
RLSNE: 74-13   **Current Use:** Commercial

The Spanish-style station in North Scituate was built by the New York, New Haven & Hartford RR ca. 1908-09. With its stucco exterior and terra cotta roof, it is similar to other NYNH&H stations including Buzzards Bay, West Barnstable, Pocasset, and Cataumet. The station has been converted into a strip mall, with a large addition on the east end. The station portion of the shopping center houses the Pipeline Salon. Although MBTA Greenbush commuter trains will pass within a few feet of the old station, they will not stop here.

North Station

135 Causeway St., Boston

Built: 1995   **Current RR:** AMTK, GRS, MBTA   **Material:** Concrete & Steel
RLSNE: 42-0, 51-0, 52-0, 58-0, 62-0   **Current Use:** Railroad/Transit/Commercial

The early history of Boston's North Station revolved around four railroads: the Boston & Lowell, the Eastern, the Fitchburg, and the Boston & Maine.

On June 23, 1835, the B&L became the first railroad to serve the north side of Boston. Their Lowell Street Station (1835-57) was an unusual wooden L-shaped structure ornamented with arches and large pillars. In 1857 the B&L built a second, larger station on Causeway Street, west of the Eastern and Fitchburg stations. The Lowell Street Station was converted to a freight house. By 1872 the B&L was planning a new grand station. It was built directly over the earlier depot, which was not torn down until the new building was completed in 1873. The new station, which included four towers and a huge train shed, was faced with brick and trimmed with Nova Scotia freestone.

The Eastern reached Lewis Wharf in 1838; it was there that they built their first East Boston Depot. Passengers were obliged to take a ferry across the Charles River to reach Boston. This depot was destroyed by fire in 1841 and was replaced the next year with a second, larger depot and a hotel. As luck would have it, on January 25, 1842, just one day after it opened, this depot also burned down. A third, less pretentious station was built the following year. Between 1852 and 1854 the Eastern constructed an extension from Revere to Boston. On April 10, 1854, the Eastern began direct rail service into Boston from their new Causeway Street Station. This station was a two-story wooden structure located between the B&L and Fitchburg stations. Only eight years later, on June 21, 1862, a fire completely destroyed the station. The Eastern immediately erected a replacement building, which opened before the year's end. It was a larger three-story brick structure with a large four-sided clock tower.

Boston & Maine Railroad

The bird's eye view of North Union Station in this antique post card image clearly shows how the Boston & Lowell's large 1872 station was merged with new facilities built to replace the Fitchburg's "Great Stone Castle," the Eastern's 1862 brick station, and the Boston & Maine's former station in nearby Haymarket Square. Designed in 1893 by Sheply, Rutan and Coolidge, the elaborate complex served the railroad for barely thirty years before it was demolished and replaced by the North Station/Boston Garden facility, which was in turn replaced by the current Fleet Center. (Courtesy of the Beverly Historical Society & Museum, Beverly, MA, Walker Transportation Collection)

For five years the Fitchburg RR's trains terminated across the Charles River in Charlestown. Construction of the Fitchburg's first and only Boston Station began on November 1, 1847, and was completed on August 9 the following year. Known as "The Great Stone Castle," it was a two-story granite structure with four tall towers, one in each corner.

The B&M opened their own station at Haymarket Square on October 20, 1845. Prior to that they had used a temporary station on the corner of Canal and Traverse Streets for three months. Designed by architect George M. Dexter, the two-story Haymarket Square Station was constructed of brick and had a large head house with ten colossal Corinthian pilasters.

By 1871 there were four railroads serving the north side of the city, each with its own station. From east to west, the stations were those of the Fitchburg, B&M, Eastern, and B&L. All were located on the north side of Causeway Street except the B&M's station, which was located two blocks south at Haymarket Square.

The B&M began its consolidation of railroads in 1884 with the lease of the Eastern, followed by the B&L just three years later. On February 13, 1893, the B&M broke ground on the Sheply, Rutan and Coolidge-designed North Union Station. This granite and brick station incorporated the 1872 B&L station on its west end. This was Boston's first Union Station, and by June 17, 1894, all north side lines—including the still independent Fitchburg—began using it. The Eastern's 1862 station and the B&M's Haymarket Square station were demolished. The Fitchburg, until also absorbed by the B&M in 1900, continued to use its station for office space. Two large B&M freight houses, located between the Fitchburg and Eastern stations, were also razed at this time.

In 1927 the former Fitchburg station, the 1894 North Union Station, and the 1872 B&L station were all demolished to make way for the North Station and Boston Garden facility, which was completed in 1928. One of the Fitchburg station towers still survives (see North Station [Fitchburg RR] in Appendix A). The 1928 North Station was a six-story concrete and steel structure faced with buff brick and artificial stone. The firm of Fellheimer & Wagner designed the building and station facilities.

The Boston Garden hosted its last game in 1995, and the new Fleet Center was opened on September 30 of that year. It was built only nine inches from the 1928 Boston Garden/North Station, which was demolished in 1998. The Fleet Center includes a small passenger waiting area that is neatly tucked away under the arena. The project was designed by Ellerbe Becket of Kansas City, Missouri.

Northampton Station   *125A Pleasant St.*

Built: 1896-97   **Current RR:** GRS   **Material:** Brick & Brownstone
RLSNE: 7-77, 7A-0, 7D-0, 33-17, 34-99   **Current Use:** Commercial

Northampton's Union Station was built in 1896-97 as part of a grade elimination project. It replaced the former Connecticut River RR and New Haven & Northampton RR stations, which were located about one-half mile north of here on Strong Avenue. The CR station was an ornate brick structure with a three-story pyramidal tower, while the NH&H was a simple structure with a low-pitched gable roof. Both of those stations were demolished as part of the project. Union Station, made of buff brick and trimmed in red Longmeadow brownstone, is shaped like a triangle and located in the junction of the NH&N and CR tracks. In 1917, and again in 1928, fire swept through a portion of the baggage room and upper offices. Despite considerable damage, the trains continued to run, and ticket sales resumed only days after the fires.

In the 1960s the Boston & Maine RR ended passenger service and sold the station. It was purchased by a machine shop, which occupied the station for many years before selling it to restaurant developers in the mid 1980s. Since 1999 the station has been home to the Union Station Steak & Seafood Restaurant. Passenger service was reinstated by Amtrak from 1972 to 1987, but passengers used a simple plexiglass shelter south of the station.

Norton Depot   *142 East Main St. (Rte. 123)*

Built: Ca. 1853   **Current RR:** None   **Material:** Brick
RLSNE: 77-4   **Current Use:** Vacant

This station was built by the Taunton Branch RR ca. 1853, replacing an earlier depot. The interior of the station included two waiting rooms separated by a central ticket office. The trackside bay window was added before the turn of the last century. In 1926 the local post office moved into one of the waiting rooms and likely took over the entire building when passenger service ended in 1938. Since 1943 the building has been home to a glue factory and a bakery. The vacant station is currently being restored.

Norwood Central Station   *164 Broadway*

Built: 1899   **Current RR:** CSXT, MBTA   **Material:** Yellow Brick
RLSNE: 67-3, 69-0   **Current Use:** Commercial

This yellow brick, slate-roofed station was erected by the New York, New Haven & Hartford RR in 1899 shortly after it took over the New England RR. It replaced a small wooden gable-roofed structure. This location was originally called Dedham Middle but was changed to Norwood Central in 1872, when the town of Norwood was officially formed, largely from a section of Dedham.

This station is similar to ones that existed in Forest Hills, Atlantic and Quincy, MA, and Warren, RI. Interestingly, the downspouts here are actually contained in channels within the building's brickwork. The former New York & New England RR shops were located across the tracks from the station until the late 1990s, when they were demolished to provide much needed additional commuter parking spaces. Today the Norwood Central Station is home to the employment offices of YCN School Transportation and Ice Cream Central.

Onset Depot   *Onset Ave. near Depot St.*

Built: Between 1893 & 1910   **Current RR:** BCLR   **Material:** Wood
RLSNE: 80-17   **Current Use:** Commercial

The Onset Station was built by the New York, New Haven & Hartford RR around the turn of the last century. The station was called Agawam, then East Wareham, Onset Bay, Onset Beach, Onset Junction, and finally Onset. The building, with its oversized hip roof, is similar to one built at Wareham in 1900. The station is now home to the Country Store, an antique shop.

Otter River Freight House   *Willow St. near Main St.*

Built: Between 1851 & 1875   **Current RR:** GRS   **Material:** Brick
RLSNE: 31-19   **Current Use:** Commercial

This former Boston & Maine RR freight house is used by the Seaman Paper Company, manufacturers of food service and wrapping tissues. The company is located north of here on Main Street and is without direct rail service. The freight house is used as a truck-to-rail transfer station. Its south wall has been rebuilt with cinder block. The station, an attractive hip-roofed, one-and-a-half-story structure, was located opposite the freight house. The close proximity of the

Baldwinsville Depot made this station redundant; passenger service to Otter River was discontinued in 1926.

Palmer Station   28 Depot St.

Built: 1884-85   **Current RR:** AMTK, CSXT, MCER, NECR   **Material:** Granite
& Brownstone   **RLSNE:** 14-65, 29-40, 36-0   **Current Use:** Commercial

The Boston & Albany RR and the New London Northern RR commissioned H. H. Richardson to design the trapezoid-shaped Palmer Station in August 1881. However, W. N. Flynt & Company, a contractor used by the NLN on several projects, did not start construction until May 1883. The station, which opened in June the following year, served both the Boston & Albany RR and the Central Vermont RY, which leased the NLN. Constructed of local Monson granite from Flynt's quarry, and trimmed with Longmeadow brownstone, it cost $53,616. A small short-lived separate granite baggage room was located east of the station. The park-like grounds were designed by Fredrick Law Olmsted.

The previous NLN station was a two-story wooden structure very similar to the one at Barretts (four miles north of Palmer). It was located almost directly across the NLN tracks from this station. The former Western RR station, almost identical to the original station surviving at West Brookfield, was located across the B&A main line from this station. After suffering for thirty-five years without a union station, the residents of Palmer finally received a station they could be proud of.

Blake & Robin Lamothe, owners of the building since 1987, have spent countless hours restoring the station. For many years it had been the home and warehouse for a flea market. On July 25, 2004, the Steaming Tender restaurant opened for take-out service, and in September of the following year the restaurant began providing elegant full service dining when it hosted the 2005 Central Vermont Railway Historical Society. The platform canopy on the B&A side was removed in the mid 1980s, but efforts are under way to build a replacement. The station was listed on the National Register of Historic Places in 1988.

Palmer [CV] Freight Office
1 Depot St.

Built: Ca. 1930s   **Current RR:** NECR   **Material:** Wood
RLSNE: 14-64.5   **Current Use:** Railroad

MICHAEL TYLICK

This simple gable-roofed building served the Central Vermont RY as a freight and train order office. Today it serves as an operations and marketing office for the CV's successor, the New England Central RR, and a sister Rail America operation, the Connecticut Southern Railroad.

Park Street [Medford] Station
121 Washington St.

Built: 1894   **Current RR:** None   **Material:** Brick & Granite
RLSNE: 52A-1.5   **Current Use:** Community

The original Park Street Station, a two-story gable-roofed structure, was located north of the tracks and east of Park Street. The Boston & Maine RR built this station in 1894 to replace it. A similar station survives in Stoneham. The Medford Branch was once double tracked to provide frequent service in response to heavy competition from streetcars and rapid transit. Passenger service on the commuter line ended in 1957. The station was added to the National Register of Historic Places in 1975, and today it is home to the Buddy Coholan Memory Loss Center, an adult day care facility for people with Alzheimer's disease.

Pepperell [Fitchburg RR] Depot   *74 Main St. (Rte. 113) at Carter St.*

Built: 1892   **Current RR:** None   **Material:** Wood
RLSNE: 44-6   **Current Use:** Commercial

This attractive depot, with its tall hip roof with flared eaves, is the original station built by the Brookline & Pepperell RR, a Fitchburg RR subsidiary, in 1892. A small wooden gable-roofed freight house once stood about 100 feet north of the station. Boston & Maine RR passenger trains last stopped here in 1931. Presently occupied by Inspirations at the Depot, a gift and flower shop, it has served a variety of commercial enterprises over the years, including a video store, caterer, and real estate office. Despite its many uses, the interior has been well preserved. The original telltales still stand behind the depot.

Pepperell [W&N] Freight House   *Groton St. (Rte. 113)*

Built: Between 1875 & 1886   **Current RR:** None   **Material:** Wood
RLSNE: 41-36   **Current Use:** Residential

RON KARR

When the Worcester & Nashua RR built their line through this area in 1848, the land east of the Nashua River was part of Groton. Soon after, the railroad built a station—then called North Groton—opposite the Pepperell paper mills. In 1851 Main Street was extended across the river to the depot. Six years later the northern part of Groton, including the bustling commercial district around Railroad Square, was annexed to Pepperell, and the station was renamed accordingly.

Between 1875 and 1886 a new wooden hip-roofed depot was erected east of Groton Street, north of this freight house, between the tracks and Tarbell Street. Passenger service ended in 1934, and the station was later demolished. This freight house was likely built by the W&N around the same time as the new depot. Although the building has been modified for use as apartments, the freight doors and slate roof tell of its prior use. The Nashua River Rail Trail passes by here on the old right of way. Pepperell was once served by two railroads; the Brookline & Pepperell RR station still survives at the corner of Main and Carter Streets.

Pine Ridge Depot   *56 Forge Village Rd., Westford*

Built: Ca. 1873   **Current RR:** N/A   **Material:** Wood
RLSNE: 46-14   **Current Use:** Residential

Originally called Westford, this station was built by the Nashua, Acton & Boston RR in 1873, when the line opened. In 1895, when the Boston & Maine RR took control, they renamed the station Pine Ridge to avoid confusion with another Westford Station located on their Stony Brook Branch. At the peak of service Westford was served by three railroads and eight train stations. The locals knew the former NA&B as the Red Line; it was never successful, and it made an early exit from the railroad scene in 1925.

The station, which was the largest intermediate station on the line, included a residence for the station master. It featured a green slate hip roof with triangular dormers on three sides. The station was located above the tracks, which were reached by walking down a set of eighteen stairs.

The depot was formerly located about two-tenths of a mile south of its current location, where Cold Spring Road intersects Patten Road. Cold Spring Road did not exist at the time, and the railroad passed under Patten Road in a small cut.

The depot, freight house, and a section house were all sold and moved after the end of service. A porch has been added to the former trackside of the building, but with careful inspection, the bay window can still be seen. Today the depot serves as a private residence, and the freight house and section house serve as outbuildings.

Pine Ridge Freight House

56 Forge Village Rd., Westford

Built: Ca. 1873   **Current RR:** N/A   **Material:** Wood
RLSNE: 46-14   **Current Use:** Private

This former Nashua, Acton & Boston RR freight house was built in 1873. It was similar to one that existed eight miles north at Dunstable. Along with the depot and the section house, the old freight house was moved to its current location after the end of service. The depot has been converted to a private residence, and the former section house and freight house serve the home as outbuildings.

Pittsfield Depot

East St.

Built: 1968   **Current RR:** AMTK, CSXT, HRR   **Material:** Wood
RLSNE: 29-104.5   **Current Use:** Railroad

This small station was built by the New York Central as a replacement for the 1914 Union Station, which was the second union station to serve Pittsfield. Declining passenger traffic and the high cost of operating led to Union Station's eventual demise. In 1960 the New Haven RR vacated it in favor of their freight house. Later, in 1968, the city of Pittsfield bought and demolished Union Station as part of an urban renewal project. The new station served passengers from 1968 until 1981, when Amtrak built a shelter for passengers near the original Union Station site. The depot is still used today as the CSX Transportation Pittsfield yard office.

Pittsfield Modern Station   *1 Columbus Ave.*

Built: 2002-05   **Current RR:** AMTK, CSXT, HRR   **Material:** Brick & Aluminum
RLSNE: 3-111, 29-106   **Current Use:** Railroad/Transit

JOHN ROY

The Berkshire Regional Transit Authority hired the Wallace Floyd Design Group as the architect for the Berkshire Intermodal Transportation Center. The groundbreaking ceremony was in held in August 2002, with construction following soon after. Originally scheduled to complete the building by summer 2003, the general contractor, David J. Tierney, Jr., was delayed by an extremely cold winter and the bankruptcy of their steel supplier. The three-story brick station finally opened on January 14, 2005. Amtrak patrons and bus travelers share the comforts of a real station located in the heart of the city, across the tracks from the site of the former Pittsfield Union Station. It's a safe bet that no one will miss the old enclosed glass shelter previously used by Amtrak.

Pleasant Lake General Store/Station   *402 Pleasant Lake Ave.*

Built: Before 1865   **Current RR:** None   **Material:** Wood
RLSNE: 80-52   **Current Use:** Commercial

When the Cape Cod RR built its extension from Yarmouth to Orleans in 1865, they used this little general store for a station. Although the railroad built a separate freight house, formerly located across the street where the Cape Cod Rail Trail parking lot is now, passengers continued to use this building until the end of service in the 1930s. The general store also served as the post office until 1972. Today the Pleasant Lake General Store is a popular stop for users of the rail-trail.

Porter Square Modern Station *Somerville Ave. near Mass. Ave., Cambridge*

Built: Ca. 1982   **Current RR:** GRS, MBTA   **Material:** Glass & Concrete
RLSNE: 42-4   **Current Use:** Railroad/Transit

Built ca. 1982 for the MBTA, when they extended the Red Line subway from Harvard Square to Alewife, this station provides convenient connections for today's commuters, who can catch a bus upstairs, an MBTA Fitchburg commuter train downstairs, and a Red Line subway in the basement. A street-level glass entryway features a steel wind-operated sculpture that resembles hot air balloons. This station was formerly called both Cambridge and Porters.

The former Boston & Maine RR Cambridge Station, built in 1937, was a Colonial-style two-level brick building. Entry and ticket sales were at street level, and the waiting room and trains were downstairs, below ground.

Prides Crossing Depot   *590 Hale St. (Rte. 27)*

Built: Between 1880 & 1899   **Current RR:** GRS, MBTA   **Material:** Wood
RLSNE: 59-4   **Current Use:** Railroad/Commercial

JIM TYLICK

The Prides Crossing stop, originally called Prides, was added to the Rockport Branch in 1880. This station was built there by the Boston & Maine RR or its predecessor, the Eastern RR, before the end of the nineteenth century. Its canopies have been shortened and enclosed, and other modifications have been made to the main structure. Today it is occupied by Prides Crossing Confections, and MBTA trains still stop here.

Provincetown Freight House   *365 Shore Rd. (Rte. 6A)*

Built: Ca. 1873   **Current RR:** N/A   **Material:** Wood
RLSNE: 80-86   **Current Use:** Private

The Old Colony RR built this freight house ca. 1873, when they opened their line to Provincetown. It once housed both the freight office and an express office. With the express business gone and the freight office relocated into an old wooden caboose, the building was sold and moved to Pilgrim Heights around 1954. It is privately owned and is currently located near the old right of way, but perpendicular to it. The station, which served as the bus terminal at least until the mid 1950s, was torn down to make room for Duarte Motors.

Reading Station   *32 Lincoln St.*

Built: Between 1865 & 1874   **Current RR:** GRS, MBTA   **Material:** Wood
RLSNE: 52-12   **Current Use:** Commercial

The Boston & Maine RR built this hip-roofed wooden station sometime after the Civil War. Similar structures were built at Melrose, Wakefield Center, Bradford, Amesbury, and Danvers East, and all of these, except Melrose, survive today. Thirty-odd years ago, the fledgling Boston & Maine RR Historical Society held their monthly meetings in this building. The attractive station, which still retains its decorative stained glass windows and slate roof, was added to the National Register of Historic Places in 1984. The station, which until 2004 was home to the Station House Restaurant, is currently occupied by Century 21 North Shore.

Renfrew Depot
Renfrew St.

Built: 1880   **Current RR:** GRS   **Material:** Brick
RLSNE: 30-14   **Current Use:** Commercial

This attractive brick station was recently purchased by the Lancaster Burke Construction Company and is being restored and used as their headquarters. The dormers and covered entranceway were added as part of the renovation. The station was built in 1880 by the Boston & Albany RR.

Rockland Station
21 East Water St.

Built: 1907   **Current RR:** None   **Material:** Brick
RLSNE: 73D-1   **Current Use:** Commercial

Rockland is located on the short Hanover Branch, which was built by the Old Colony & Newport RR in 1868. The first Rockland Depot was a small structure located on the south side of the tracks. It was replaced by a second wooden station with a hip roof, on the north side of the tracks. The current brick station was erected in 1907 by the New York, New Haven & Hartford RR on the same site as the second structure.

The station has been incorporated into a strip mall, roughly triple its original size. The central hip-roofed portion of the mall is the former depot. Today the complex is home to S & H Liquor and a Dunkin' Donuts.

Rockport Freight House

Built: Between 1861 & 1884   **Current RR:** GRS, MBTA   **Material:** Wood
RLSNE: 59-17   **Current Use:** Commercial

This former Eastern RR freight house is located at the far end the MBTA's layover yard. For many years the freight house has been used for storage by a Blue Seal Feeds dealer. The Rockport Station, formerly located east of the freight house, was a large, hip-roofed structure similar to the one surviving at Hudson, MA.

Rosemont Station
179 Rosemont St.

Built: Between 1915 & 1925   **Current RR:** AMTK, GRS, MBTA
Material: Wood   **RLSNE:** 52-35   **Current Use:** Commercial/Residential

MBTA and Amtrak trains pass by here every day, but they no longer stop at this former Boston & Maine RR station. The building has been substantially altered, with a second story added, as well as a large two-story addition in the rear. It has served a variety of commercial occupants and has an apartment upstairs. Until April 2006 the building was the home of Rosemont Station, a gift shop, and Designs by Angelo, a florist. The new owners are expected to open a tea shop and consignment shop for gifts and crafts.

Rosemont passengers were originally served by a small shelter, which was replaced by the 1890s with an eight-foot by twelve-foot shanty. Although larger, the conveniences were limited to a potbelly stove, which was used primarily to keep the B&M flagman warm between trains. That structure, located caddy corner to the current station, was considered by the local residents to be woefully inadequate. They petitioned the railroad for a better station, similar to the one their neighbors to the north in Westville, NH, had recently received. The current station, which was originally a simple one-story hipped-roof structure with a small bay window on the trackside, was the result of their efforts.

Route 128 [Westwood] Modern Station   *50 University Ave.*

Built: 2000   **Current RR:** AMTK, CSXT, MBTA   **Material:** Glass & Aluminum
RLSNE: 27-12   **Current Use:** Railroad/Commercial

Route 128 Station was the brain-child of then New Haven RR president Frederic C. Dumaine, Jr. The New Haven was the first railroad in this country to build a train station completely oriented toward motorists. The station, located north of the current Route 128, opened in February 1953. The buildings (eastbound and westbound) were adapted from prefabricated metal home automobile garages. Station improvements were slow in coming, but by 1965 a new pair of brick stations were built south of Route 128. Construction of the current MBTA station, with a huge multi-level parking garage, was completed in 2000. The old brick stations were demolished.

Ruggles Modern Station   *1150 Tremont St., Boston*

Built: Ca. 1987   **Current RR:** AMTK, CSXT, MBTA   **Material:** Concrete, Glass & Aluminum   **RLSNE:** 27-2   **Current Use:** Railroad/Transit/Commercial

RON KARR

The Southwest Corridor Project (see Forest Hills Modern Station) was completed in the summer of 1987, and this modern station was built for the MBTA as part of this project. Designed by the Boston firm of Stull and Lee, it features an angled concrete entrance and long arched glass walkway. The facilities here provide connecting services to buses, the commuter rail, and the MBTA Orange Line.

Salem Station   *89 Margin St.*

Built: 1959   **Current RR:** GRS, MBTA   **Material:** Stucco & Brick
RLSNE: 56A-0, 57-0, 58-16   **Current Use:** Community

RON KARR

The original station in Salem was built in 1838 to serve the Eastern RR. It was a multi-story wooden depot with ionic columns and a train shed. A replacement station designed by Gridley J. F. Bryant was built in 1846-47. In addition to serving passengers, this huge Norman-style granite building with two medieval-looking towers on either side of the train shed, also served as the Eastern RR's headquarters. Although severely damaged by fire on April 7, 1882, the station survived until 1954, when it was razed as part of the $7-million grade elimination project that created the Salem Tunnel.

In 1959 the Boston & Maine RR built this flat-roofed brick station to replace the razed granite station. Unfortunately, the tracks and covered platforms were only accessible by a long flight of stairs. With the introduction of the Americans with Disabilities Act in 1990, extensive modifications would have been required to permit continued use of the station. Instead, the MBTA built a new "station" off Bridge Street on the bank of the North River. Today's MBTA commuters are provided only a platform and canopy for shelter; however, there are more parking spaces.

The station was extensively remodeled in 2003 for use by Brujitos, a playground/restaurant along the lines of Chuck E. Cheese's restaurant. The brick exterior was replaced with a contemporary southwest-design stucco exterior on all but the back side, and it received new windows and doors. The restaurant closed in June 2006, and the building was taken over by a new occupant, the Phoenix School, a private alternative single-classroom school.

Salisbury Point Depot   *270 Main St.*

Built: 1848   **Current RR:** N/A   **Material:** Wood
RLSNE: 58G-3   **Current Use:** Museum

The only intermediate stop on the Eastern RR's short branch to Amesbury was Salisbury Point Station, which served until passenger service ended in 1936. Two years later an Amesbury resident moved the eleven-by-twenty-foot building to his property and converted it to an aviary to raise canaries.

In 1980 the depot, by then in bad shape, was purchased and moved to the Bartlett Museum on Main Street in Amesbury, where it was restored and dedicated in 1983. It is presently owned by the Salisbury Point Railroad Historical Society, which pays a token rent to the Bartlett Museum, a former school house featuring an extensive collection of local history.

Saugus Depot   *344 Central St.*

Built: Ca. 1853   **Current RR:** None   **Material:** Wood
RLSNE: 60-7   **Current Use:** Commercial

The Saugus Branch RR built this station ca. 1853. The depot has received a major addition on the west end, which is occupied by All City Glass & Mirror Company. A dance school occupies the original portion of the structure. The building, which is similar to the one surviving at Cliftondale, as well as the recently demolished Maplewood Depot, still retains some of its arched windows.

Saundersville Station
74 Elmwood St.

Built: Between 1870 & 1889   **Current RR:** PW   **Material:** Wood
RLSNE: 25-34   **Current Use:** Residential

The Saundersville Station has been moved south one-quarter mile from its original location and turned 180 degrees. It was placed on a foundation overlooking the railroad tracks, where it serves as a private residence. The depot originally had a gabled-hip roof; the hip portion has been removed and an addition added on the north side. The Providence & Worcester RR likely built this station some time between 1870 and 1889 to replace an earlier structure.

Sharon Station
Chestnut St.

Built: 1936   **Current RR:** AMTK, CSXT, MBTA   **Material:** Brick
RLSNE: 27-18   **Current Use:** Railroad/Commercial

Sharon once had a wooden Victorian-style station like those still surviving at East Greenwich and Kingston, RI. The current single-story Colonial-style brick station was designed by Engineer F. J. Pitcher, who worked for the New Haven RR. Built in 1936, it is similar to other New Haven stations including Quincy Adams, Yarmouth, and Route 128 in Massachusetts, and Meriden in Connecticut, none of which survive today. The railroad maintained a ticket agency here until the 1970s. Today the station is home to Chuu Chuu Donuts.

Sharon Passenger Shelter   Buckland Rd.

Built: 1936   **Current RR:** AMTK, CSXT, MBTA   **Material:** Brick & Wood
RLSNE: 27-18   **Current Use:** Railroad

This three-sided shelter was built at the same time as the station across the tracks. Then, as now, more commuters waited for trains into Boston, so this simple shelter served outbound riders, while better facilities were placed on the inbound side, where the most passengers would benefit.

Shawsheen Station   Haverhill St. (Rte. 133), Andover

Built: Ca. 1908   **Current RR:** AMTK, GRS, MBTA   **Material:** Brick
RLSNE: 52-24   **Current Use:** Commercial

Shawsheen Village, a planned community, was built to house the American Woolen Company mill workers and their families. The Boston & Maine RR built this station there around 1908. It is strikingly similar to, but smaller than, the Methuen Station. No longer serving passengers, the building is used for storage, and most of its windows are boarded up for security. The westbound passenger canopy still stands, although it is in bad shape. The entire village is listed on the National Register of Historic Places.

Sheffield Combination Depot   Rte. 7A near Rte. 7

Built: Ca. 1850   **Current RR:** N/A   **Material:** Wood
RLSNE: 3-79   **Current Use:** Residential

The Sheffield Combination Depot was built by the Stockbridge & Pittsfield RR ca. 1850 and was very similar to the one built at Housatonic (still extant) and the original ones at South Lee and Lenox. The station, sold to a private party in the 1970s, has been moved about two miles south to Route 7A. Formerly occupied by a bed and breakfast, the depot was recently purchased by a private party.

Sheffield Freight House   *Main St. (Rte. 7)*

Built: Ca. 1909 **Current RR:** HRR **Material:** Wood
RLSNE: 3-79 **Current Use:** Commercial

This former New York, New Haven & Hartford RR freight house is located off Route 7 behind the Sheffield town offices. A garage door has been added to this ca. 1909 building, which is currently used for commercial purposes.

Shelburne Falls Freight House   *14 Depot St.*

Built: 1867 **Current RR:** GRS **Material:** Wood
RLSNE: 31-69 **Current Use:** Museum

This is the original freight house built in 1867 by the Troy & Greenfield RR when they reached Shelburne Falls from Greenfield. The Shelburne Falls Trolley Museum operates the restored Shelburne Falls & Colrain Street RY trolley on a short stretch of track in the former freight yard. On June 16, 2004, the trolley museum purchased the entire freight yard, including the freight house, which it will preserve as an historic landmark.

Shirley Passenger Shelter *Front St. near Church St.*

Built: 1993   **Current RR:** GRS, MBTA   **Material:** Wood
RLSNE: 42-39   **Current Use:** Railroad

This structure is not the original depot; it was built by the MBTA in 1993. The attractive hip-roofed building, with its decorative copper ridge flashing, replaced a plexiglass "bubble" erected in 1981 by the MBTA, when service was restored here. Shirley was once served by a modest-sized wooden structure with a hip roof and a buggy port.

Silver Hill Passenger Shelter *Merriam St.*

Built: 1979   **Current RR:** GRS, MBTA   **Material:** Wood
RLSNE: 42-15   **Current Use:** Railroad

Silver Hill, a turn-of-the-twentieth-century neighborhood in Weston, which comprises many Queen Anne and Colonial Revival homes, was added to the National Register of Historic Places in August 2004. Although this eighty-nine-lot subdivision was created from former farm land, Silver Hill was an established flag stop well into the Fitchburg RR era. This small three-sided shelter was built by the MBTA in 1979. It is reminiscent of old-fashioned flag stop shelters and resembles the eastbound Mystic, CT, shelter. The flag stop was discontinued in 1981 but was later reinstated. Today two weekday trains stop here in each direction, but passengers are no longer required to display a flag. Most passengers who use this station, which is located in a residential neighborhood and provides extremely limited parking on site, probably walk to the station.

South Athol Combination Depot   *Rice Rd. near Hackett St.*

Built: Ca. 1871   **Current RR:** None   **Material:** Wood
RLSNE: 35-40   **Current Use:** Residential

The South Athol Combination Depot was built by the Athol & Enfield RR ca. 1871, when they extended their line from Barretts Junction to Athol. The railroad had planned to erect only a flag stop, but the village residents insisted on a regular station, and the railroad obliged them. Similar structures were built at Collins, North Dana, and New Salem, the latter still extant. Passenger service here ended in 1935, and the station now serves as a private residence.

South Bolton Combination Depot   *484 South Bolton Rd.*

Built: Between 1882 & 1899   **Current RR:** None   **Material:** Wood
RLSNE: 34-25   **Current Use:** Residential

RON KARR

The small gable-roofed South Bolton Station was built soon after the Central Massachusetts RR extended its line to Hudson in 1881-82. It was originally located on South Bolton Road, north of the tracks and west of the road. The agency was discontinued on January 10, 1921. Around 1943 the building was sold to Christian Lee and moved a short distance on a flatbed truck to 484 South Bolton Road. After being placed on a foundation and enlarged with the addition of a second story, it became the Lee family's home.

South Deerfield [B&M] Freight House   *7 Railroad St.*

Built: Between 1846 & 1875   **Current RR:** GRS   **Material:** Wood
RLSNE: 33-28   **Current Use:** Commercial

This former Boston & Maine RR freight house is now occupied by the Nutri-Systems Meals-on-Wheels Store, an on-line supplier of equipment for Meals-on-Wheels providers. The depot, no longer extant, was located between the freight house and Elm Street. It was a simple gable-roofed wooden structure with a trackside bay window.

South Hanson Depot   *1120 Main St. (Rte. 27)*

Built: Ca. 1845   **Current RR:** MBTA   **Material:** Wood
RLSNE: 73-25   **Current Use:** Vacant

The original Hanson station burned down just two weeks after opening. This exact duplicate was built ca. 1845. Originally called Hanson, the name was changed to South Hanson on June 24, 1878. This station is similar in style to other Old Colony RR stations, including one at Scituate that no longer survives. A separate freight house was located just north of the depot. The Anderson Hay & Grain Store formerly occupied the depot, but today it appears to be vacant. Across the tracks, the MBTA has constructed a high-level platform for today's commuters.

South Lawrence Freight House

Andover St.

Built: Between 1870 & 1900   **Current RR:** AMTK, GRS, MBTA
Material: Metal Siding & Wood   **RLSNE:** 52-25.5   **Current Use:** Railroad

This large old freight house is used by Guilford Rail System as their Lawrence yard office. The building has received metal sheathing and has been enlarged.

South Lee Depot

40 Willow St.

Built: 1890   **Current RR:** HRR   **Material:** Brick
RLSNE: 3-96   **Current Use:** Commercial

This Gothic-style brick station was built by the New York, New Haven & Hartford RR to replace an earlier wooden structure similar to the ones surviving at Cornwall Bridge, CT, and Housatonic, MA. It was located just west of the Willow Street grade crossing before it was moved westward to its current location. Many of the doors and windows have been closed off with brick, and the building has received a small addition. Today Mead Specialty Paper uses it for storage.

South Middleton Depot   *Maple St. (Rte. 62), Middleton*

Built: Ca. 1866   **Current RR:** N/A   **Material:** Wood
RLSNE: 56-7   **Current Use:** Vacant

RON KARR

This depot was originally located across the street from what is now the Bostik industrial property on Boston Street in South Middleton. Also known as Oakdale, Paper Mills, and Middleton, it was on the Salem & Lowell RR line, which opened in 1850. Passenger service in South Middleton ended in September 1932, and the depot was moved out of town and appended to a residence.

After being lost for decades, this station reappeared when a developer was preparing to demolish it to build a larger house on property located at 36 North Street in North Reading. The porcelain "South Middleton" station sign and the previous owner's insistence that this was an old station prompted the developer to investigate the history of the structure. The Middleton Historical Society and town officials were able to confirm that this was indeed the old depot from South Middleton.

On April 19, 2006, with private and town funds, the depot was moved to it current location. It sits on blocks in a wooded area at the end of an unmarked driveway accessible from Maple Street, about a block and a half from Route 114, just before King Street splits off of Maple. It can also be reached via a short walk from the parking lot behind Memorial Hall (on Route 114), by walking downhill through the woods toward Maple Street. The town hopes to restore the station, but its final location and use have yet to be determined.

South Station   *Dewey Square, Boston*

Built: 1896-98   **Current RR:** AMTK, CSXT, MBTA   **Material:** Stone
RLSNE: 27-0, 62-2, 64-0, 68-0, 73-0   **Current Use:** Railroad/Commercial/Transit

The early history of Boston's South Station revolved around four railroads: Boston & Worcester, Boston & Providence, Old Colony, and New York & New England. The B&W was eventually consolidated into the Boston & Albany, while the remaining three became part of the New York, New Haven & Hartford.

The B&W was the first railroad to serve Boston. Their original station, located on Washington Street at the corner of Indiana Place (later Corning Street), opened April 16, 1834. It served until November 7, 1836, when a second station was built at Beach and Lincoln Streets on land recently reclaimed by filling the former South Cove tidal basin. The city of Boston paid a $75,000 bonus to the railroad for moving its station here. The new two-story brick structure had passenger facilities on one side and tracks on the other side of the ground floor. The building's second story was used for offices and featured a cupola with a weathervane on top. The station was expanded to a length of 290 feet in 1841.

In March 1846 a new station was opened adjacent to the existing one. Built by the B&W on their property, it was erected for use by the Old Colony. This arrangement was short-lived, since the OC opened a station on Kneeland Street on May 19, 1847. With the departure of the OC, the B&W began using both structures for its trains, and in 1863 the B&W remodeled and modernized them, including separate sections for inbound and outbound trains.

In 1867 the B&W was consolidated with the Western RR as the B&A, and planning for a new station began in fall 1878. The following year, the railroad commissioners recommended the B&A use the newly built B&P station, but the B&A deemed it impractical and undesirable to share that facility. Instead they erected a new station across the street from the former one, on the south side of Kneeland Street. The three-story structure, with a six-track train shed, was constructed of brick with granite trimmings. Though not quite finished, it opened on September 4, 1881. The first floor was used for passenger services and the upper floors for company offices. The old station was converted to handle freight and express until its removal in 1918. The Kneeland Street Station served passengers until July 23, 1899, when all services were transferred to the new South Station. The building was converted to a cold storage warehouse, but was torn down in the early 1960s to make way for a highway interchange.

Meanwhile, the B&P had begun service on June 4, 1834, from a brick station located on Pleasant Street (now part of Broadway). This two-story structure with an attached train shed was expanded in 1842 with the addition of a four-story clock tower and a single-story wing. It served until 1875, when the city of Boston, as part of the Columbus Avenue improvement project, forced the railroad to build a new station across the street at Park Square.

The new station, which opened January 4, 1875, was designed by Peabody and Stearns. It was a large Gothic-style, three-story brick and sandstone structure. It included a six-story, four-sided clock tower and a

Dewey Square Station, Boston, ca. 1890. This small attractive station was built on the site of Boston's present South Station by the New York & New England RR in 1880-81, next door to their railroad offices. It was used for only sixteen years before being demolished to make way for South Station. (Courtesy of the Beverly Historical Society & Museum, Beverly, MA, Walker Transportation Collection)

six-hundred-foot long, five-track train shed. At the time it was claimed to be the world's largest station and probably the most elegant of all Boston's stations. It was closed on September 10, 1899, when all trains were transferred to the new South Station. The building continued to serve other commercial purposes until it was damaged by fire and torn down in 1909.

The OC began service on November 10, 1845. Their first station was located south of the Fort Point Channel at South Boston. In March 1846 their line was extended to Albany Street, and they opened their new station adjacent to the B&W station. This arrangement required a grade crossing of both companies' lines, and this difficulty led to the construction of the station on Kneeland Street, which opened on May 19, 1847. It was a three-story rectangular brick station, which had a 544-foot-long train shed and cost a little over $39,000. The ground floor was used for passengers, and the upper floors served as the railroad's headquarters.

In 1867 the Kneeland Street Station was remodeled in accordance with plans from noted architect Gridley J. F. Bryant, who also designed the 1846-47 Salem Station. The new look included a bay window, a large clock facing South Street, which was illuminated at night, and an extension on the east end. Passenger traffic was transferred to the new South Station on December 31, 1898. The station was then turned over to the B&A, which used the head house for a freight office. Having fallen into disrepair and deemed unsafe, it was torn down in May 1918.

The Boston & New York Central RR, a predecessor to the NY&NE, began serving Boston on January 1, 1855, from its depot located at the foot of Summer Street. That station was destroyed on November 9, 1872, in Boston's Great Fire. A replacement wooden station consisting of a head house and two-track train shed was built on the same site to serve both passengers and freight. It proved to be too small, so two separate freight houses were constructed in 1880, and the station was completely rebuilt in 1880-81. It was a single-story gable-roofed structure featuring a center gable with a clock and a two-track train shed. The station served passengers until August 22, 1896, when passengers were transferred to the former OC station, and this structure was torn down in preparation for construction of South Station on the same site.

By 1895 politicians, the media, and the public were all pressuring the NYNH&H and the B&A to build a union station. In fact it was mandated by a bill passed in 1896. Union Station would consolidate the NYNH&H's former OC (Kneeland Street), B&P (Park Square), and New England RR stations as well as the B&A's Kneeland Street Station. Construction costs were split: 80% for the NYNH&H and 20% for the B&A. The building was dedicated on December 30, 1898. On New Years Day 1899 the former OC and NE route trains began using it. They were soon followed by the B&A

This early twentieth–century post card depicts Boston's South Station in its prime. The jewel of twenty-three New England stations designed by Sheply, Rutan and Coolidge, it was the region's most prominent rail station and one of the largest in the nation until a large portion of it was demolished in the 1970s. (Ron Karr collection)

trains on July 23, and finally, by the former B&P line trains on September 10.

The Classical Revival-style stone building was designed by Sheply, Rutan and Coolidge. It included a large waiting room with a 28½-foot-high ceiling, marble floors, two parcel areas, two baggage areas, a restaurant, and a large triple-span train shed containing 28 tracks. Until 1913 it was the largest and busiest station in the country.

South Station was built with a little-known innovation. It had two underground loop tracks to expedite rush hour loading and unloading. This loop was the first of its kind in this country. Although later successfully incorporated into Grand Central Terminal, the loop here was only used for one day. Despite having been designed with an elaborate exhaust system, steam locomotive fumes were too dense to continue use.

The train shed was removed in the early 1930s, and between 1972 and 1973 the express building on Atlantic Avenue and about half the Summer Street façade were removed. After a long period of decline, in 1984 South Station was closed for complete rebuilding. From 1984 to 1988 a temporary station served the public while most of the station interior was gutted. Although little more than the central portion of the original L-shaped station remains, it still provides travelers with modern conveniences, such as a food court and shops, along with the traditional ticket counters, baggage check, and waiting areas. Above the main entrance at Dewey Square is the only remaining hand-wound tower clock in New England. The building, now owned by the MBTA, was placed on the National Register of Historic Places in 1975.

South Sudbury Depot   37 Union Ave.

Built: Ca. 1952   **Current RR:** None   **Material:** Wood
RLSNE: 34-16, 47-5   **Current Use:** Commercial

The original Framingham & Lowell RR station and freight house, built before the Massachusetts Central RR reached South Sudbury, were located just north of the Boston Post Road (Route 20). After the arrival of the MC, the Old Colony RR built a beautiful Victorian-style union station with a three-story tower. That station, built ca. 1887-91, was located in the southeast corner of the diamond. Passenger service on the F&L, then under the flag of the New York, New Haven & Hartford, was suspended in 1933, leaving only the Boston & Maine RR in the large station. The costs to maintain the old building were too high, so the B&M erected this simple depot ca. 1952 to serve South Sudbury. Despite attempts to move and preserve the Victorian-era station, it was demolished after the new one opened.

The sign on the station reads "Sudbury," although the original name of this station was South Sudbury; Sudbury (see Sudbury Depot) was located one mile north on the Framingham & Lowell RR. The South Sudbury Depot currently houses a limousine service.

South Truro Depot
Old County Rd. near Prince Valley Rd.

Built: 1873   **Current RR:** None   **Material:** Wood
RLSNE: 80-74   **Current Use:** Residential

DOUG SCOTT

This depot was built to serve the extension of the Old Colony RR's Cape Cod Branch from Wellfleet to Provincetown, which opened in 1873. Similar stations existed at North Eastham, Truro, North Truro, and West Falmouth. Passenger service on the branch east of Yarmouth ended in 1938, with a temporary restoration during 1940. The station was moved a few feet east around the middle of the last century. It now serves as a summer cottage, which is hard to find because of its location off a dirt road one-tenth of a mile south of the intersection of Old County and Prince Valley Roads.

South Walpole Depot
44 Summer St.

Built: Ca. 1912   **Current RR:** CSXT   **Material:** Wood
RLSNE: 72-16   **Current Use:** Government

This former New York, New Haven & Hartford RR depot served passengers until 1933, when service on this line was dropped. The freight agency remained in the station until 1941. Except for the removal of its order boards, the South Walpole Depot has not changed much since it was built ca. 1912. Today it is used by the United States Postal Service.

South Weymouth Depot   85 Pond St.

Built: 1845   **Current RR:** CSXT, MBTA   **Material:** Wood
RLSNE: 73-15   **Current Use:** Commercial

This clapboard-sided, hip-roofed station served the traveling public for 110 years before service was abandoned. Built in 1845, it is the original depot constructed by the Old Colony RR. After passenger service ended in 1959, the depot was used by a drywall company for about twenty years. Like other former Old Colony stations, the South Weymouth Depot was not used by the MBTA when it restored service. Vacant and in danger of being demolished, it was purchased in 2001 by a private party. In 2005 the station was turned away from the tracks and towards the road; it has been renovated and today is home to the Olde Depot General Store. The new MBTA stop is located adjacent to the former South Weymouth Naval Air Station.

Southbridge Station   6 Larochelle Way

Built: Ca. 1910-11   **Current RR:** None   **Material:** Stone & Brick
RLSNE: 16A-18   **Current Use:** Municipal

The original Southbridge Station was completed in November 1866. It was a wooden gable-roofed structure with circular eave windows and a train shed. This Spanish-style station, which included a waiting room, baggage room, and ticket office, was built ca. 1910-11 by the New York, New Haven & Hartford RR. During the early 1900s the NYNH&H built many Spanish-style stations throughout their system. Other survivors include West Barnstable, Buzzards Bay, North Scituate, and Nantasket in Massachusetts, Rowayton and Naugatuck in Connecticut, and Westerly in Rhode Island.

The last passenger train to serve Southbridge was a Mack rail bus on August 30, 1930. The former brick freight house burned down in the

1980s. Today the station is home to the Causabon Senior Center. It was added to the National Register of Historic Places in 1989.

Southville Combination Depot　　　　　　　　　260 Parkerville Rd.

Built: 1835　**Current RR:** N/A　**Material:** Wood
RLSNE: 64-28　**Current Use:** Residential

This Carpenter Gothic combination depot was built by the Boston & Worcester RR in 1835. It was moved across Southville Road to its current location with a team of horses around 1905. The station's passenger canopies and covered buggy port were removed and it was converted to general store, which lasted until the late 1960s. The former depot was purchased and converted to a private residence in 1973. The replacement station, a stone structure similar to those designed by H. H. Richardson, no longer survives.

Spencer Station　　　　　　　　　　　　　　　　62 Wall St.

Built: 1879　**Current RR:** None　**Material:** Brick
RLSNE: 29C-2　**Current Use:** Commercial

MICHAEL TYLCK

This hip-roofed structure is the original station erected when the Spencer RR built the line in 1879. All 2.2 miles of the line from the Boston & Albany RR junction to the station are up-hill. The freight house and a small yard were located south of the station. Passenger service here ended in 1932-33. Today the station is occupied by Artie's Restaurant. Plans are underway to create a rail-trail between here and South Spencer.

Springfield Station   55 Frank B. Murray St.

Built: 1926   **Current RR:** AMTK, CSO, CSXT, GRS   **Material:** Brick
RLSNE: 8-62, 18-29, 29-54, 33-0   **Current Use:** Vacant

The original Springfield Station, built for the Western RR, opened in 1839. It was a unique wooden Egyptian-style building with towers on both sides and a train shed in the middle. Unfortunately, in 1851 sparks from a locomotive ignited a fire that destroyed it. A replacement station was built later that year, a brick union station with a large five-track arched train shed.

Nearly four decades later, the Boston & Albany RR, successor to the Western, hired the Boston architectural firm of Shepley, Rutan and Coolidge to design a new union station as part of a grade crossing elimination project. Construction was started in August 1888 with the demolition of the old Union Station. Norcross Brothers of Worcester, the contractor on many Shepley, Rutan and Coolidge stations, completed the building in March 1891. The combined cost of the granite station and arched bridge over Main Street was nearly a half million dollars.

The new Union Station was actually two structures on opposite sides of the tracks, connected by a massive one-story battered stone base under the tracks. Although owned by the B&A, both the New York, New Haven & Hartford and the Boston & Maine RRs paid rent to use it. This station was torn down in 1920 to make room for construction of its successor; the arched bridge over Main Street still survives.

Completed in 1926, this brick station was built by the B&A, and like its predecessor, was shared by the NYNH&H and the B&M. In addition to passenger facilities, the station contained Signal Tower 40 and the main offices of the B&A. The offices were used until 1987, when Conrail consolidated its New England and Albany Divisions at Selkirk, NY. For ten years the deteriorating building remained unused. In 1998 the city of Springfield received federal funding to restore the building, and work is under way to transform it into an intermodal center with retail and office space. The three strange-looking towers are baggage elevators; when originally built there were four of them. Similar baggage elevators were also used at Worcester's Union Station, but no longer exist.

Today's Amtrak patrons use a small modern station located across the tracks from the 1926 station (see Springfield Modern Station).

Springfield Modern Station
66 Lyman St.

Built: 1994   **Current RR:** AMTK, CSO, CSXT, GRS   **Material:** Cast Concrete
RLSNE: 8-62, 18-29, 29-54, 33-0   **Current Use:** Railroad

RON GALLANT

This simple station, which provides a waiting room, ticket office, and baggage check, was opened on Thanksgiving Day 1994. Prior to that Amtrak's ticket office was located in the pedestrian tunnel that connected the 1926 Union Station's grand concourse to Lyman Street. Plans are underway to restore Union Station, located across the tracks from here.

State Line [CV] Depot
90 Palmer Rd. (Rte. 32), Monson

Built: Between 1850 & 1875   **Current RR:** N/A   **Material:** Wood
RLSNE: 14-56   **Current Use:** Commercial

This diminutive station, with its fancy gabled-hip roof with flared eaves, is similar to the one that existed at Kittemaug, CT, and to several section houses found elsewhere on the Central Vermont. It was moved to the Quaboag Country Club in Monson prior to 1950 and is currently used for storage. The depot was formerly located on Route 32 on the northeast side of the grade crossing, just north of the Connecticut-Massachusetts border.

Sterling Freight House   *13 Waushacum Ave.*

Built: Between 1848 & 1875   **Current RR:** None   **Material:** Wood
RLSNE: 40-12   **Current Use:** Commercial

Now used for storage, this gable-roofed building was likely the original Fitchburg & Worcester RR freight house. The station, a simple gable-roofed structure, was located south of the freight house. Freight service to Sterling was abandoned in 1962. A large factory building located nearby has been recycled and is now home to the Cider Mill Building Arts & Antiques. The short but scenic Sterling Rail-Trail begins in the parking lot south of the old freight house.

Sterling Junction Freight House   *4 Campground Rd.*

Built: Between 1848 & 1888   **Current RR:** GRS   **Material:** Wood
RLSNE: 40-14, 41-12   **Current Use:** Commercial

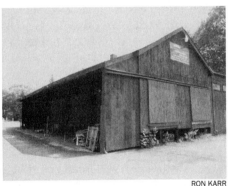

RON KARR

The Sterling Freight House was purchased by Richard Blanchflower in 1954. By that time the depot and express office had already been removed. They were located west of the freight house and in between the tracks of the Boston & Maine RR and the New York, New Haven & Hartford RR. The depot was a simple gable-roofed structure, and the express office was a small hip-roofed building. Over the years, the owner has added a full length lean-to on the trackside of the freight house as well as the three connected buildings on the street side. The main building still has its original slate roof, and its lines are clearly visible in spite of the additions. Today the freight house is home to Sterling Storage and Sterling Plumbing & Heating Contractors.

Stockbridge Station

Depot St.

Built: 1893   **Current RR:** BSRM, HRR   **Material:** Blue Dolomite Stone
RLSNE: 3-94   **Current Use:** Railroad

In the late 1880s the Laurel Hill Civic Association got tired of badgering the Housatonic RR for a new depot and began raising funds to erect one. The group eventually paid for half of this English Gothic Revival-style building, which was designed by Frank Waller of New York City and built for the New York, New Haven & Hartford RR in 1893. It replaced the original depot, which was similar to the one surviving at Housatonic.

The New Haven RR leased the building for use as a night club in the mid 1960s. A few years later, a late-night fire gutted the interior. The railroad wanted to raze the structure, but it yielded to public pressure and sold it instead. The depot was reconstructed and turned into a gift shop. Since then it has been home to several restaurants and other commercial enterprises, but today the beautifully restored station is once again serving railroad passengers. The town of Stockbridge is the final southbound stop for the Berkshire Scenic RY's tourist trains. Stockbridge is well known for the many rich and famous people who have called it home, including Nathaniel Hawthorne and Norman Rockwell.

Stoneham Station

40 Pine St.

Built: Ca. 1896   **Current RR:** None   **Material:** Brick & Granite
RLSNE: 51B-2.5   **Current Use:** Commercial

This Boston & Maine RR station was opened in September 1896. It replaced an earlier wooden structure erected in 1863. This brick station is very similar to the one surviving at Park Street in Medford. It was added to the National Register of Historic Places in 1984 and is home to the Stoneham Municipal Employees Federal Credit Union.

Stoughton Station

45 Wyman St.

Built: 1887-88   **Current RR:** CSXT, MBTA   **Material:** Granite
RLSNE: 27B-4, 76A-2   **Current Use:** Railroad/Commercial

The Boston & Providence RR first came to Stoughton in the spring of 1845. Their original wooden depot stood at the end of Railroad Avenue. A second station was built the same year, after the original one burned down. The second station was blown down in a heavy gale and replaced by a third structure. That building was a combination station, freight house, and engine house located south of Wyman Street at the end of Railroad Avenue.

In the late 1880s the B&P commissioned noted Boston architect Charles Brigham, who also designed the first Boston Museum of Fine Arts and the B&P's Dedham Station, to design a new station. Construction of this handsome station, with its sixty-two-foot, four-sided clock tower, was started in May 1887 and completed the following March. Some 850 tons of granite, hauled from the nearby Myron Gilbert quarry, were used in its construction. The predecessor station was torn down later that year.

Declining demand for rail service forced service cutbacks, and in 1958 service to North Easton was dropped, so Stoughton once again became a terminal station. In the 1960s this Victorian-style building, which had survived a direct hit from an express train in 1924, faced its greatest threat: urban renewal. Plans called for a complete revamping of Stoughton's business district and included the station's demolition.

Fortunately, the Stoughton Historical Society stepped in and helped save the only remaining example of a towered terminal built in the late nineteenth century. The station was listed on the National Register of Historic Places in 1974. Today's MBTA commuters can still take refuge from the weather inside the beautifully restored historic structure. Inside the old station a vendor sells limited convenience items to the morning's commuters.

Sudbury Depot   40 Hudson Rd.

Built: Between 1871 & 1899   **Current RR:** None   **Material:** Wood
RLSNE: 47-6   **Current Use:** Residential

The Sudbury Depot, now located about two-tenths of a mile west of its former location, is a private residence. The T-shaped, hip-roofed structure was originally located east of the grade crossing and north of the tracks. It has received additions but is well cared for and still has a great deal of charm.

Sudbury Freight House   51 Hudson Rd.

Built: Between 1871 & 1889   **Current RR:** N/A   **Material:** Wood
RLSNE: 47-6   **Current Use:** Private

The former Sudbury Freight House has been moved a quarter mile west along Hudson Road to a private residence, where it has been modified for use as a garage. Although it is difficult to see from the road, the sign over the garage door still says "Sudbury."

Swampscott Depot   10 Railroad Ave.

Built: 1868   **Current RR:** GRS, MBTA   **Material:** Wood
RLSNE: 58-13, 58C-0   **Current Use:** Community

The Swampscott Depot was built by the Eastern RR in 1868. It was designed by George W. Cram, who worked for the railroad. The contractor was Charles Nathan Ingalls, who also built the Danvers East and Chelsea Stations for the Eastern. The station features a hip roof and a four-sided awning, which gives it the appearance of a double roof. This was a standard design similar to others built throughout New England during this time period, including those surviving at Danvers East, Bradford, Amesbury, and Ossipee, NH. The station no longer sports its fancy clock tower and ten gabled roof dormers. It is owned by the MBTA and leased to a community service group, which helps with its upkeep. Modern commuter patterns and the depot's location on the outbound track make this an unattractive location for commercial enterprises. In 1998 the station was placed on the National Register of Historic Places.

Tapleyville Passenger Shelter   *195 Log Cabin Rd., Kennebunkport, ME*

Built: Between 1900 & 1920   **Current RR:** N/A   **Material:** Wood
RLSNE: 54-8.5   **Current Use:** Museum

MATT COSGRO

The former Tapleyville Passenger Shelter was moved to the Seashore Trolley Museum in 1964, three years after passenger service ended. The shelter was purchased from the Boston & Maine RR for one dollar and moved by truck to Kennebunkport, ME. It replaced a frame structure with a gabled-hip roof. Today the small three-sided structure is located near the museum's Visitors Center and has been renamed "Arundel."

Tewksbury Center Depot   *44 North St.*

Built: 1900   **Current RR:** N/A   **Material:** Wood
RLSNE: 51D-3   **Current Use:** Residential

RON KARR

This former Boston & Maine RR depot was built in 1900. It is similar to one that existed nearby at Wamesit. Passenger service ended here in 1924. The hip-roofed building has been moved to a nearby location and is now a private residence.

Thayer Depot
Mill St., Lancaster

Built: Mid 1800s   **Current RR:** GRS   **Material:** Wood
RLSNE: 41-18   **Current Use:** Abandoned

When built by the Worcester & Nashua RR, this depot was called South Lancaster. In 1909 the name was changed to Prescott, only to be renamed Thayer the following year. The agency here was closed in 1952. Today the gable-roofed building is boarded up and looks as though it has not been cared for in years, but the decorative king post and the gabled bay window certainly reveal its past use.

Topsfield Depot
16 Summer St.

Built: 1853-54   **Current RR:** N/A   **Material:** Wood
RLSNE: 54-15   **Current Use:** Residential

RON KARR

This is the original Topsfield Depot built in 1853-54 by the Danvers & Georgetown RR. It was replaced in 1897 by a larger station with a flared-eaves hip roof, located on Park Avenue midway between Main and Summer Streets and east of the railroad tracks. That station was torn down in the early 1950s. Originally located at the Main Street railroad crossing, the older depot was later moved to the Main Street location that is now occupied by the post office, then moved again to Summer Street, where it resides today. When originally constructed, it had a one-and-a-half-story station section and two-story tenement section for the station agent and his family. The apartment portion of the building is no longer extant. The remaining section serves as a private residence.

Topsfield Freight House (1 of 2) — *South of 11 Grove St.*

Built: Between 1854 & 1875   **Current RR:** None   **Material:** Wood
RLSNE: 54-15   **Current Use:** Vacant

This former Boston & Maine RR freight house stands vacant. It is the first of two freight houses still extant in Topsfield. Even though the rails to Topsfield were abandoned in 1981, the MBTA still owns it.

Topsfield Freight House (2 of 2) — *11 Grove St.*

Built: Between 1875 & 1900   **Current RR:** None   **Material:** Wood
RLSNE: 54-15   **Current Use:** Private

This freight house was built by the railroad to supplement the first freight house (located nearest to Main Street). Around 1944 the railroad leased it to the Essex County Co-op, who used it for a grain warehouse. The co-op eventually bought the building from the railroad and later sold it to a private party. It was common practice for railroads to construct additional warehouse space and lease it to consignees. It made good business sense: the railroad earned revenue from the building and from the handling of freight for the consignee.

Touisset Depot   *727 Pearse Rd.*

Built: 1860s   **Current RR:** None   **Material:** Wood
RLSNE: 26A-3   **Current Use:** Residential

The former Touisset Depot has received several additions and today serves as a private residence. The station is located on a rise; the tracks passed behind it and crossed Pearse Road on a double-tracked girder bridge. The western abutment and concrete pedestrian stairs leading up to the station identify the bridge's former location.

Townsend Combination Depot/Freight House   *Railroad St.*

Built: Ca. 1848   **Current RR:** None   **Material:** Wood
RLSNE: 43-10   **Current Use:** Commercial

This former combination depot was built by the Fitchburg RR ca. 1848, when the line was opened. The small building was woefully inadequate, and in the early 1880s the townspeople voted to build Depot Street and advise the president of the Fitchburg of their desire to have better passenger facilities. A Victorian-style replacement station was erected west of the old building, and the old station was used for freight after that. Formerly occupied by Townsend Grain, which has been out of business for several years, the building's current use is not clear. The depot is deteriorating, with vegetation encroaching on all sides, but it still sports the Townsend Grain sign.

Townsend Station   *Railroad St.*

Built: Ca. 1882   **Current RR:** None   **Material:** Wood
RLSNE: 43-10   **Current Use:** Commercial

RON KARR

This Victorian-style station was erected by the Fitchburg RR around 1882 to replace the first station (see Townsend Combination Depot/Freight House), which was too small to accommodate the growing town. The heavily modified station was similar to one surviving in Littleton and one that existed in Orange. Today it is occupied by a NAPA Auto Parts store that uses the addition on the west end for retail and the station portion for parts storage.

Uxbridge Station   *20 South Main St.*

Built: 1890s   **Current RR:** PW   **Material:** Brick & Stone
RLSNE: 25-24   **Current Use:** Commercial

The Providence & Worcester RR built this granite and brick Queen Anne-style station in the 1890s. It is similar to one that existed in Millville just four miles south of here. It replaced the original station, which was a large combination depot with a low-pitched gable roof. There used to be a large wooden water tower just north of the station. The freight house, which still survives, is located off a long spur that leaves the main line one-third of a mile south of the station.

The station has been the home of Savers Bank's Uxbridge branch for many years. Unfortunately, the trackside windows and doors have all been closed off and a glass foyer added in the front for the ATM. In 1983 it was added to the National Register of Historic Places.

Uxbridge Freight House
46 Depot St.

Built: Between 1847 & 1875   **Current RR:** PW   **Material:** Wood
RLSNE: 25-24   **Current Use:** Commercial

The former Providence & Worcester RR freight house is located on a long siding off the main line. A propane gas dealer has occupied it for many years. Located nearby are the former Capron Mills, where in 1820 the first-ever power looms for weaving of woolen cloth were used.

Wakefield Depot/Freight House
68 North Ave.

Built: Ca. 1845   **Current RR:** GRS, MBTA   **Material:** Wood
RLSNE: 52-10   **Current Use:** Commercial

This station and the town were originally called South Reading until both were renamed Wakefield in 1868. This is the original depot built by the Boston & Maine RR ca. 1845, when that company completed its own line to Boston from North Wilmington. Prior to 1890 it was located across the tracks from the current brick station. When the newer station was built, the depot was moved to its current location and converted to a freight house. As part of the conversion, the building width was increased to the overhang of the roof eaves, and freight doors were added. The freight house is currently occupied by L. Addison & Associates. Although it has been slightly modified, it still looks much like it did when the railroad converted it.

Wakefield Station *25-29 Tuttle St.*

Built: 1889   **Current RR:** GRS, MBTA   **Material:** Brick
RLSNE: 52-10   **Current Use:** Commercial

The Boston & Maine RR built this brick station and one nearly identical to it in Marblehead in 1889. The former express office, which once stood south of the station, no longer exists. The station's roof has been modified to create additional second-story space. The original depot, which still survives, was moved and converted to a freight house when this one was opened.

Today's MBTA commuters board trains here, but they are not afforded the convenience of the station building itself. The former depot is now occupied by several commercial enterprises. This structure, which still retains its unique chimney pots, was added to the National Register of Historic Places in 1989.

Wakefield Centre Depot *57 Water St.*

Built: Early 1900s   **Current RR:** None   **Material:** Wood
RLSNE: 54-0.5   **Current Use:** Commercial

RON KARR

This station was built to a standard Boston & Maine RR design just after the turn of the century. The former Wakefield Junction Depot was almost identical, and the nearby Reading Station is a larger version of this structure, with an oversized hip roof. The depot is now home to the Omelette Headquarters restaurant. The building was added to the National Register of Historic Places in 1989.

Walpole Station   *99 West St.*

Built: 1883   **Current RR:** CSXT, MBTA   **Material:** Wood
RLSNE: 67-7.5, 72-13   **Current Use:** Railroad/Commercial

Walpole Union Station was built in 1883 to serve the Old Colony and New York & New England RRs. This unique structure features two wings connected in the center by a two-story tower, each wing sporting a hip roof with flared eaves. It included an operator tower facing the junction, which, until discontinued in the 1990s, was one of the last operating towers on the MBTA. Walpole had many railroad structures. The freight house and express buildings were located north of the station on the NY&NE line, the express office within the wye, and the freight house just beyond the wye track. A wooden tower (SS 232) was located in the southeast corner of the diamond. Today the Choo-Choo Stop, a coffee shop that sells train tickets and caters to commuters, occupies the station.

Waltham Highlands Combination Depot   *100 Hammond St.*

Built: Ca. 1881   **Current RR:** None   **Material:** Wood
RLSNE: 34-6   **Current Use:** Commercial

This former Boston & Maine RR combination depot was built by the Massachusetts Central RR ca. 1881. This standard gable-roofed station still retains its roof bracing and king post. Having been given a second story on the west end, the building is now home to Regan Real Estate & Insurance. A similar station once existed at Coldbrook.

Wampum Depot   *6 West St. (Rte 121), Wrentham*

Built: 1893   **Current RR:** None   **Material:** Wood
RLSNE: 69-13   **Current Use:** Residential

This Old Colony RR depot was built in 1893. Similar stations once existed nearby at Pondville, Waltham Heights, Titicut, West Stoughton, and West Bridgewater. It was last used for passenger service in 1938. The station has been moved, and the hip roof was raised to add a second story. The single-story section nearest the road was part of the station and likely served as the baggage room. Today the depot is home to Wampum Station Apartments.

Ware [B&A] Freight House/Depot   *1 Mechanic St.*

Built: Between 1870 & 1886   **Current RR:** MCER   **Material:** Wood
RLSNE: 34-70, 36-12   **Current Use:** Commercial

Knapps Beverage Depot currently occupies the original Ware River RR freight house. It has been moved twice; the first time, it was relocated 200 feet south around 1901, when the highway underpass was built. Ironically, the freight house was returned to its original location, where it stands today, in the 1920s. The Boston & Maine RR freight house was located north of the highway underpass.

The Ware Station, a Gothic wooden structure, was located west and north of the former Maple Street crossing. Originally built to serve the Ware River Branch, which was operated by the Boston & Albany RR as of 1873, it was later moved one track-width north to make room for the track of the Boston & Maine RR, which came to town ca. 1887. Union Station was torn down in 1940, and the freight house served passengers until the end of service in 1948.

Wareham Depot

Built: Ca. 1985-86   **Current RR:** BCLR   **Material:** Wood
RLSNE: 80-15   **Current Use:** Municipal

This station was built around 1985-86 to serve Amtrak and Cape Cod & Hyannis RR patrons. Ironically, the CC&HR stopped providing service in 1988, and even Amtrak's summer-only service was discontinued in 1996. This is the third station to serve Wareham. Its predecessor, built by the New York, New Haven & Hartford RR in 1900 and similar to the one surviving at Onset, was torn down in 1965.

Warren Depot

63 Bacon St.

Built: 1839   **Current RR:** N/A   **Material:** Wood
RLSNE: 29-29   **Current Use:** Residential

Although it has received alterations, this two-family residence located on upper Bacon Street is believed to be the original Western RR depot that was formerly located on Main Street. A wooden Greek Revival-style structure, it was erected when the line opened from Worcester to Springfield in October 1839. The station was replaced sometime between 1845 and 1870 with a wooden Gothic Revival-style building. That station was similar to others built by the Western, such as Chester and West Warren, the latter no longer extant. In 1892, when the Boston & Albany RR completed the current station, the second station was also moved, but it has since been demolished.

Warren's freight house, with its beautiful brick dentil trim, is a good example of the early standard style of red brick freight houses built by the Boston & Albany RR at their larger stations. Other examples survive at Dalton, West Brookfield, and West Springfield. A fine one in Westborough that featured large arched freight doors was torn down between summer 2005 and spring 2006 (see Westboro Freight House in Appendix B).

Warren Station *47 Main St. (Rte. 67)*

Built: 1891-92   **Current RR:** AMTK, CSXT   **Material:** Granite & Brownstone
RLSNE: 29-29   **Current Use:** Commercial

The Boston & Albany RR commissioned the firm of Sheply, Rutan and Coolidge to design the Warren Station. It was constructed as part of a grade crossing elimination project. Norcross Brothers began construction in July 1891, and the station was completed the following February at a cost of $10,097. Today this station, which features two small eyelid dormers and one large hooded arch dormer on each of the long sides, is now the home of Fontaine Insurance and Financial Services Agency.

This was the third station to serve Warren. The original 1839 station was a wooden Greek Revival-style structure. The second was a wooden Gothic Revival-style, gable-roofed structure similar to one built at West Warren.

Warren Freight House *Maple St. (Rte. 19)*

Built: 1840s   **Current RR:** AMTK, CSXT   **Material:** Brick
RLSNE: 29-29   **Current Use:** Commercial

Warren Freight House is another of the Boston & Albany RR's standard red brick freight houses. It replaced a small wooden gable-roofed structure, which survived until 1891, when it was torn down as part of the same grade elimination project that produced the current station. Originally located on the south side of the Maple Street railroad underpass, the freight house was moved about 500 feet west on June 20, 1891, as part of the project.

Wayland Depot   *1 Cochituate Rd (Rte. 27)*

Built: 1881   **Current RR:** None   **Material:** Wood
RLSNE: 34-12   **Current Use:** Community

RON KARR

The Central Massachusetts RR built this depot in 1881, when service to Wayland began. It was built to their standard gabled-hip roof style, featuring an oversized roof with large brackets reaching more than half way down the walls. It is similar to others on the line (see Weston Combination Depot). Purchased by the town in the early 1970s, the attractive station is leased to the nonprofit Wayland Depot, Inc. The station is now occupied by their gift shop, which is run by volunteers.

Wayland Freight House   *Concord Rd. (Rte. 126)*

Built: 1881   **Current RR:** None   **Material:** Wood
RLSNE: 34-12   **Current Use:** Municipal

The Central Massachusetts RR built the Wayland Freight House in 1881, the same year as the depot (see Wayland Depot). Owned by the town, it used to hold deliveries of leather for Cochituate shoe factories, groceries, clothing, and hardware; it now houses books for library sales, park and recreation equipment, and unused fire hoses. The freight house is as original as it gets, never having received improvements; it lacks a foundation and has no insulation or lighting. At one point Wayland was the terminus of the railroad. There used to be an engine house, round water tower, and a turntable located west of the station.

Webster [B&A] Depot   *10 Oxford Ave., Dudley (Pleasant St. in Webster)*

Built: Ca. 1886   **Current RR:** None   **Material:** Wood
RLSNE: 29A-11   **Current Use:** Commercial

This depot was likely built in 1886, when the Providence, Webster & Springfield RR (then operated by the Boston & Albany RR) extended its line one mile south from Webster Mills to Webster. Passenger service ended ca. 1919, and the line was abandoned in 1958 as part of a flood control project that dammed the French River in Hodges Village four and one-half miles north of here. A grain dealer used the station for many years. Today the depot, with its clipped gable roof, has been modified with the addition of a garage on the north end and a cinder block addition on the east side for commercial purposes. Although the station was called Webster, it is technically located just over the town line in Dudley.

The B&A freight house, a wooden structure with a low-pitched gable roof, was located in the former yard area to the east of the station. The New York, New Haven & Hartford RR station, a Gothic wooden building, was located on Main Street until it was torn down in May 1936.

Wedgemere Station   *Mystic Valley Pky. near Bacon St., Winchester*

Built: Ca. 1957   **Current RR:** AMTK, GRS, MBTA   **Material:** Brick & Concrete
RLSNE: 51-7.5   **Current Use:** Railroad

RON KARR

This simple flat-roofed brick station was opened in 1957 as part of a joint project between the Boston & Maine RR and the town of Winchester to eliminate troublesome grade crossings here and in downtown Winchester. The grade was raised on an embankment, and two new stations were built, this one and Winchester. Although the ticket office was closed just three years after the station opened, most MBTA trains still stop here.

Wellesley Station   *279 Linden St.*

Built: Ca. 1850   **Current RR:** AMTK, CSXT, MBTA   **Material:** Wood
RLSNE: 64-15   **Current Use:** Commercial

This standard Boston & Worcester RR station, which was built ca. 1850, is the last of this type to survive. A granite Sheply, Rutan and Coolidge-designed station, which featured rounded projections with conical roofs at the trackside corners, replaced it in 1889. The depot has been moved a half mile east of its original location near Grove Street, and it is now home to Captain Mardens Seafood, a wholesale seafood market and restaurant. It has had many additions, but the slate hip roof and brackets are still very prominent features when viewed from trackside. A similar depot existed in nearby Natick.

Wellesley Farms Station   *Croton St. Ext.*

Built: 1893-94   **Current RR:** AMTK, CSXT, MBTA   **Material:** Stone
RLSNE: 64-12.5   **Current Use:** Railroad

The Boston & Albany RR commissioned the firm of Sheply, Rutan and Coolidge to design this station. The firm received a reduced fee since it was a near copy of the Richardson-designed station at Eliot (no longer extant). The Norcross Brothers started construction in 1893 and completed it in May the following year at a cost of $6,516.

Around 1970 the Penn Central RR tried to have the station demolished, raising the ire of local residents. In order to appease the community, the PC left the stone exterior and roof intact. The depot is the only B&A station that retains its approximate original landscaping, which was designed by Frederick Law Olmsted, the designer of New York's Central Park. The station was added to the National Register of Historic Places in 1986. Today it provides MBTA passengers some shelter from the elements.

Wellesley Hills Station   *339 Washington St.*

Built: 1885-86   **Current RR:** AMTK, CSXT, MBTA   **Material:** Granite &
Brownstone   **RLSNE:** 64-13.5   **Current Use:** Commercial/Railroad

RON KARR

This station was the last of nine commissions H. H. Richardson received from the Boston & Albany RR. It was completed on March 13, 1886, shortly before his death the following month. The building, which cost $10,054, included attractive park-like grounds designed by Fredrick Law Olmsted. It was remodeled in 1958, when the roof and front were altered for a dry cleaner, and again in 1978 for a bank. It is now home to Jaylin Cleaners and Antique Time Machines, an antique clock store. Today's MBTA passengers still board trains here, but they no longer are afforded the protection of the station.

West Barnstable Station   *2469 Meetinghouse Way (Rte. 149)*

Built: 1911   **Current RR:** BCLR, CCCR   **Material:** Wood & Stucco
RLSNE: 80-35   **Current Use:** Museum/Railroad

This distinctive Spanish-style station has a red tile roof and a stucco exterior. It is the same style as those in Buzzards Bay and Sagamore. It was built in 1911 by the New York, New Haven & Hartford RR to replace an earlier station that had burned. Last used for passenger service by the New Haven in 1964, train service was reinstated by the Cape Code & Hyannis RR in 1982 (discontinued 1988) and by Amtrak from 1985 to 1996. Amtrak passengers used a new mini-high platform just west of the station, however.

On October 14, 2001, the town of Barnstable, state officials, and the Cape Cod chapter of the National Railway Historical Society signed a lease for the chapter to restore the station and open it as a museum. The station is now listed on the National Register of Historic Places.

West Boylston Freight House   *Goodale St. near Prospect St.*

Built: Ca. 1848   **Current RR:** GRS   **Material:** Wood
RLSNE: 41-9   **Current Use:** Commercial

This location was originally called South Boylston. The name was changed to West Boylston when the former West Boylston Station, located on the Massachusetts Central RR, was abandoned and the area flooded to form the Wachusett Reservoir in 1903. The Worcester & Nashua RR constructed this freight house ca. 1848 when it built this line. The original depot, a small wooden gable-roofed structure built ca. 1848, was located just north of the original Prospect Street underpass on the west side of the tracks. Having fallen victim to local vandals, it was torn down in the 1960s. Today the old freight house is occupied by a construction company, which uses it for storage.

Built: Between 1839 & 1847   **Current RR:** AMTK, CSXT   **Material:** Wood
RLSNE: 29-26   **Current Use:** Commercial

Built by the Western RR, this Gothic Revival station is one of the oldest still in existence in New England. It was possibly the second station to serve West Brookfield. In the days before dining cars, this station, with its 75-foot-long dining area, was a regular meal stop for the Western's trains. Formerly located just east of the 1884 stone station, it was moved to its current location and turned 180 degrees after that station was built. Here it began a second career as a station for the trolley line between Palmer and Worcester. After the trolley line shut down, the building was used for grain storage by Wirthmore Feeds. Although the interior of the station has been remodeled, many of the exterior details remain, including the three ogee arches on the west end. Purchased ca. 1970 by the Sherman Oil Company, the old depot is currently used as a warehouse. A similar station once existed at Palmer.

Built: 1884   **Current RR:** AMTK, CSXT   **Material:** Granite
RLSNE: 29-26   **Current Use:** Historical Society/Museum

This well-cared-for depot was occupied by the West Brookfield Senior Center until recently, when the town built a new senior center across the street. Ironically, the new building looks a lot like a train station. In September 2006, after some renovations to electrical, mechanical, and security systems, the Quaboag Historical Society moved into the old station. For the first time in its 111-year existence, the society has a permanent museum.

West Brookfield Freight House   14 Freight House Rd.

Built: 1840s   **Current RR:** AMTK, CSXT   **Material:** Brick
RLSNE: 29-26   **Current Use:** Commercial

This large brick freight house is typical of many Boston & Albany RR freight houses built in the mid-1800s. A testament to their substantial construction, three others are still extant; they can be found in Warren, West Springfield, and Dalton. Similar freight houses existed in nearby South Spencer and, until 2005, in Westboro. Today the West Brookfield Freight House is used for commercial purposes.

West Chelmsford Freight House   School St.

Built: Between 1848 & 1870   **Current RR:** GRS   **Material:** Wood
RLSNE: 45-2   **Current Use:** Vacant

This former Boston & Maine RR freight house was modified to include the agent's office after the railroad retired the station in the 1930s. The station was an elaborate two-story structure with a large ell located across the street from the freight house. Passenger service ended in 1953. The freight house was occupied for many years by Stan's Model Train Shop, but it is currently empty.

West Concord Depot/Baggage Room   *20 Commonwealth Ave.*

Built: Ca. 1893-94   **Current RR:** GRS, MBTA   **Material:** Wood with Brick
Façade   **RLSNE:** 42-22, 46-24, 47-12   **Current Use:** Commercial/Railroad

Although the Fitchburg RR built its line through Concord in 1844, this section of town did not receive a station until 1871 when the Framingham & Lowell RR built its line. Two years later, Concord Junction (renamed West Concord in 1928) became the southern terminus of the Nashua, Acton & Boston RR. A small depot was erected ca. 1871, and within three years a freight house, engine house, and turntable were added. All of these are gone today.

This station was built in 1893-94 on the site of the original depot. This unique Queen Anne-style station was constructed with three separate sections under one L-shaped hip roof. The freight office, located in the northwest portion of the building, and the roof extending over it were demolished in 1933, and the eight-foot gap between the waiting room and baggage room was enclosed in 1982. In 1984 the building's exterior was covered by brick face siding. The town-owned building, occupied by the Club Car Cafe since 1990, was added to the National Register of Historic Places in 1989.

West Springfield Freight House   *38 Front St.*

Built: Between 1870 & 1875   **Current RR:** AMTK, CSXT   **Material:** Brick
RLSNE: 29-57   **Current Use:** Community

This was at least the second freight house built by the Boston & Albany RR to serve West Springfield (also called Mittineague). An earlier structure was located south of the tracks and on the opposite side of Bridge Street. The depot, a brick gable-roofed structure similar to the B&A station surviving at Gilbertville, was located along Front Street near the foot of Second Street, but it is no longer extant. Today the freight house is home to the Emmanuel Baptist Deaf Chapel.

West Stockbridge Station   *6 Depot St.*

Built: Between 1880 & 1905   **Current RR:** None   **Material:** Wood
RLSNE: 3C-7   **Current Use:** Commercial

This former New Haven RR station was built to their standard New England saltbox style. These stations could be found almost everywhere on the New Haven. After the station closed, it was bought by A. W. Baldwin, the owner of the local hardware store, who used it for storage. Although the building has been altered, the classic lines are still visible. A similar station survives at nearby Lee, MA. The station was enlarged by enclosing the canopy around 1967, and it now provides retail space for local businesses.

West Wrentham Freight House   *11 Wrentham Rd., Grants Mill, RI*

Built: Ca. 1877   **Current RR:** N/A   **Material:** Wood
RLSNE: 67B-4   **Current Use:** Residential

This freight house was likely built in 1877 when the New York & New England RR opened its Valley Falls Branch. It was moved to its current location by the grandfather of its current owner in the 1930s. A locally owned lowboy flatbed truck was used to move it. It has received significant additions and modifications, but the original lines can still be discerned. Today it is a private residence.

Westboro Station   *31 East Main St. (Rte. 30)*

Built: 1888-89   **Current RR:** AMTK, CSXT, MBTA   **Material:** Granite & Brownstone   **RLSNE:** 64-32   **Current Use:** Commercial

RON KARR

Construction on this Boston & Albany RR station began in 1898 and was completed the following year. It was erected as part of a grade crossing elimination project that rerouted the B&A main line, which used to pass right through town, just north of the town center. The station housed a combined freight and express section, as well as a passenger and ticket services. It replaced an earlier station that was located at the junction of East Main and Brigham Streets. Although its Romanesque style and the pink Milford granite used in this station would have many believe it is an H. H. Richardson design, this structure, with its decorative trefoil dormers, was actually designed by a B&A architect.

The station was last used for passenger service in 1960. It was eventually purchased by Bay State Abrasives, but it was unused for the most part; by the late 1990s it had fallen into deplorable condition. Waterman Design Associates, a civil engineering firm, purchased the station from Tyrolit, successor to Bay State Abrasives, in January 2000. The firm completely restored the station from top to bottom and opened it as their new offices in February 2001. They received the 2003 Massachusetts Historical Commission Preservation Award for their achievement.

Westfield [B&A] Station   *16 North Elm St.*

Built: 1879   **Current RR:** AMTK, CSXT, PVR   **Material:** Brick   **RLSNE:** 7-61, 29-63   **Current Use:** Commercial

The Boston & Albany RR's Westfield Station, a handsomely restored brick structure, was built in 1879. It features a cross-gabled roof with Jerkin head ends and decorative roof brackets. This station and a smaller brick Italianate station used by the New Haven

& Northampton RR were both situated in the northeast corner of the former grade crossing of the B&A and the New York, New Haven & Hartford RR's Canal Line. Passenger service on the NH&N ended in 1928, and its station was removed in the 1940s.

The current station replaced an earlier grade-level station built by the Western RR, which was similar to the one surviving in West Brookfield. Westfield, like many other locations on the B&A, had a standard red brick freight house, which was located east of here along Railroad Avenue until it burned down in the 1960s. The station is now the Westfield Financial Center.

Westfield [NYNH&H] Freight Office   *One Depot St.*

Built: Between 1852 & 1875   **Current RR:** PVR   **Material:** Wood
RLSNE: 7-61, 29-63   **Current Use:** Railroad

This building, which features a Jerkin-head roof, was formerly located south of the Pochassic Street Bridge in the northwest quadrant of the railroad crossing. It was moved by the New Haven RR and used as a freight office. It has received a small addition, but continues to serve as the operating offices of the Pioneer Valley RR.

Weston Combination Depot   *55 Church St.*

Built: Ca. 1881   **Current RR:** None   **Material:** Wood
RLSNE: 34-9   **Current Use:** Residential

RON KARR

The Weston Combination Depot was built by the Central Massachusetts RR ca. 1881. It features a standard gabled-hip roof, similar to the station surviving in Wayland. In 1912 the station was moved about two hundred feet east as part of a grade crossing elimination project. The depot, which is still owned by the MBTA, appears to be occupied by a private party.

Whately Freight House   *110 Christian Ln.*

Built: Between 1846 & 1890   **Current RR:** GRS   **Material:** Wood
RLSNE: 33-26   **Current Use:** Commercial

RON KARR

Whately's former Boston & Maine RR freight house is now home to Samson Manufacturing, whose chief product line is a plastic container system used by emergency service agencies to store and transport oxygen tanks. The name of this street was changed to Depot Road when the railroad came to town in 1846, but in 1971 a successful town referendum changed it back to Christian Lane. The freight house has been recently renovated, with the addition of diagonal siding and new windows.

Whitins Station   *683 Linwood Ave., Northbridge*

Built: 1901   **Current RR:** PW   **Material:** Wood with Brick Façade
RLSNE: 25-26   **Current Use:** Commercial

RON KARR

This station was erected by the New York, New Haven & Hartford RR in 1901. It replaced the original Whitins Depot built by the Providence & Worcester RR. That station was made of brick and was located across the tracks from this one, approximately where the highway overpass is today.

Whitins was the home of Whitins Machine Works, which had their own narrow-gauge, and later standard-gauge, railroad to bring freight to and from their mill buildings nearby. The freight house, a good-sized wooden gable-roofed structure, stood north of the station at least into the late 1960s.

Originally built with a saltbox-style roof, a common design used throughout the NYNH&H, the station has been enlarged by equalizing the front and rear rooflines. Today it is home to the China Pacific Restaurant.

Wilkinsonville Depot
                                                              2 Follette St.

Built: Between 1847 & 1878   **Current RR:** PW   **Material:** Wood
RLSNE: 25-35   **Current Use:** Private

This depot was built by the Providence & Worcester RR and is likely the original depot to serve Sutton (later renamed Wilkinsonville). The tiny depot was moved when it was replaced with a gable-roofed combination depot on the same site. The replacement station is long gone, but the tiny depot, albeit in poor shape, still survives nearby, where it is used for storage by a local resident.

Williamsburg Station
                                                              4 Depot St.

Built: Ca. 1867-68   **Current RR:** None   **Material:** Brick
RLSNE: 7D-8   **Current Use:** Commercial

RON KARR

The New Haven & Northampton RR built the Williamsburg Station, which opened on February 1, 1868. The Italianate brick structure is similar to ones that existed in nearby Florence and Holyoke as well as others on the NH&N. Today Lashaway Logging uses the building for storage.

Williamstown Station   *370 Cole Ave.*

Built: 1898   **Current RR:** GRS   **Material:** Granite & Marble
RLSNE: 31-98   **Current Use:** Private

The Gifford-Wood Company built this Romanesque-style station of Blue Quarry Vermont Stone for the Fitchburg RR. It replaced the original wooden depot built in 1859, which was destroyed by fire. This unique stone station is shaped like an elongated hexagon, with a long midsection parallel to the tracks and the shorter triangular points at either end. The station still has its original passenger canopy, which extends about the length of a passenger car from each end of the station and connects with the stone baggage building on the east end. The station has a bay window in the center of the trackside portion of the building and a triangle-shaped dormer on the street side. The architect employed deep brackets and a stone arch to support the extended roof on the west end of the building.

Shortly after being built, the station was damaged by fire, but it was rebuilt the following year. Passenger service to Williamstown ended in November 1958. The privately-owned building has been listed on the National Register of Historic Places since 1994.

Williamstown Baggage Office/Room   *370 Cole Ave.*

Built: 1898   **Current RR:** GRS   **Material:** Granite & Marble
RLSNE: 31-98   **Current Use:** Private

This baggage room is located just east of the station and is connected to it by the passenger canopy. The rectangular building, with its hip roof, is relatively simple compared to the unusually shaped station.

Williamstown Freight House   *361 Cole Rd.*

Built: Between 1860 & 1880   **Current RR:** GRS   **Material:** Wood
RLSNE: 31-98   **Current Use:** Abandoned

This former Boston & Maine RR freight house has received some additions over the years. The rear portion with the slate roof is the old freight house. The whole complex is abandoned. Two large coal silos from Thomas McMahon & Sons still stand as testament to how busy the freight agent must have been here at Williamstown.

Wilmington Station   *35 Church St.*

Built: Ca. 1844-1850   **Current RR:** N/A   **Material:** Wood
RLSNE: 51-15, 51C-0   **Current Use:** Residential

This Greek Revival-style station was built between 1844 and 1850 to serve the Boston & Lowell and Boston & Maine RRs. Records indicate that by 1836 the town of Wilmington had begun petitioning the directors of the B&L to provide a stop in their town. The B&L was originally built without intermediate stops and was very slow to add more. By 1887 the town had become disenchanted with what they considered to be a worn-out and homely structure, and they petitioned the railroad for a new one. A replacement was erected ca. 1887, and this one was moved nearby to Church Street and used for a residence.

Wilmington Depot   *433 Main St. (Rte. 38/129)*

Built: Ca. 1887   **Current RR:** AMTK, GRS, MBTA   **Material:** Wood with Brick Façade   **RLSNE:** 51-15, 51C-0   **Current Use:** Commercial

This depot was built by the Boston & Maine RR ca. 1887 to replace the original Wilmington Station. That building was moved to nearby Church Street and is still used as a private residence. The B&M erected almost identical stations elsewhere on their system, including West Street (Everett) and Bennett Hall (North Billerica), neither of which survive today. A small wooden hip-roofed express office, which survived at least to the 1970s, was located just north of the station.

The depot was sold by the Boston & Maine RR in 1962 and has served several commercial enterprises since then, but it has been home to Big Joe's, a pizza and sub restaurant, for many years. The MBTA opened a new commuter platform in 2003, located just north of the station on the opposite side of the tracks.

Wilmington Freight House   *Main St. (Rte. 38/129)*

Built: Between 1835 & 1875   **Current RR:** AMTK, GRS, MBTA   **Material:** Wood   **RLSNE:** 51-15, 51C-0   **Current Use:** Railroad

This is the original freight house built by the Boston & Lowell RR. Over the years it has received several "improvements," and only the brick chimney leads one to believe this is actually an historic structure. Today the MBTA's signal department uses the old building.

Winchester Station   27 Watefield Rd.

Built: Ca. 1957   **Current RR:** AMTK, GRS, MBTA   **Material:** Brick & Concrete
RLSNE: 51-8, 51A-0   **Current Use:** Railroad/Commercial

This station was opened in 1957 as part of a joint project between the Boston & Maine RR and the town of Winchester to eliminate troublesome grade crossings here and in Wedgemere. The grade was raised on an embankment, and two new stations were built, this one and Wedgemere. This station replaced a wooden structure that had a large hip roof with flared eaves. The operator's tower, located at the south end of the station, is at the original grade level. The ticket agency remained open well into the 1960s, but today the station is used for office and retail space.

Woodland Depot   1897 Washington St.

Built: 1886   **Current RR:** None   **Material:** Granite & Brownstone
RLSNE: 64B-1   **Current Use:** Commercial

In 1886 the Boston & Albany RR built a 3.5-mile connection between the Riverside Line and Newton Highlands to allow trains to travel in a circuit. As part of that project, the B&A commissioned H. H. Richardson in October 1884 to design the three intermediate stations, Waban, Eliot, and Woodland, of which only the latter survives. Richardson's master builder, Norcross Brothers of Worcester, was hired to construct all three stations. Waban was completed in July 1886, Woodland that September, and Eliot in late 1888. Richardson, who died in April 1886, never saw any of these stations finished.

The depot is located on property that is now part of the Woodland Golf Club, where it is used for storage of tools and equipment. It was placed on the National Register of Historic Places in 1976. Today's commuters wait for their light rail vehicles at a nondescript shelter south of the Washington Street Bridge.

Worcester Station   *2 Washington Square*

Built: 1909-11   **Current RR:** AMTK, CSXT, MBTA, PW   **Material:** Terra Cotta & Granite   **RLSNE:** 15-71, 25-43, 29-0, 37-0, 41-0, 64-44   **Current Use:** Railroad/Commercial/Transit

RON KARR

Worcester's Union Station was built from 1909 to 1911. It served the Boston & Albany RR, the New, York, New Haven & Hartford RR, and the Boston & Maine RR, whose names it still bears. Union Station, which opened on June 4, 1911, was built as part of a grade separation project. It replaced the previous union station, which was designed by Ware and Van Brunt and opened in 1875. Located on the opposite side of Washington Square, that station was made of stone and modeled after a Roman basilica in an exuberant Beaux Arts/Classical style. It included a 212-foot clock tower and a 120-foot-wide arched train shed, and it cost $750,000 to build.

The present station was designed by Samuel Huckel, Jr. of the Philadelphia firm Watson and Huckel. The French Renaissance-style station originally featured two 175-foot towers made of white marble. Each tower had a lion's head and many ornamental features. The original towers were torn down in 1926 because they were too heavy. The main waiting room was covered by an elliptical roof lined with stained glass. The station was home to one of the B&A railroad restaurants; others were located in the Springfield and Pittsfield stations.

Union Station was owned by the Boston & Albany RR; the NYNH&H and B&M paid rent based on revenues. In its heyday over 100 trains a day stopped here. With its takeover of passenger service in 1971, Amtrak stopped using Union Station and by 1975-76 had built the small brick station just east of the highway overpass. By 1972 the last business, a barbershop, had moved out of Union Station, and the building was abandoned.

The Worcester Redevelopment Authority purchased the derelict station in 1994. They installed a temporary roof to dry out the structure while the firm of Finegold, Alexander & Associates developed plans for a $24.8-million historical renovation based entirely on old photographs. Restoration of the station, including replicated fiberglass towers, began in 1997. The interior highlight is the Grand Hall, which features a large elliptical ceiling made of glass.

Worcester Union Station once agin began hosting rail passengers on June 20, 2000, when the MBTA—and after a bit of controversy, Amtrak—began using the renovated station. Since May 2003 the station has been occupied by Union Station The Restaurant, and in February 2004 they were joined by the Union Blues Jazz & Blues Showroom, an upscale club. Construction began in June 2004 on a new intercity bus terminal, which, when completed, will make Union Station a true intermodal facility. In 1980 the structure was listed on the National Register of Historic Places.

Worcester Modern Station   45 Shrewsbury St.

Built: Ca. 1975-76   **Current RR:** AMTK, CSXT, MBTA   **Material:** Brick
RLSNE: 15-71, 25-43, 29-0, 37-0, 41-0, 64-44   **Current Use:** Vacant

Amtrak built this small brick station just east of Union Station when they took over passenger service from Penn Central. When the MBTA restored commuter service to Worcester, they also used this facility. After the restoration of Union Station, the MBTA, and then Amtrak, moved to Union Station. Since that time, this station has been vacant. There are plans to build a parking garage on this site, which would result in demolition of this building. There is a plaque on the station dedicated to the memory of Duncan J. McCrea, a former Amtrak employee who designed this station.

Zylonite Depot   *Park St. (Rte. 8), Adams*

Built: Ca. 1845-46   **Current RR:** N/A   **Material:** Wood
RLSNE: 30-15   **Current Use:** Municipal

This tiny Boston & Albany RR depot is similar to, but much smaller than, the one surviving at Cheshire. Sometime ago it was moved adjacent to the Renfrew Station. After many years in Renfrew, the structure was moved again in 1999 or 2000, this time to Adams, where it was restored for use as a tourist information booth. It is now located just west of the Ashuwillticook Rail Trail, which opened in the fall of 2003. Zylonite was named for a mineral used in celluloid that was once mined locally.

Rhode Island

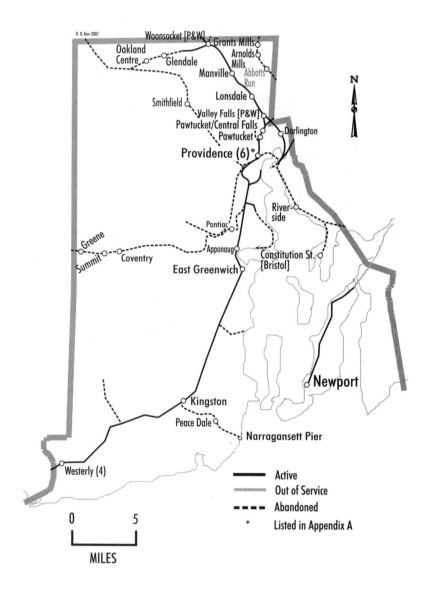

R. D. Karr 2007

Woonsocket [P&W]
Grants Mills
Oakland Centre
Arnolds Mills
Glendale
Manville
Abbotts Run
Smithfield
Lonsdale
Valley Falls [P&W]
Pawtucket/Central Falls
Pawtucket
Darlington
Providence (6)*
River-side
Pontiac
Greene
Apponaug
Constitution St. [Bristol]
Summit
Coventry
East Greenwich
Newport
Kingston
Peace Dale
Narragansett Pier
Westerly (4)

N

Active
Out of Service
Abandoned
* Listed in Appendix A

0   5
MILES

Rhode Island

Abbotts Run Freight House   *11 Wrentham Rd. (Rte. 121), Grants Mills*

Built: Ca. 1877   **Current RR:** None   **Material:** Wood
RLSNE: 67B-9   **Current Use:** Private

This small freight house was likely built ca. 1877, when the New York & New England RR opened its Valley Falls Branch. It was moved to its current location by the grandfather of its current owner in the 1930s, using a lowboy flatbed truck. It would appear that the New Haven was happy to sell off the depots and freight houses which formerly served this line. No less than four on the Valley Falls Branch were sold and moved, the others being Arnolds Mills, West Wrentham, MA, and Adamsdale, MA, all still extant. Abbotts Run was a busy station, with a separate freight house and a siding that directly served a mill.

Apponaug Freight House   *3666 West Shore Rd.*

Built: Between 1837 & 1900   **Current RR:** AMTK, PW   **Material:** Wood
RLSNE: 19-10.5   **Current Use:** Commercial

A former New Haven RR freight house, this building is currently home to Apponaug Auto Supply. The old New Haven station sign can still be seen above the entrance. The Apponaug Station, formerly located across the tracks and a little south, was a frame structure with a hip roof and flared eaves. A large building has been erected adjacent to the old freight house and connected to it.

Arnolds Mills Freight House
690 Nate Whipple Hwy. (Rte. 120)

Built: Ca. 1877   **Current RR:** N/A   **Material:** Wood
RLSNE: 67B-8   **Current Use:** Community

The former Arnolds Mills Freight House has had a second calling. It was moved in 1933 when the New Haven RR sold it to the Arnold Mills United Methodist Church. It is located behind the church, where it is used to store equipment for the local Boy Scout troop. The New York & New England RR built the freight house ca. 1877.

Constitution Street [Bristol] Depot
5 Thames St.

Built: Before 1904   **Current RR:** None   **Material:** Wood
RLSNE: 26-16.5   **Current Use:** Residential

The Providence, Warren & Bristol RR first reached Bristol in 1855. A commuter railroad with many closely spaced stops, the PW&B had four stations within the town of Bristol. The main station was a large brick structure with a Quonset-style curved roof. That station was located on Main Street where Independence Park is now.

Between 1905 and 1926, the PW&B and the Newport & Providence Street RY provided connecting service between Providence and Newport via a ferry from Constitution Street to Bristol Ferry on Aquidneck Island. The New York, New Haven & Hartford extended their line one-half mile to reach the ferry landing and purchased this building from Dr. Eugene LeClair to use as the depot. The tracks were located in Thames Street, and the ferry landing was directly opposite the station. Today the depot is a private residence, the former passenger cano0py serving as the front porch.

Coventry Depot   *21 Hill Farm Rd.*

Built: Early 1850s   **Current RR:** N/A   **Material:** Wood
RLSNE: 10-18   **Current Use:** Commercial

The Hartford, Providence & Fishkill RR opened the line through Coventry Centre (later renamed Coventry by the railroad) in the early 1850s. This structure was the first and only depot to serve this area. It was built to a standard design, similar to others that still survive at Greene and Summit. Formerly located on the northeast side of the Hill Farm Road grade crossing, it was moved to its current location in the mid 1970s. With several additions, the station is now home to Pete's Pizza Plus. The Trestle Trail, an unpaved rail-trail, runs along the old HP&F right of way from here to the Connecticut border, where it continues to Moosup, CT, as the Moosup Valley State Park Trail.

Darlington Freight House   *330 Cottage St.*

Built: Ca. 1874   **Current RR:** PW   **Material:** Brick
RLSNE: 25A-2   **Current Use:** Commercial

The Providence & Worcester RR built this freight house ca. 1874. At one point Darlington had a good-sized freight yard to help serve the many customers here. Even today an interesting array of main-line tracks and sidings crisscross and run alongside Industrial Highway. The recently restored building is now home to a medical office.

East Greenwich Station   *146 Duke St.*

Built: Ca. 1870   **Current RR:** AMTK, PW   **Material:** Wood
RLSNE: 19-13   **Current Use:** Commercial

This Victorian station was built by the New York, Providence & Boston RR around 1870, replacing an earlier station. It is similar to the one in Kingston; however, it no longer sports its four-sided overhang like its brethren some fourteen miles west of here. Today it is the home of the London Bridge Child Care and School Age Center.

Glendale Depot   *1916 Old Victory Hwy.*

Built: Ca. 1891   **Current RR:** N/A   **Material:** Wood
RLSNE: 66C-7   **Current Use:** Government

This former New Haven depot has been moved west along Old Victory Highway. It used to be located just east of the Branch River. This is the original depot built by the New York & New England RR ca. 1891. Today it is occupied by the Glendale Post Office.

Greene Station   *6091 Flat River Rd. (Rte. 117)*

Built: 1854   **Current RR:** N/A   **Material:** Wood
RLSNE: 10-24   **Current Use:** Residential

Until the railroad was built there was no village called Greene; railroad officials chose the name in honor of General Nathaniel Greene, a native Rhode Islander of Revolutionary War fame. The original Greene Depot was built by the Hartford, Providence & Fishkill RR in 1854. It was a small single-story wooden structure. Two years later this two-story station was built to replace the original, which was moved nearby and became a home. The new station included a tenement in the second story for the station agent and his family. It was moved in the early 1880s from the south side of the right of way, west of Hopkins Hollow Road, to the north side, east of the road. Today an historical marker indicates the former station site.

Passenger service ended in the early 1930s, and the line was abandoned in 1967. The depot was almost torn down, but a local man bought it and moved it to its present location on Flat River Road. For many years the depot continued to serve the community in its present location as a small store and gas station. Today it is a private residence.

Kingston Station   *1 Railroad Ave.*

Built: 1875   **Current RR:** AMTK, PW   **Material:** Wood
RLSNE: 19-27, 21-0   **Current Use:** Railroad/Museum

The New York, Providence & Boston RR built this beautiful Victorian station in 1875, two years after the line was double tracked. It replaced a small gable-roofed frame depot of standard design, similar to those surviving in West Mystic, Noank, Stony Creek, and Westbrook, CT. The original depot was located about one mile east of here. The new location was chosen to better serve the Narragansett Pier RR.

In 1974 a group of local residents formed the Friends of Kingston Station to restore the aging station and preserve its history. Working with the owner, the Rhode Island State Department of Transportation, the Friends completed an initial restoration in 1976, and after a disastrous fire in 1988, initiated a $3.5-million restoration and modernization that was completed in February 1998. As part of the renovation, the station was moved back from the tracks and placed on a new foundation.

The station is currently occupied by Amtrak and the Rhode Island Railroad Museum. The museum, which opened on June 22, 2002, is operated by the Friends and is open on weekend afternoons. Visitors can see displays of local railroad history, then step out on the platform and watch an Amtrak Acela speed by at 130 miles per hour. On weekends the parking lot is full of cars belonging to users of the very popular William C. O'Neil Bike Path. The building was placed on the National Register of Historic Places in 1975. A similar station exists in East Greenwich.

Lonsdale Freight House   *5 Ann Hope Way*

Built: 1909-10   **Current RR:** PW   **Material:** Brick
RLSNE: 25-7   **Current Use:** Abandoned

Seemingly lost and forgotten, the Lonsdale Freight House, which has been exposed to the elements for many years, lingers on to remind us of the important role the railroad once played in this formerly heavily industrialized area. The building still sits on its original stone foundation, but the windows and doors have been closed off with cinder blocks, and the roof has collapsed. The freight house was built by the New York, New Haven & Hartford in 1909-10. The Lonsdale Depot, also made of brick, was located catty-cornered from the depot.

Manville Freight House   *50 New River Rd.*

Built: 1850   **Current RR:** PW   **Material:** Wood
RLSNE: 25-12   **Current Use:** Commercial

The Manville Freight House was built by the Providence & Worcester Railroad in 1850. The station, a stylish structure with a steep hip roof with flared eaves, was located north of this building. Today the freight house provides office space for Planned Environments Management Corporation.

Narragansett Pier Station   *145 Boon St.*

Built: Ca. 1876   **Current RR:** None   **Material:** Wood
RLSNE: 21-8   **Current Use:** Commercial/Residential

The Narragansett Pier RR built this station in 1876 at the end of an eight-mile branch to the isolated resort community of Narragansett Pier. It is one of three surviving stations along the branch, the others being Peace Dale and Kingston. Today the old depot is used primarily for commercial purposes, with some apartments.

Newport Depot
19 America's Cup Ave.

Built: Early 1900s   **Current RR:** OCN   **Material:** Wood
RLSNE: 81-19   **Current Use:** Railroad

The Old Colony & Newport Scenic Railway has been serving the public since 1979 as a restorer and operator of historic railroad equipment. Today's passengers are provided a ten-mile scenic train ride along Narragansett Bay. The little depot began life in the early 1900s as an office for the nearby Island Cemetery. The building was moved in 1915, when it was replaced with a larger brick office building and relegated to use as the monument showroom. In the 1970s the cemetery had little use for this tiny building and was planning to tear it down before it was sold to a private party and moved to 18 Elm Street. The OC&N later purchased it and relocated it to a site south of Bridge Street to serve as its depot. The building was restored by 1982, and by 1985 it was again moved, to its present location, to make way for the visitor information center. The old Newport station was razed in 1939, passenger service on the New York, New Haven & Hartford RR having ended the year before. It, too, was located where the visitor information center now stands.

Oakland Centre Depot
1496 Old Victory Hwy.

Built: Ca. 1891   **Current RR:** N/A   **Material:** Wood
RLSNE: 66C-8   **Current Use:** Commercial

This original New York & New England RR depot was built ca. 1891 and was originally located near Recreation Hall, just east of the intersection of Oakland School Street and Old Victory Highway. It has been relocated behind the Brown Funeral Home, where it has received additions and has been converted to a garage.

Pawtucket Freight House   *Pine St. near Goff St.*

Built: 1882   **Current RR:** AMTK, MBTA, PW   **Material:** Brick
RLSNE: 25-4.25, 27-39.75   **Current Use:** Commecial

Having outgrown a smaller wooden freight house, in 1882 the Providence & Worcester RR constructed this large brick replacement. The New York, New Haven & Hartford RR enlarged it by one hundred feet in 1907 and moved it slightly south when they relocated the main line. Today it is used for storage by a steel supplier, who receives its product via rail.

Pawtucket/Central Falls Station   *309 Broad St.*

Built: 1915-16   **Current RR:** AMTK, MBTA, PW   **Material:** Brick & Granite
RLSNE: 25-4.5, 27-39.5   **Current Use:** Community

This station was part of an imaginative solution to eliminate problematic grade crossings in the Pawtucket and Central Falls area. Understandably, the New York, New Haven & Hartford RR wanted to build only one new station to replace the two stations, which were less than a half-mile apart. However, neither community wanted to lose their station. After almost two decades of debate and intervention by the governor of Rhode Island, an agreement was reached. A single station would be built right on the town line. The old Central Falls station was razed as part of the project; the Pawtucket station survived at least into the 1980s.

F. W. Mellor, a New Haven RR architect, designed the new Pawtucket/Central Falls Station. Work was begun in early 1915, and the station was opened on June 16, 1916. It comprised a large waiting room, ticket office, baggage office, express office, restaurant, and barbershop. The station, which featured a copper roof, stained glass skylights, and an iron and glass porte-cochere similar to Providence Union Station, was built by the

Norcross Brothers. The station was probably more than was required for this location; Providence was only 4.5 miles from here, and most long distance trains only stopped at Providence. The majority of the trains stopping here were local trains for Providence, Boston, or Worcester.

Today the 35,000-square-foot Beaux Arts station is the topic of a study for possible restoration, including MBTA passenger service (last service was Feb 20, 1981). It is currently the home of an Iglesia Pentecostal church, but was purchased in July 2005 by a Memphis-based developer.

Peace Dale Depot   43 Railroad St.

Built: 1876   **Current RR:** None   **Material:** Wood
RLSNE: 21-4   **Current Use:** Commercial

This is the original Peace Dale Depot built by the Narragansett Pier RR in 1876. This depot and one that existed in Wakefield each had flat roofs with a decorative partial hip roof that went around all four sides (also known as a monitor-on-hip roof). In the early 1900s the NP added center dormers to both stations. The nearby Wakefield Depot was razed in April 1948. Peace Dale was the short line's headquarters, and the NP general offices were located upstairs. The old Peace Dale Roundhouse still survives and is located behind the depot. The brick roundhouse has been renovated to complement the depot, and We Lease It Trucking occupies both.

Users of the William C. O'Neil Bike Path pass by here on their way from Kingston to Wakefield. Because the trestle just west of the station was removed when the line was abandoned, trail builders had to route the bike path past the depot on city streets.

Pontiac Combination Depot

Built: Ca. 1879   **Current RR:** None   **Material:** Wood
RLSNE: 23-4.5   **Current Use:** Municipal

The Pontiac Depot was built by the New York, Providence & Boston RR ca. 1879. Passenger service to Pontiac ended in 1926. The depot was later moved to the Great House Restaurant on Post Road (Route 1) in Warwick, where it became their cocktail lounge. After serving the restaurant for a couple of decades, however, the depot was returned to its home. The top part of the gabled-hip roof was removed to transport the structure, and for a few years only a tarp protected the interior from the weather. Happily, today it has been renovated and placed on a foundation in the Pontiac Village Community Park, a few hundred yards north of its original location at the corner of Greenwich Avenue and Reed Street. The ell in the rear of the depot was added as part of the renovation.

Providence Station   *One Union Station (formerly 40 Exchange Ter.)*

Built: 1894-98   **Current RR:** None   **Material:** Brick & Stone   **RLSNE:** 10-0, 19-0, 24-0, 25-0, 26-0, 27-44   **Current Use:** Commercial/ Community

The first union station in Providence was built in 1847-48 for use by the Providence & Worcester, the New York, Providence & Boston, and the Boston & Providence RRs. Two years later the Providence and Springfield also began using the station. It was designed by twenty-two-year-old Thomas Tefft, a Brown-educated architect, in a Romanesque style with two identical six-story towers and was, at the time, the longest building in America. As a presidential candidate, Abraham Lincoln once gave a speech from Railroad Hall, located inside the station.

Started in 1873, planning for a new Union Station was studied and debated for many years due to the number of rail routes involved and the need to reach a compromise between the various railroads and the city of Providence. Site preparation began in 1894 with the demolition of existing structures, grading, and foundation pile driving, as well as the relocation of roads, bridges, and the Mill and Woonasquatucket Rivers, and filling of the Cove Basin. However, construction of the station's superstructure did not begin until early in 1896. Shortly thereafter, on February 21, 1896, the original Tefft-designed station, still in use during construction, was destroyed by fire. Due to delays caused by controversy in the final design of the train shed, the new station was not opened until September 18, 1898.

Stone, Carpenter, and Willson of Providence designed this Renaissance-style station. By the time construction began, the New York, New Haven & Hartford RR controlled all rail lines into the new Union Station. Providence, Warren & Bristol trains continued to use the Fox Point Station until the East Providence Tunnel was opened in 1909, thus bringing all rail lines to a single location for the first time in Providence's history.

Union Station comprised five buildings. The middle building was the central terminal; the two buildings west of the terminal contained the station restaurant and railroad offices, while those to the east contained the baggage and express buildings. Until 1952 a large train shed was located on the north side of the station near the current Water Place Park and the Riverwalk. The central terminal was connected to the buildings on either

Union Station in its heyday was a popular subject for early twentieth-century post cards of Providence. Built in sight of Rhode Island's Capital Building, this complex included five buildings connected by columned porticos, a large central clock tower, and a huge glass entrance canopy, as well as a large train shed. (Courtesy of the Beverly Historical Society & Museum, Beverly, MA, Walker Transportation Collection)

side of it by colonnades. The main entrance, located under a large clock tower, was protected by a glass roof that covered the entire street in front of it. This canopy was removed and replaced with a much smaller one in 1954.

In 1986 the tracks were moved to a new alignment, and passengers began using the new Amtrak station on Gaspee Street (see Providence Modern Station). On April 26, 1987, the westernmost of the five Union Station buildings was damaged by fire. Despite this setback, Union Station was eventually transformed into Union Station Plaza, and today all of the buildings are utilized for office and retail purposes. The central terminal became home to the Rhode Island Foundation, a philanthropical organization established in 1916.

Union Station occupies a prominent location in the middle of what arguably has become New England's finest city center. The entire complex has been listed on the National Register of Historic Places since 1975. (See also Providence Office Building, Station Restaurant, Baggage Building, and Express Office [Appendix A].)

Providence Railroad Office   *30 Exchange Ter.*

Built: 1894-98   **Current RR:** None • **Material:** Brick & Stone • **RLSNE:** 10-0, 19-0, 24-0, 25-0, 26-0, 27-44 • **Current Use:** Commercial/Community

This building is the western-most building of the five comprised by Union Station Plaza. Today the Greater Providence Chamber of Commerce and other offices occupy it. Interestingly, the Marriott Courtyard hotel, located near this building where the tracks used to be, was built to match the Renaissance style of the five original Union Station buildings.

Providence Station Restaurant   *36 Exchange Ter.*

Built: 1894-98   **Current RR:** None   **Material:** Brick & Stone
RLSNE: 10-0, 19-0, 24-0, 25-0, 26-0, 27-44   **Current Use:** Commercial

This building is located just west of the Union Station central terminal and originally housed a large restaurant. Around 1920 the restaurant was closed, having been replaced by a smaller one added to the waiting area of the main building. Later the baggage handling was transferred here. Today it is occupied by the Union Station Brewery, a popular nightclub, and other commercial enterprises.

Providence Baggage Office   *50 Exchange Ter.*

Built: 1894-98   **Current RR:** None   **Material:** Brick & Stone
RLSNE: 10-0, 19-0, 24-0, 25-0, 26-0, 27-44   **Current Use:** Commercial

Located just east of the Union Station central terminal, this building was used to meet travelers' baggage needs. From 1939-44 it was used as the express office. In addition to various offices, today the building is home to RI RA, an authentic Irish pub and restaurant.

Providence Modern Station   *100 Gaspee St. (Rte. 1)*

Built: 1986   **Current RR:** AMTK, MBTA, PW   **Material:** Concrete & Stone
RLSNE: 10-0, 19-0, 24-0, 25-0, 26-0, 27-44   **Current Use:** Railroad/Commercial

As part of a national trend, Amtrak phased out several old large underutilized stations in favor of smaller, easier-to-maintain buildings. Providence was one of these. The new Amtrak Providence Station was opened on June 16, 1986. Fortunately for Providence—other cities were not so lucky—this station was built with some interesting aesthetic features, like the three-story clock tower and an overhead glass dome. The station project included relocating the main line to pass underneath the new station.

Ironically, this is not the first station to be located on Gaspee Street. The Providence & Springfield had built a station here in 1880 to avoid paying expensive rental fees for its two daily trains to use the Tefft-designed Union Station (see Providence Station).

Riverside Depot   *250 Bullocks Point Ave.*

Built: Between 1853 & 1891   **Current RR:** None   **Material:** Brick
RLSNE: 26-6   **Current Use:** Commercial

Today this former New Haven RR station is home to Elite Tanning. The East Bay Bike Path, a 14.5-mile paved rail-trail that attracts over a million users each year, passes within several feet of this recently restored depot.

Smithfield Depot   *220 Stillwater Rd.*

Built: Ca. 1873   **Current RR:** None   **Material:** Wood
RLSNE: 24-12   **Current Use:** Museum

AMANDA ROY

This station is the original Providence & Springfield RR depot, likely built when the line was opened in 1873. An almost identical station existed at Primrose, and one that was similar but slightly larger existed at Stillwater. The tiny two-room station has been moved to the grounds of the Smith-Appleby House Museum, which is owned and operated by the Historical Society of Smithfield. The museum is open for special events and by arrangement only, but the depot can be viewed from the parking lot when the museum is closed.

Summit Depot   *25 Log Bridge Rd.*

Built: Early 1850s   **Current RR:** None   **Material:** Wood
RLSNE: 10-22   **Current Use:** Residential

This station was built in the early 1850s by the Hartford, Providence & Fishkill RR. It was almost identical to Coventry Depot and similar to the two-story station at Greene. The station, now moved southeast about 100 feet, has become one of several additions to a much larger building. The nearby Summit General Store has on display some great old photos and maps of this area's stations, including those at Greene and Coventry. The Trestle Trail, an unpaved rail trail, runs along the old HP&F right of way from Coventry to the Connecticut border, where it continues to Moosup, CT, as the Moosup Valley State Park Trail.

Valley Falls [P&W] Freight House   *60 Mill St.*

Built: Between 1847 & 1900   **Current RR:** PW   **Material:** Wood & Metal Siding
RLSNE: 25-6, 25A-0, 67B-13.5   **Current Use:** Railroad

Valley Falls once had two depots, one built by the Providence & Worcester RR and the other by the New York & New England RR. Although neither of these survives today, the P&W's Valley Falls Freight House does. Today's P&W, reincarnated in 1973, operates all local freight service from the yard here at Valley Falls, and the former freight house is home to their transportation center.

Westerly Station   *14 Railroad Ave.*

Built: 1912-13   **Current RR:** AMTK, PW   **Material:** Stucco
RLSNE: 19-44   **Current Use:** Railroad

This Spanish Colonial Revival station, with its terra cotta roof, was built by the New York, New Haven & Hartford RR as part of a curve reduction project. When it opened in 1913, the former wooden Victorian-style station was demolished. Similar to the surviving stations in Kingston and East Greenwich, that station was built in 1872 and was located just east of the current station in the area now occupied by the parking lot. This is the third station to serve Westerly since the line opened in 1837. The original station was a simple gable-roofed structure similar to nearby Noank and West Mystic, CT. The current station, which features ornate terra-cotta decorations with the initials NYNH&H, was completely restored in 1998.

Westerly Station, Westbound   *14 Railroad Ave.*

Built: 1912-13   **Current RR:** AMTK, PW   **Material:** Stucco
RLSNE: 19-44   **Current Use:** Railroad

This enclosed structure provides shelter for Amtrak's westbound patrons in Westerly. It was built in conjunction with the station and the pedestrian subway, which allows passengers access to the westbound platform without crossing the tracks. The 1872 predecessor station also had a subway and westbound shelter. When the station was renovated in 1998, a lift system was installed on both sides of the subway to comply with current requirements of the Americans with Disabilities Act (ADA).

Westerly Passenger Subway   14 Railroad Ave.

Built: 1912-13   **Current RR:** AMTK, PW   **Material:** Stucco
RLSNE: 19-44   **Current Use:** Railroad

This structure is actually the eastbound headhouse of the passenger subway. The westbound station serves as the other subway headhouse. The 1912-13 station project comprised four structures: the main station building, westbound station building, this eastbound headhouse, and the subway.

Westerly Freight House   31 Friendship St.

Built: 1913   **Current RR:** AMTK, PW   **Material:** Brick
RLSNE: 19-44   **Current Use:** Commercial

This standard brick freight house was built by the New York, New Haven & Hartford RR in 1913. Part of a curve reduction project, it was completed the same year as the station. The large freight house features a two-story office section and a one-story warehouse area. The New Haven had similar freight houses throughout their system. The ones in Wallingford and Waterbury, Connecticut, still survive. The building has been occupied by Westerly Agway for many years.

Woonsocket [P&W] Station   *1 Depot Square*

Built: 1882   **Current RR:** PW   **Material:** Brick & Granite
RLSNE: 25-16   **Current Use:** Government

This Queen Anne-style station was built by the Providence & Worcester RR in 1882, replacing an earlier wooden depot which had burned. The design is attributed to the railroad's chief engineer, John Waldo Ellis, who lost his office when the previous station was destroyed. A cement casting above the street entrance proclaims "Providence & Worcester MDCCC LXXXII." Due to the elevation differences in Woonsocket, passengers for the Charles River Line and Pascoag extension utilized a separate station located north of here at the corner of Arnold Street and Harris Avenue.

The new P&W used the station as their general offices from 1976 until 1990, when they completed their transition to Worcester. The station has been listed on the National Register of Historic Places since 1991 and now serves as a visitor center and headquarters for the John H. Chafee Blackstone River Valley National Heritage Corridor Commission. It is currently undergoing a $1.8 million renovation.

Appendix A
Other Passenger and Freight-Related Structures

THIS appendix contains those structures which did not meet the criteria established in the section of the introduction titled "Types of Structures Included," but which I deemed worthy of mention in this book. There are twelve structures, which fall into the following categories: three replicas of former railroad buildings; three structures enclosed within larger buildings; two that have been modified so much they are unrecognizable; two that are only partial remains of former stations; and one that was built as an intermodal station but has yet to provide rail service. One is a house that, according to local legend, once served as a train station.

Structures in this appendix are identified in italics on the maps located at the beginning of the chapters for each state.

Madison, CT   Freight House/Depot   9 Old Rte. 79

Built: Ca. 1980s   **Current RR:** N/A   **Material:** Wood
RLSNE: 12-19   **Current Use:** Municipal

This building is a replica of the Madison Freight House/Depot, which was located three-tenths of a mile southeast of this location. It was built as the Depot Meeting Center/Madison Senior Center. A former railroad caboose has been attached to the rear of the freight house. (See Madison Station for more information.)

Salisbury, CT Freight House   *15 Academy St.*

Built: Between 1869 & 1900   **Current RR:** None   **Material:** Wood
RLSNE: 17-63   **Current Use:** Commercial

JOHN ROY

The former Salisbury Freight House is located north of the station's current location on the west side of the right of way. It has been modified beyond recognition except for the brick chimney that protrudes from the conglomeration that includes it. The structure is occupied by Arts in Motion, an artists' cooperative.

Black Rock, MA Depot   *44 Beechwood St., Cohasset*

Built: Ca. 1890   **Current RR:** N/A   **Material:** Wood
RLSNE: 74-10   **Current Use:** Residential

This former Old Colony RR depot, built ca. 1890, was moved two miles to Beechwood Street, likely after the suspension of passenger service. Over the years it was remodeled and given additions for use as a residence. The depot and its additions were torn down ca. 2005 and replaced with a much larger two-story colonial home. The owner did retain the former ticket office as a bay window on his new kitchen. This tiny remnant of the old depot cannot be seen from the road.

Howes, MA Depot   *17 East St., Middleton*

Built: 1873   **Current RR:** N/A   **Material:** Wood
RLSNE: 57-8   **Current Use:** Residential

RON KARR

The Eastern RR added this station stop in 1873. It was named Howes after Benjamin Howe, a state representative who lived nearby and regularly used the railroad for his trips to the state capital. Sometime after the railroad ended passenger service in 1926, this former station was moved a quarter mile north from Gregory Street to East Street. Today the depot is a private residence, but it has been extensively remodeled and no longer resembles its former appearance.

Hyannis, MA Modern Station   *215 Lyannough Rd.*

Built: 2001-02   **Current RR:** BCLR, CCCR   **Material:** Wood
RLSNE: 80C-3   **Current Use:** Commercial/Transit/ Community

Palladium Construction built the Hyannis Transportation Center for the Cape Cod Regional Transit Authority. Construction began in 2001, and the facility was dedicated on September 23, 2002. It was designed by HTNB Architecture to serve as an intermodal center to provide all forms of ground transportation, with connecting ferry shuttles. The center includes a community meeting room, administrative offices for the RTA, a visitor information area, and 220 parking spaces. Although the station was built with a rail passenger mini-high platform, the Cape Cod Central RR still uses the wooden depot across the tracks. Since Amtrak no longer serves the Cape, there is currently no regular train service from this station.

Millbury [P&W], MA Station   *1 River St.*

Built: 1995-97   **Current RR:** PW   **Material:** Wood
RLSNE: 25-35   **Current Use:** Municipal

The original Millbury Station was built by the Providence & Worcester RR ca. 1847, when the line was opened. That station was replaced in 1874 by a large brick station with a clipped gable roof. The brick station was sold to the town of Millbury in 1949 and modified for use by its highway department. The then deteriorating station was torn down around 1973. When the town built its new senior center (1995-97), they had it designed to look like the old station. The replicated depot, made of wood, is the southern portion of the building. Located roughly where the old one was, it is oriented perpendicular to the tracks. The attractive structure, designed by JCA Architects of Boston, is in a park-like setting with a manicured landscape and beautiful gardens.

Natick, MA Station   *2 South Ave.*

Built: Ca. 1897   **Current RR:** AMTK, CSXT, MBTA   **Material:** Stone
RLSNE: 64-18, 64D-0   **Current Use:** Commercial/Railroad

RON KARR

The Natick Station was designed by A. W. Longfellow, Jr., in 1897 for the Boston & Albany RR. Longfellow served under H. H. Richardson, himself an architect of several New England stations, from 1882-86 before starting his own firm. The station replaced an earlier wooden depot of standard design, similar to the ca. 1850 station extant in nearby Wellesley. The new station was part of a grade crossing elimination project started in the mid 1890s.

The once attractive granite and brownstone building was literally built over in the 1960s; it still exists inside the newer building. It has become the wine cellar of Powers Wine Merchants, a liquor store established in 1933. Today's MBTA commuters are afforded only a platform and the old station canopy. A mural on the wall of the outer building depicts the historic structure, but it is doubtful that any passengers realize how close the former B&A station is.

North Station [Fitchburg RR], MA *Cape Cod Nat. Seashore, N. Truro*

Built: 1847-48   **Current RR:** N/A   **Material:** Granite
RLSNE: 42-0, 62-0   **Current Use:** Vacant

DOUG SCOTT

Located on a bluff in North Truro, this fifty-five-foot tower is all that remains of the Fitchburg's 1848 Boston station. Known as "The Great Stone Castle," the station was a two-story granite structure with four ninety-foot towers, one in each corner. That station was demolished in 1927 to make room for the North Station and Boston Garden facility (see North Station in the Masschusetts chapter for complete history).

On October 12, 1850, the famous soprano Jenny Lind, also know as the Swedish Nightingale, performed from this very same tower. After a successful first night, her promoter, P. T. Barnum, had oversold the second night's performance by over a thousand tickets. The station's grand hall was packed, and many restless fans could not enter the building. To appease the crowds in the street, many of whom had tickets, the singer performed from this tower.

Harold Aldrich, who owned the land on which the tower was eventually placed, convinced the Boston & Maine RR to let him save one of the four towers. It was disassembled stone by stone and transported on a railroad flat car to North Truro. From there it was moved to its current location by truck and by horse and wagon. The abbreviated tower can be found near the Coast Guard's Highland Light in North Truro. Owned by the United States Government since the 1960s, it is now part of the Cape Cod National Seashore.

Parker Mills, MA Depot   *Wedgewood Pl.*

Built: Between 1846 & 1873   **Current RR:** N/A   **Material:** Wood
RLSNE: 80-14   **Current Use:** Residential

Parker Mills in Wareham, MA, was served by a small board-and-batten, hip-roofed depot. The station was established to serve the Parkers Mills, named after a New Bedford industrialist. The mill later became the Tremont Nail Company. The New Haven RR closed this agency in 1925. The depot, originally located in Wareham Center, is now located nearby, on Wedgewood Place in Wareham. Unfortunately, the former depot has been incorporated within a private residence and is unrecognizable.

Sherborn, MA Depot   *20 Lake St.*

Built: 1870   **Current RR:** N/A   **Material:** Wood
RLSNE: 72-4   **Current Use:** Residential

RON KARR

It was common for paper railroads like the Mansfield & Framingham RR to obtain a charter and build a line, then lease it to another railroad company to operate. The M&F, which was immediately leased to the Boston, Clinton & Fitchburg RR, built Sherborn Station in 1870. The station was originally located at the end of Powderhouse Lane (then called Railroad Avenue). Passenger service to Sherborn ended in 1933, and the building was sold in 1935 and moved the following year to its current location at 20 Lake Street. The depot, which originally was a single-story structure with a hip roof, has been extensively remodeled and bears no resemblance to its original appearance.

Silver Lake, MA Depot   *279 Lake St.*

Built: Before 1844   **Current RR:** MBTA   **Material:** Wood
RLSNE: 73-29   **Current Use:** Residential

This farmhouse on Lake Street was once used as a station by the Old Colony RR. Local legend has it that during construction of the Plymouth Line, about 1844, an agreement was made with the owner of the house for part of the structure to be used as a ticket office/waiting room, presumably for a fee.

Providence, RI Express Office   *56 Exchange Ter.*

Built: 1989   **Current RR:** N/A   **Material:** Brick & Stone
RLSNE: 10-0, 19-0, 24-0, 25-0, 26-0, 27-44   **Current Use:** Commercial

The easternmost building of the original five comprised by Union Station, most of this structure was demolished in 1941. The first floor was paved over to provide a loading and parking area for trucks. As a result, the express business was moved to the former baggage building, and baggage handling was moved to the former restaurant building, the restaurant having been relocated to the central terminal in the 1920s.

As part of a renovation project in 1989, this replica of the express building was erected to restore the symmetry of the Union Station complex. It is currently used for office space. Among other tenants, the building houses the home office of the National Collegiate Athletic Association's (NCAA) Big East Conference.

Appendix B
Recently Lost Structures

THIS appendix contains brief notes on structures which have only recently met their demise. Most of these were either demolished or burned down. Some of them were included in the state chapters and had to be removed before we went to press. Others were lost in the last two decades since I first began to research this book in the late 1980s. This appendix contains no photos, and the locations of the lost structures are not indicated on the chapter maps. For the reader's convenience, references to relevant chapters and mileages in *The Rail Lines of Southern New England* are given.

Connecticut

Beckleys Depot   *Beckley Rd.*
Built: Between 1848 & 1900   **Material:** Wood   **RLSNE:** 8B-3

Sometime before the 1950s, this small station was moved and added to the rear of a private residence on Beckley Road. The home and the depot building looked abandoned and in sad shape when I last saw them standing in November 1997. When I returned to photograph the station for my book on December 28, 2001, the building and the depot were gone; only an empty lot remained.

Botsford Depot   *Swamp Rd. near Botsford Hill Rd.*
Built: 1894   **Material:** Wood   **RLSNE:** 3-15, 3A-0

Botsford Station was a typical New York, New Haven & Hartford RR saltbox-style station. Built in 1894, it was damaged by fire in 1931 but was rebuilt. No longer used for passenger service, the station was sold in October 1952. The station, freight house, and a wooden water tower all survived long past their useful prime and slowly deteriorated. The station was destroyed in an arson fire in the early 1990s. The water tower was disassembled and moved to the Danbury Railway Museum in 2002.

Cottage Grove Depot   *Cottage Grove Rd. (Rte. 218)*

Built: Between 1871 & 1900   **Material:** Wood   **RLSNE:** 17-4

In the mid 1990s, the tiny Cottage Grove Depot was moved about a tenth of a mile east of its original location, to the Copaco Center shopping plaza entrance, directly beneath the shopping center sign. The station had been only a flag stop on the former Central New England RR. Last seen in November 1997, it was gone when I returned in May 2006. The depot was small and may have been moved again, but it is not known what actually happened to it.

Darien Station, Eastbound   *Squab Ln. near Boston Post Rd.*

Built: Early 1930s   **Material:** Brick   **RLSNE:** 1-38

This tiny hip-roofed brick depot was razed as part of the station renovation project in 2002. Prior to being removed, it was occupied by Darien Taxi.

Guilford Depot   *Old Whitfield St.*

Built: 1852   **Material:** Wood   **RLSNE:** 12-15

Guilford Depot was built in 1852 by the Shore Line RR. An attempt was made to preserve this building in 1979, but it failed. Amtrak removed the roof overhangs in the fall of 1979. The station lingered on for another twenty-one years, but met its end unceremoniously on February 23, 2000.

Mansfield Combination Depot   *57 Middle Tpke. (Rte. 44)*

Built: 1927-28   **Material:** Wood   **RLSNE:** 14-38

Around 3:30 AM on July 2, 2003, the Mansfield Combination Depot was engulfed by an horrific fire that left very little standing. Although it was still owned by the railroad, it had been occupied by a restaurant since 1978, and at the time of the fire it was home to the Depot Restaurant. The depot was built by the Central Vermont RY and opened on June 16, 1930, replacing a smaller wooden depot. Similar combination depots were built at nearby Eagleville and South Willington, although neither of these survives today.

Moosup Freight House
Ward Ave. (Rte. 14) near Railroad Ave.

Built: Between 1849 & 1878   **Material:** Wood   **RLSNE:** 10-32

This former Hartford, Providence & Fishkill RR freight house was located behind the old Western Auto building in downtown Moosup. Unfortunately, the property on which both Western Auto and the freight house resided was purchased for the development of a new Cumberland Farms convenience store. The Connecticut Eastern Railroad Museum attempted to save the freight house; sadly, they did not have enough time and resources to accomplish that. The freight house, which was in good shape, was demolished in 2005.

New London Freight House
Walbach St.

Built: 1899   **Material:** Wood   **RLSNE:** 12-49, 14-0, 19-62

The old New London Freight House, which had been used by Amtrak maintenance-of-way crews, was torn down in 2001 or early 2002. This was part of large-scale redevelopment effort spearheaded by the New London Development Corporation, a public-private partnership. The freight house was built by the New York, New Haven & Hartford RR in 1899. A similar freight house was located at Mystic.

Plainfield Freight House/Depot
Railroad Ave.

Built: Between 1930 &1948   **Material:** Concrete Block   **RLSNE:** 10-35, 15-28

This former New Haven RR structure served first as a freight house and later as a depot. The Providence & Worcester RR used it as an office until the late 1980s. The author last saw this building in 1993. It is not known when it was removed.

Pomfret Station
Railroad St.

Built: Early 1900s   **Material:** Brick   **RLSNE:** 16-30

This station was built in the early 1900s by the New York, New Haven & Hartford RR, whose initials—NYNH&H RR—were proudly inscribed on the fireplace. Unfortunately, it was severely damaged by fire on October 27, 2000, and was torn down shortly thereafter.

South Norwalk Station, Westbound *Monroe St.*

Built: 1890s **Material:** Brick **RLSNE:** 1-41, 2-0, 2A-0

The westbound 1890s South Norwalk Station was demolished in the mid 1990s to make room for a modern station. See South Norwalk Westbound and Eastbound Stations for more information.

South Norwalk Freight House *33 North Water*

Built: Ca. 1891 **Material:** Wood **RLSNE:** 1-41, 2-0, 2A-0

The South Norwalk Freight House was built ca. 1891. It was last seen by the author on March 19, 1995. When I returned in May 2002, the Maritime Aquarium had replaced the freight house with a paved parking lot.

Stamford Station, Eastbound *Station Pl.*

Built: Ca. 1893 **Material:** Wood **RLSNE:** 1-33, 1A-0

This station was built ca. 1893 by the New York, New Haven & Hartford RR. It was razed in November 1987, when the current modern station was completed. See Stamford Modern Station for more details.

Stamford Station, Westbound *State St.*

Built: Ca. 1893 **Material:** Brick **RLSNE:** 1-33, 1A-0

This station was built ca. 1893 by the New York, New Haven & Hartford RR. It was razed in March 1983, when construction of a modern station was started. See Stamford Modern Station for more details.

Suffield Depot *115 Mountain Rd.*

Built: 1835 **Material:** Wood **RLSNE:** 8C-5

This Grecian-Doric building was built ca. 1835 as a house of worship to serve the First Congregationalist Church in Suffield. It was designed by local architect Henry A. Sykes, who also designed the Second Baptist Church, which still stands in Suffield. About 1867, parishioners decided to move the structure and erect a new brick meeting house, which was completed in 1869. The old church became a railroad station in 1870, when the first train arrived at Suffield. When the last passenger train pulled out of the station in 1926, the building continued to be used for other purposes. The station was last used by Suffield Auto Sales, but was razed sometime between November 1995 and July 2002.

Thomaston Combination Depot/Freight House   *East Main St.*

Built: Ca. 1848   **Material:** Wood   **RLSNE:** 5-36

This was the original combination depot built for the Naugatuck RR ca. 1848. It was similar to ones erected at East Litchfield and Waterville. The combination depot was converted to a freight house in 1881, when it was replaced by a brick station (see Thomaston Station). After years of neglect, it partially collapsed in 1994 during a winter storm that dumped fifteen inches of snow on Thomaston. Two years later the entire structure was removed.

Massachusetts

Athol Freight House   *South St.*

Built: Late 1800s   **Material:** Brick   **RLSNE:** 31-32, 35-45

The Athol Freight House, which was last used by Agway for storage, was destroyed by fire in the late 1990s or early 2000s. The Boston & Maine RR closed the freight agency and transferred the work to nearby Orange in the early 1960s. The freight house was last seen by the author on September 1, 1996.

Charlemont Freight House   *Rte. 8A*

Built: Between 1870 & 1900   **Material:** Wood   **RLSNE:** 31-78

The Charlemont Freight House was demolished in 1996. It was last used by Homgas, a propane dealer.

Egypt Depot   *Captain Pierce Rd. near Curtis St.*

Built: Ca. 1910   **Material:** Wood   **RLSNE:** 74-15

The small Egypt Depot was built ca. 1910 by the New York, New Haven & Hartford RR. The building was unoccupied and falling down in the mid 1990s and didn't make it to this century. It was last used as a general store.

Gardner Freight House   *Main St. near Chestnut St.*

Built: Between 1870 & 1900   **Material:** Wood   **RLSNE:** 31-15, 37-26

The Gardner Freight House was heavily damaged by fire on July 15, 2002, and was demolished shortly thereafter. It was used by the Boston & Maine RR as a freight office until the early 1980s.

Greenfield Freight House   *Bank Row (Rte. 5)*

Built: 1900   **Material:** Wood   **RLSNE:** 31-55, 33-36

The Greenfield Freight House burned down some time between July 1998 and 2002. The large freight house was last used by an automobile dealer.

Hamilton-Wenham Freight House   *Maine St. (Rte. 1A)*

Built: 1862   **Material:** Wood   **RLSNE:** 58-23, 58E-0

The small Hamilton-Wenham Freight House was built in 1862 by the Eastern Railroad. It burned in late 2000; a modern commuter platform now sits in its place.

Hudson [Fitchburg RR] Freight House   *Broad St. near South St. Ext.*

Built: Ca. 1850   **Material:** Wood   **RLSNE:** 42B-9

The former Fitchburg RR freight house was likely built when this line was opened in 1850. Originally located west of Broad Street and north of South Street Extension, it had been moved to Sawyer Lane and placed on a foundation. Unfortunately the freight house, which had a clipped gable roof, was torn down in the summer of 2003.

Jefferson [Fitchburg RR] Freight Houses   *Quinapoxet St.*

Built: Early 1900s   **Material:** Wood   **RLSNE:** 37-10

Jefferson once boasted two wooden freight houses. Both of these were located north of Quinapoxet Street, on the west side of the tracks. When last observed in June 1998, they were in poor shape, and by May 2002 they were gone.

Mansfield Depot   *Crocker St.*

Built: 1954   **Material:** Wood   **RLSNE:** 72-21, 77-0

The New Haven RR built this temporary station in 1954 as part of a grade separation project (see Mansfield Modern Station for more information). Its predecessor was the original two-story frame station, which was torn down as part of the project. Replaced by the new Mansfield Station, it was demolished in the first two weeks of January 2004.

Maplewood Depot   *Maplewood St.*

Built: 1853   **Material:** Wood   **RLSNE:** 60-3

In 2001 this old depot stood in the way of the expanding Maplewood Street Welding Shop. The shop's owner put off construction to give preservationists a chance to organize. The newly formed Friends of the Maplewood Depot quickly raised the necessary $15,000 to move the depot before the deadline expired. On April 4, 2002, the small depot was moved about a half mile down the tracks to 662 Cross Street, behind the Charles Ro Supply Company. Unfortunately, after it sat abandoned on blocks for over two years, the city of Malden took legal action, and it was razed in October 2004. The depot was very similar to other stations surviving at Cliftondale and Saugus.

Nantasket Junction Freight House   *190 Summer St.*

Built: Between 1880 & 1900   **Material:** Wood   **RLSNE:** 74-8, 74A-0

Nantasket's freight house was last used by the Hingham Lumber Company for storage. Both the freight house and the lumber company were removed by August 2006, and a new MBTA station was being constructed in its place.

Route 128 [Westwood] Stations   *University Ave.*

Built: 1965   **Material:** Brick   **RLSNE:** 27-12

The Route 128 Eastbound and Westbound Stations were erected in 1965 by the New York, New Haven & Hartford RR. Amtrak demolished them in November 2000, when the current modern station opened.

Russell Freight House   *Carrington Rd.*

Built: Between 1875 & 1900   **Material:** Wood   **RLSNE:** 29-71

The Russell Freight House was a gable-roofed board-and-batten structure. It last served as a loading dock for transferring freight from rail to truck. The freight house was last seen by the author in October 2001, but it was gone by May 2006.

Templeton Combination Depot   *658 Patriots Rd. (Rte. 2A)*

Built: Ca. 1873   **Material:** Brick   **RLSNE:** 36-39

Forgotten and abandoned, the former Boston & Albany RR combination depot was literally falling down when last seen, the south end having collapsed. At one point the local aggregate company was using the building, but these facilities were also abandoned. The station may have been built while the line was leased by the New London Northern RR in the early 1870s. It was similar to ones built in Williamsville, Barre Plains, and Old Furnace, MA, and the brick stations on the NLN such as South Coventry, South Windham, and Monson (see South Coventry and South Windham, CT, Combination Depots). Regular passenger service here ended in 1935, but mixed service lasted until 1948. The station was torn down in the fall of 2002.

Westboro Freight House   *Brigham St. near Cottage St.*

Built: 1840s   **Material:** Brick   **RLSNE:** 64-32

In 1899 the Boston & Albany RR relocated the railroad tracks north to their current location and away from the center of town, leaving this freight house off the main line. It was one of the large brick freight houses common on the B&A; similar structures still exist at Dalton, Warren, West Brookfield, and West Springfield. Although the rails had been removed and the arched freight doors on the street side had been walled in with concrete block, it was used for storage by Tyrolit, a manufacturer of abrasive wheels, discs, and hones. Sometime between mid 2005 and mid 2006, the freight house and the industrial complex were demolished as part of a major mixed-use development project for downtown Westborough.

Winchendon [B&A] Freight House   *Central St. (Rte. 202)*

Built: Between 1873 & 1899   **Material:** Wood   **RLSNE:** 36-49, 37-36, 38-8, 39-0

Winchendon was once the home of two depots and two freight houses. The former Boston & Albany RR freight house was last used by a lumber company for storage. Formerly located southeast of Central Street, it was razed sometime between August 1996 and April 2005.

Winchendon [B&M] Freight House   *Central St. (Rte. 202)*

Built: Between 1890 & 1899   **Material:** Wood   **RLSNE:** 36-49, 37-36, 38-8, 39-0

This large freight house was likely built after 1890, when the Fitchburg RR, a Boston & Maine RR predecessor, consolidated three of the original four railroads serving Winchendon. Formerly located northwest of Central Street, it was razed sometime between August 1996 and April 2005. A Brooks Pharmacy now stands at its former location.

Rhode Island

Centredale Depot   *Putnam Pike (Rte. 44)*

Built: Between 1872 and 1915   **Material:** Wood   **RLSNE:** 24-6.5

The Centredale Depot was occupied by a restaurant in the early 1990s, but it was torn down sometime after that to make room for a Burger King restaurant.

Oakland Depot   *Old Victory Hwy. near Whipple Ave.*

Built: Ca. 1873s   **Material:** Wood   **RLSNE:** 24-19

The original Oakland Depot, built by the Providence & Springfield RR ca. 1873, was last used by the Remington Lumber Company. When that company went out of business, the old depot was acquired by the local historical society but remained unused and vacant. The new property owner demolished the depot in October 2003.

Appendix C
Cross Reference to *The Rail Lines of Southern New England*

THIS appendix provides a cross-reference to Ronald Dale Karr's *The Rail Lines of Southern New England* to help readers easily locate all the structures included in this guide that are associated with rail lines in that book. The rail lines are listed alphabetically by the chapter titles used for them in *The Rail Lines of Southern New England*, with chapter numbers in parentheses after the names of the lines. Branch lines are sorted under the lines with which they are associated. Structures that are located on both the main line and a branch are repeated once for the branch and once for the main line. Likewise, union stations are listed once for each line they served. The numbers in front of the structure names indicate the mileposts at which the structures can be found along each line.

Agricultural Branch (Chap. 65)

MA	0	Framingham Station, Baggage Office/Room
	23	Clinton Station

Air Line (Chap. 11)

CT	11	East Wallingford Combination Depot
	17	Middlefield Combination Depot
	24	Portland Combination Depot
	31	East Hampton Depot

Air Line - Colchester Branch (Chap. 11A)

CT	4	Colchester Depot, Freight House

Billerica & Bedford (Chap. 49)

MA	0	Bedford Depot, Engine House/Freight House
	8.5	North Billerica Depot, Freight House

Billerica & Bedford - B&B Narrow Gauge (Chap. 49A)

MA	0	Bedford Depot, Engine House/Freight House
	9	North Billerica Depot, Freight House

Boston & Lowell (Chap. 51)

MA   0   North Station, North Station [Fitchburg RR] (Appendix A)
       7.5   Wedgemere Station
       8   Winchester Station
       12.9   Anderson RTC Modern Station
       15   Wilmington Station, Depot, Freight House
       22   North Billerica Depot, Freight House
       26   Lowell [B&L] Modern Station

Boston & Lowell - Lowell & Lawrence Branch (Chap. 51D)

MA   3   Tewksbury Center Depot
       10.5   Lawrence Station, Modern Station

Boston & Lowell - Stoneham Branch (Chap. 51B)

MA   1.5   Farm Hill Depot
       2.5   Stoneham Station

Boston & Lowell - Wilmington [Wildcat] Branch (Chap. 51C)

MA   0   Wilmington Station, Depot, Freight House

Boston & Lowell - Woburn Loop (Chap. 51A)

MA   0   Winchester Station

Boston & Maine (Chap. 52)

MA   0   North Station, North Station [Fitchburg RR] (Appendix A)
       4.5   Malden Station, Modern Station
       10   Wakefield Depot/Freight House, Station
       12   Reading Station
       20.5   Ballardvale Station
       23   Andover Station, Freight House
       24   Shawsheen Station
       25.5   South Lawrence Freight House
       26   Lawrence Station, Modern Station
       27   North Andover Depot, Freight House
       32.5   Bradford Depot
       33   Haverhill Freight Houses (3)
       35   Rosemont Station

Boston & Maine - Lowell Branch (Chap. 52C)

MA   9   Lowell [B&M] Station

Boston & Maine - Medford Branch (Chap. 52A)

MA   1.5   Park Street [Medford] Station

Boston & Maine - Wilmington Branch (Chap. 52B)

MA   0   Wilmington Station, Depot, Freight House

Boston & Providence (Chap. 27)

MA	0	South Station
	1	Back Bay Station
	2	Ruggles Modern Station
	5	Forest Hills Modern Station
	12	Route 128 [Westwood] Modern Station
	15	Canton Junction Station
	18	Sharon Station, Passenger Shelter
	32	Attleboro Stations, Freight House
RI	39.5	Pawtucket/Central Falls Station
	39.8	Pawtucket Freight House
	44	Providence Station Complex (4 structures), Modern Station, Express Office (Appendix A)

Boston & Providence - Attleboro Branch (Chap. 27C)

MA	0	Attleboro Stations, Freight House
	4	Chestnut St. [North Attleboro] Depot

Boston & Providence - Dedham Branch (Chap. 27A)

MA	0	Forest Hills Modern Station

Boston & Providence - Stoughton Branch (Chap. 27B)

MA	0	Canton Junction Station
	4	Stoughton Station

Boston & Worcester [Boston & Albany] (Chap. 64)

MA	0	South Station
	1	Back Bay Station
	4	Allston Station
	12.5	Wellesley Farms Station
	13.5	Wellesley Hills Station
	15	Wellesley Station
	18	Natick Station (Appendix A)
	21	Framingham Station, Baggage Office/Room
	24	Ashland Station
	28	Southville Combination Depot
	32	Westboro Station
	38	North Grafton Freight House
	44	Worcester Station, Modern Station

Boston & Worcester [Boston & Albany] - Highland Branch (Chap. 64B)

MA	1	Woodland Depot
	3.5	Newton Highlands Station

Boston & Worcester [Boston & Albany] - Milford Branch (Chap. 64E)

MA	0	Framingham Station, Baggage Office/Room

```
        4    East Holliston Depot
        5    Holliston Depot
       12    Milford [B&A] Station
```

Boston & Worcester [Boston & Albany] - Millbury Branch (Chap. 64F)

```
MA      3    Millbury [B&A] Freight House
```

Boston & Worcester [Boston & Albany] - Saxonville Branch (Chap. 64D)

```
MA      0    Natick Station (Appendix A)
```

Boston, Barre & Gardner (Chap. 37)

```
MA      0    Worcester Station, Modern Station
        8    Holden Depot, Freight House
       10    Jefferson [Fitchburg RR] Depot
```

Boston, Revere Beach & Lynn (Chap. 61)

```
MA    8.5    Lynn Modern Station
```

Brookline & Pepperell (Chap. 44)

```
MA      6    Pepperell [B&P] Depot
```

Cape Cod (Chap. 80)

```
MA      0    Middleboro Freight House
       14    Parker Mills Depot (Appendix A)
       15    Wareham Depot
       17    Onset Depot
       20    Buzzards Bay Station
       31    East Sandwich Depot
       35    West Barnstable Station
       52    Pleasant Lake General Store/Station
       58    East Brewster Depot
       74    South Truro Depot
       86    Provincetown Freight House
```

Cape Cod - Chatham Branch (Chap. 80D)

```
MA      7    Chatham Depot, Freight House
```

Cape Cod - Fairhaven Branch (Chap. 80A)

```
MA      5    Marion Combination Depot
```

Cape Cod - Hyannis Branch (Chap. 80C)

```
MA      3    Hyannis Station, Combination Depot, Modern Station (Appendix A)
```

Cape Cod - Woods Hole Branch (Chap. 80B)

```
MA      0    Buzzards Bay Station
        1    Gray Gables Depot
        2    Monument Beach Station
```

Connecticut Valley (Chap. 13)

CT	0	Hartford Station
	6	Wethersfield Freight House/Depot
	9	Rocky Hill Depot, Freight House
	15	Cromwell [CV] Freight House
	32	Goodspeeds Freight House
	35.5	Chester Depot, Combination Depot
	36	Deep River Freight House
	40	Essex Freight House/Depot
	44	Old Saybrook Station, Freight House

Connecticut Western (Chap. 17)

CT	0	Hartford Station
	6	Bloomfield Freight House
	23	High St. Jct. [Collinsville] Combination Depot
	35.5	Winsted Freight House
	46	Norfolk Station
	52	East Canaan Combination Depot
	55	Canaan Station
	63	Salisbury Depot, Freight House (Appendix A)
	65	Lakeville Depot

Danbury & Norwalk (Chap. 2)

CT	0	South Norwalk Stations
	7.5	Wilton Combination Depot, Depot
	9	Cannondale Combination Depot
	13	Branchville Depot
	17	Redding General Store/Station
	21	Bethel Combination Depot, Modern Station
	24	Danbury Depot, Station, Modern Station

Danbury & Norwalk - Hawleyville Branch (Chap. 2C)

CT	0	Bethel Combination Depot, Modern Station

Danbury & Norwalk - Ridgefield Branch (Chap. 2B)

CT	0	Branchville Depot
	4	Ridgefield Depot

Danbury & Norwalk - Wilsons Point Branch (Chap. 2A)

CT	0	South Norwalk Stations

Dighton & Somerset (Chap. 76)

MA	10	North Easton Station
	22	Dean St. [Taunton] Station

Dighton & Somerset - Stoughton Branch (Chap. 76A)

MA   2   Stoughton Station

Eastern (Chap. 58)

MA   0   North Station, North Station [Fitchburg RR] (Appendix A)
      11.5   Lynn Modern Station
      12   East Lynn Station
      13   Swampscott Depot
      16   Salem Station
      18   Beverly Station
      28   Ipswich Freight House
      37   Newburyport Modern Station

Eastern - Amesbury Branch (Chap. 58G)

MA   3   Salisbury Point Depot
      4   Amesbury Station

Eastern - Essex Branch (Chap. 58F)

MA   5.5   Essex Freight House
      6   Conomo Depot

Eastern - Newburyport City Branch (Chap. 58H)

MA   0   Newburyport Modern Station

Eastern - Swampscott Branch (Chap. 58C)

MA   0   Swampscott Depot

Essex (Chap. 57)

MA   0   Salem Station
      5   Danvers East Depot
      8   Howes Depot (Appendix A)
      10   Middleton Depot
      19.5   North Andover Depot, Freight House

Fall River (Chap. 78)

MA   6   Avon Station
      16   Bridgewater Station
      23   Middleboro Freight House
      25   Lakeville Station

Fitchburg (Chap. 42)

MA   0   North Station, North Station [Fitchburg RR] (Appendix A)
      4   Porter Square Modern Station
      6   Belmont Depot, Station
      13   Kendal Green Depot
      15   Silver Hill Passenger Shelter

20	Concord Station, Express Office
22	West Concord Depot/Baggage Room
31.5	Littleton Station
39	Shirley Passenger Shelter
50	Fitchburg Modern Station

Fitchburg - Marlboro Branch (Chap. 42B)

MA	13	Marlboro [B&M] Combination Depot

Fitchburg & Worcester (Chap. 40)

MA	0	Fitchburg Modern Station
	5	Leominster Station
	12	Sterling Freight House
	14	Sterling Junction Freight House

Framingham & Lowell (Chap. 47)

MA	5	South Sudbury Depot
	6	Sudbury Depot, Freight House
	12	West Concord Depot/Baggage Room
	27	Lowell [B&L] Modern Station

Gloucester & Rockport Branch (Chap. 59)

MA	4	Prides Crossing Depot
	4.5	Beverly Farms Depot
	7	Manchester Freight House
	17	Rockport Freight House

Grafton & Upton (Chap. 70)

MA	0	North Grafton Freight House
	11	Hopedale Combination Depot
	12	Milford [B&A] Station

Grand Junction (Chap. 63)

MA	0	Allston Station

Hartford & New Haven (Chap. 8)

CT	0	New Haven Station
	0.4	State Street [New Haven] Modern Station
	4	Quinnipiak Depot
	7	North Haven Station, Freight House
	12	Wallingford Station, Freight House
	19	Meriden Station
	26	Berlin Station
	32	Newington [H&NH] Freight House
	37	Hartford Station
	43	Windsor Station, Freight House
	49	Windsor Locks Station

| | 50 | Warehouse Point Freight House |
| MA | 62 | Springfield Station, Modern Station |

Hartford & New Haven - Middletown Branch (Chap. 8B)

| CT | 0 | Berlin Station |
| | 4 | East Berlin Depot |

Hartford & New Haven - New Britain Branch (Chap. 8A)

| CT | 0 | Berlin Station |

Hartford & New Haven - Suffield Branch (Chap. 8C)

| CT | 0 | Windsor Locks Station |

Hartford, Providence & Fishkill (Chap. 10)

RI	0	Providence Station Complex (4), Modern Station, Express Office (Appendix A)
	18	Coventry Depot
	22	Summit Depot
	24	Greene Station
CT	58	Willimantic [NY&NE] Express Office
	63	Hop River Station
	82	Buckland Combination Depot
	89	Hartford Station
	95	Newington [HP&F] Depot
	103	Plainville Freight House
	105	Forestville Depot
	112	Terryville Depot, Freight House
	122	Waterbury Station, Freight Houses

Hartford, Providence & Fishkill - Danbury Extension (Chap. 10C)

CT	0	Waterbury Station, Freight Houses
	30	, Danbury Depot, Station, Modern Station
	35	Mill Plain Depot

Housatonic (Chap. 3)

CT	0	Bridgeport Modern Station
	10	Stepney Combination Depot
	19	Newtown Depot
	29	Brookfield Combination Depot
	36	New Milford Depot
	42	Gaylordsville Hotel/Station, Freight House/Depot, Combination Depot
	48	Kent Combination Depot
	57	Cornwall Bridge Combination Depot
	61	West Cornwall Combination Depot
	66	Lime Rock Freight House/Depot

	67	Falls Village Combination Depot
	73	Canaan Station
MA	79	Sheffield Combination Depot, Freight House
	85	Great Barrington Station
	90	Housatonic Depot, Freight House
	94	Stockbridge Station
	96	South Lee Depot
	100	Lee Depot, Freight House
	103	Lenox Station
	106	New Lenox General Store/Station
	111	Pittsfield Modern Station

Housatonic - Danbury Branch (Chap. 3B)

CT	4	Danbury Depot, Station, Modern Station

Housatonic - Derby Branch (Chap. 3A)

CT	13	Shelton Freight House

Housatonic - State Line Branch (Chap. 3C)

MA	7	West Stockbridge Station

Lexington & Arlington (Chap. 50)

MA	8	Lexington Station
	12	Bedford Depot, Engine House/Freight House

Manchester & Lawrence (Chap. 53)

MA	0	Lawrence Station, Modern Station
	2	Methuen Station, Freight House

Mansfield & Framingham (Chap. 72)

MA	0	Framingham Station, Baggage Office/Room
	4	Sherborn Depot (Appendix A)
	13	Walpole Station
	16	South Walpole Depot
	21	Mansfield Modern Station

Meriden, Waterbury & Connecticut River (Chap. 9)

CT	0	Waterbury Station, Freight Houses

Midland (Chap. 68)

MA	0	South Station

Milford & Woonsocket (Chap. 71)

MA	0	Franklin Junction Freight House
	2.5	Forge Park Modern Station
	15	Hopkinton Depot

20   Ashland Station

Narragansett Pier (Chap. 21)

RI   0   Kingston Station
        4   Peace Dale Depot
        8   Narragansett Pier Station

Nashua & Lowell (Chap. 48)

MA   0   Lowell [B&L] Modern Station

Nashua, Acton & Boston (Chap. 46)

MA   14   Pine Ridge Depot, Freight House
       24   West Concord Depot/Baggage Room

Naugatuck (Chap. 5)

CT   15   Seymour Passenger Shelter, Freight House
       22   Naugatuck Station
       27   Waterbury Station, Freight Houses
       36   Thomaston Station
       47   Torrington Station
       56   Winsted Freight House

New Bedford & Taunton (Chap. 77)

MA   0   Mansfield Modern Station
       4   Norton Depot

New Bedford & Taunton - Attleboro Branch (Chap. 77A)

MA   5   Barrowsville Depot
       9   Attleboro Stations, Freight House

New Bedford & Taunton - Middleboro & Taunton Branch (Chap. 77B)

MA   8   Middleboro Freight House

New Haven & Derby (Chap. 6)

CT   0   New Haven Station
      11   Derby-Shelton Station

New Haven & Northampton (Chap. 7)

CT   0   New Haven Station
       8   Mount Carmel Station, Freight House
      20   Milldale Combination Depot
      27   Plainville Freight House
      37   Avon Combination Depot
      42   Simsbury [NH&N] Combination Depot, Depot
      47   Granby Combination Depot

MA   61   Westfield [NYNH&H] Freight Office

72   Easthampton Station
77   Northampton Station

New Haven & Northampton - New Hartford Branch (Chap. 7B)

CT   3   Unionville Depot, Freight House
      8   Collinsville [NH&N] Freight House
   14   New Hartford [NH&N] Freight House

New Haven & Northampton - Shelburne Falls Extension (Chap. 7A)

MA 0   Northampton Station

New Haven & Northampton - Tariffville Branch (Chap. 7F)

CT   0   Simsbury [NH&N] Depot, Combination Depot

New Haven & Northampton - Williamsburg Branch (Chap. 7D)

MA 0   Northampton Station
     8   Williamsburg Station

New London Northern (Chap. 14)

CT   0   New London Station, Baggage/Express Office
   26   South Windham [CV] Combination Depot
   35   South Coventry Combination Depot
   44   West Willington Combination Depot
   50   Stafford Station

MA 56   State Line [CV] Depot
  64.7 Palmer [CV] Freight Office
   65   Palmer Station
   85   Amherst [CV] Depot

New York & New Haven (Chap. 1)

CT 28   Greenwich Modern Station, Station
  29.5 Cos Cob Station
   30   Riverside Depot
   31   Old Greenwich Station
   33   Stamford Modern Station
   37   Noroton Heights Station, Modern Station
   38   Darien Station
   39   Rowayton Depot
   41   South Norwalk Stations
   42   East Norwalk Depot
   44   Westport Stations
   47   Greens Farms Depot
   49   Southport Stations, Freight House
   51   Fairfield Stations
   56   Bridgeport Modern Station
   59   Stratford Stations

63   Milford Stations
72   New Haven Station

New York & New Haven - New Canaan Branch (Chap. 1A)

CT   0   Stamford Modern Station
      8   New Canaan Station

New York, Providence & Boston (Chap. 19)

RI   0   Providence Station Complex (4 structures), Modern
           Station, Express Office (Appendix A)
      10.5   Apponaug Freight House
      13   East Greenwich Station
      27   Kingston Station
      44   Westerly Station Complex (3), Freight House

CT   53   Mystic Combination Depot, Passenger Shelter
      54   West Mystic Depot
      55   Noank Depot
      61   Groton Freight House
      62   New London Station, Baggage/Express Office

Newburyport (Chap. 54)

MA   0.5   Wakefield Centre Depot
      3   Lynnfield Centre Depot
      8.5   Tapleyville Passenger Shelter
      9.5   Danvers [Newburyport RR] Freight House
      15   Topsfield Depot, Freight Houses
      18   East Boxford Station, Freight House
      30   Newburyport Modern Station

Newport & Fall River (Chap. 81)

RI   19   Newport Depot

Norfolk County (Chap. 67)

MA   3   Norwood Central Station
      7.5   Walpole Station
      16   Franklin Station
      16.5   Franklin Junction Freight House

Norfolk County - Valley Falls Branch (Chap. 67B)

MA   4   West Wrentham Freight House

RI   8   Arnolds Mills Freight House
      9   Abbotts Run Freight House

MA   12   Adamsdale Depot

RI   13.5   Valley Falls Freight House

Norwich & Worcester (Chap. 15)

CT	0	Groton Freight House
	12	Norwich [N&W] Station
	45	Putnam Station, Express Office
MA	66	Auburn Combination Depot
	71	Worcester Station, Modern Station

Norwich & Worcester - Norwich Connection (Chap. 15A)

CT	0	Norwich [N&W] Station

Old Colony (Chap. 73)

MA	0	South Station
	15	South Weymouth Depot
	18	North Abington Station
	25	South Hanson Depot
	29	Silver Lake Depot (Appendix A)
	33	Kingston Station, Freight House

Old Colony - Hanover Branch (Chap. 73D)

MA	0	North Abington Station
	1	Rockland Station

Old Colony - Milton Branch (Chap. 73B)

MA	3	Mattapan Depot

Pawtuxet Valley (Chap. 23)

RI	4.5	Pontiac Combination Depot

Peterborough & Shirley (Chap. 43)

MA	10	Townsend Station, Combination Depot/Freight House

Pittsfield & North Adams (Chap. 30)

MA	8	Cheshire Depot, Freight House
	12	Maple Grove Freight House
	13	Adams Station, Express Office
	14	Renfrew Depot
	15	Zylonite Depot
	18	North Adams Freight House

Plymouth & Middleborough (Chap. 79)

MA	0	Middleboro Freight House

Providence & Springfield (Chap. 24)

RI	0	Providence Station Complex (4 structures), Modern Station, Express Office (Appendix A)
	12	Smithfield Depot

Providence & Worcester (Chap. 25)

RI   0   Providence Station Complex (4 structures), Modern
             Station, Express Office (Appendix A)
     4.3   Pawtucket Freight House
     4.5   Pawtucket/Central Falls Station
     6   Valley Falls [P&W] Freight House
     7   Lonsdale Freight House
     12   Manville Freight House
     16   Woonsocket [P&W] Station

MA   24   Uxbridge Station, Freight House
     26   Whitins Station
     34   Saundersville Station
     35   Wilkinsonville Depot
     37   Millbury [P&W] Station (Appendix A)
     43   Worcester Station, Modern Station

Providence & Worcester - East Providence Branch (Chap. 25A)

RI   0   Valley Falls Freight House
     2   Darlington Freight House

Providence, Warren & Bristol (Chap. 26)

RI   0   Providence Station Complex (4 structures), Modern
             Station, Express Office (Appendix A)
     6   Riverside Depot
     16.5 Constitution St. [Bristol] Depot

Providence, Warren & Bristol - Fall River Branch (Chap. 26A)

MA   3   Touisset Depot

Salem & Lowell (Chap. 56)

MA   7   South Middleton Depot
     9   North Reading Depot

Salem & Lowell - Salem Harbor Branch (Chap. 56A)

MA   0   Salem Station

Saugus Branch (Chap. 60)

MA   5.5   Cliftondale Depot
     7   Saugus Depot

Shepaug (Chap. 4)

CT   12   Roxbury Combination Depot
     19   Washington Combination Depot
     32   Litchfield Station

Shore Line (Chap. 12)

CT 10   Stony Creek Depot
    19   Madison Station, Freight House (Appendix A)
    23   Clinton Depot
    27   Westbrook Combination Depot
    31   Old Saybrook Station, Freight House
    49   New London Station, Baggage/Express Office

South Reading Branch (Chap. 55)

MA 0.5   Wakefield Centre Depot

South Shore (Chap. 74)

MA 7   Hingham Stations
    10   Black Rock Depot (Appendix A)
    11   Cohasset Station
    13   North Scituate Station
    32   Kingston Station, Freight House

South Shore - Nantasket Branch (Chap. 74A)

MA 2   Nantasket Station
    5   Allerton Freight House

Southbridge & Blackstone (Chap. 16)

CT 25   Putnam Station, Express Office
    38   Hampton Freight House
    42   Clarks Corner [Chaplin] Depot

Southbridge & Blackstone - Southbridge Branch (Chap. 16A)

MA 18   Southbridge Station

Springfield, Athol & Northeastern (Chap. 35)

MA 37   New Salem Combination Depot
    40   South Athol Combination Depot
    45   Athol Station

Stony Brook (Chap. 45)

MA 2   West Chelmsford Freight House

Union Freight (Chap. 62)

MA 0   North Station, North Station [Fitchburg RR] (Appendix A)
    2   South Station

Vermont & Massachusetts (Chap. 31)

MA 0   Fitchburg Modern Station
    19   Otter River Freight House
    32   Athol Station

	41	Erving Depot, Freight House
	69	Shelburne Falls Freight House
	93	North Adams Freight House
	98	Williamstown Station, Baggage Office/Room, Freight House

Walpole & Wrentham (Chap. 69)

MA	0	Norwood Central Station
	2	East Walpole Freight House
	13	Wampum Depot

Ware River (Chap. 36)

MA	0	Palmer Station
	12	Ware [B&A] Freight House
	16	Gilbertville [B&A] Depot, Freight House

Western [Boston & Albany] (Chap. 29)

MA	0	Worcester Station, Modern Station
	20	East Brookfield Station
	26	West Brookfield Stations, Freight House
	29	Warren Depot, Station, Freight House
	40	Palmer Station
	54	Springfield Station, Modern Station
	57	West Springfield Freight House
	63	Westfield [B&A] Station
	82	Chester Combination Depot
	98	Hinsdale Combination Depot
	101	Dalton Station, Freight House
	104.5	Pittsfield Depot
	106	Pittsfield Modern Station

Western [Boston & Albany] - Chester & Becket Branch (Chap. 29E)

MA	0	Chester Combination Depot

Western [Boston & Albany] - North Brookfield Branch (Chap. 29D)

MA	0	East Brookfield Station
	4	North Brookfield Combination Depot

Western [Boston & Albany] - Spencer Branch (Chap. 29C)

MA	2	Spencer Station

Western [Boston & Albany] - Webster Branch (Chap. 29A)

MA	11	Webster [B&A] Depot

Worcester & Nashua (Chap. 41)

MA	0	Worcester Station, Modern Station
	9	West Boylston Freight House
	12	Sterling Junction Freight House

17   Clinton Station
18   Thayer Depot
19   Lancaster Freight House
32   Groton Freight House
36   Pepperell [W&N] Freight House

Appendix D

Depots and Freight Houses on Rail-Trails

FOR ABOUT twenty years now, there has been a growing movement to reuse abandoned railroad rights of way as recreational trails. The charge has been led by both local groups and the Rails-to-Trails Conservancy, a national organization. The RTC tries to preserve abandoned rail corridors by turning them into linear parks, thus preventing the piecemeal sale of the rights of way to abutters and the permanent loss of these corridors.

This appendix is broken down into three sections, one for each state. Within states, rail-trails are listed alphabetically by name. There are numerous rail-trails, but only those with structures identified in this book are listed. The listings provide the names of the towns in which the trails begin and end. Some rail-trails have been developed in distinct, non-contiguous sections; such trails may be listed multiple times, once for each section that contains railroad structures identified in this book. Applicable structures are listed in the order they appear when traveling between the endpoints listed. All structures are within sight of the rail-trail unless identified as "nearby." Nearby structures were either moved away from the right of way/trail, the trail was diverted so the structure cannot be viewed from the trail, or the trail comes close to but does not reach the structure. These buildings can be viewed by taking a short detour from the trail, as indicated in the descriptive text for the structure.

Connecticut

Trail Name	Trail End Points	Structures on or near Trail
Airline North State Park Trail	Windham to Putnam	Hampton Freight House (½ mile off trail)
Airline South State Park Trail	Cobalt to Willimantic	Easthampton Depot

Trail Name	Trail End Points	Structures on or near Trail
Airline South State Park Trail (Colchester Spur)	Amston to Colchester	Colchester Depot ColchesterFreight House
Farmington Canal Greenway	Hamden to Cheshire	Mount Carmel Depot Mount Carmel Freight House
Farmington Canal Greenway	Simsbury	Simsbury [NH&N] Depot Simsbury [NH&N] Combination Depot (nearby)
Farmington Canal Greenway	Simsbury to Avon	Avon Combination Depot (nearby)
Farmington Canal Greenway	Suffield to East Granby	Granby Combination Depot
Farmington River Trail	Burlington to Collinsville	Collinsville [NH&N] Freight House
Hop River State Park Trail	Manchester to Willimantic	Hop River Station (nearby)
Housatonic Railbed Trail	Stepney to Newtown	Stepney Combination Depot (nearby)
Railroad Ramble	Lakeville to Salisbury	Salisbury Depot Salisbury Freight House
Ridgefield Rail Trail	Ridgefield to Branchville	Branchville Station (nearby)
Stillwater Greenway (Winsted Riverfront Recapture)	Winsted	Winsted Freight House (nearby)

Massachusetts

Trail Name	Trail End Points	Structures on or Near Trail
Ashuwillticook Rail Trail	Lanesborough to Adams	Adams Express Office Adams Station Zylonite Depot Maple Grove Freight House Cheshire Depot Cheshire Freight House
Assabet River Rail Trail	Marlborough to Hudson	Marlboro Combination Depot
Bedford Narrow-Gauge Rail Trail	Bedford	Bedford Depot
Cape Cod Rail Trail	Dennis to South Wellfleet	Pleasant Lake General Store/Depot East Brewster Depot (nearby)
Fitchburg-Leominster Rail Trail	Fitchburg to Leominster	Leominster Station
Harwich-Chatham Trail	Harwich to Chatham	Chatham Depot (nearby)
Manhan Rail Trail	Easthampton to Mt. Tom	Easthampton Station
Marblehead Bicycle Path	Marblehead to Swampscott	Swampscott Depot (nearby)
Minuteman Bikeway	Bedford to Alewife	Bedford Depot Bedford Engine House/ Freight House Lexington Station
Nashua River Rail Trail	Ayer to Nashua, NH	Groton Freight House Pepperell [W&N] Freight House Pepperell [B&P] Depot (nearby)
Northampton Bikeway	Northampton to Florence	Northampton Station (nearby)

Trail Name	Trail End Points	Structures on or Near Trail
Norwottuck Rail Trail	Belchertown to Northampton	Amherst [B&M] Depot Hadley Freight House Northampton Station (nearby)
Reformatory Branch Trail	Bedford to Concord	Bedford Depot Bedford Engine House/Freight House (nearby)
Shining Sea Bikeway	Falmouth to Woods Hole	Falmouth Station
Sterling Rail-Trail	Sterling Center	Sterling Freight House
Upper Charles Trail	Holliston to Milford	Holliston Depot East Holliston Depot Milford [B&A] Station (nearby)

Rhode Island

Trail Name	Trail End Points	Structures on or Near Trail
Trestle Trail	Coventry to Connecticut Border	Coventry Depot Summit Depot Greene Station (nearby)
William C. O'Neill Bike Path	Kingston to Wakefield	Kingston Station Peace Dale Depot
East Bay Bike Path	Providence to Bristol	Riverside Depot Constitution St. [Bristol] Depot (nearby)

Selected Bibliography

1785-1935: 150th Anniversary of Easthampton, Massachusetts. Easthampton, MA: Easthampton News, 1935.

Alexander, Edwin P. *Down at the Depot: American Railroad Stations from 1831 to 1920.* New York: Bramhill House, 1970.

"B&M to Build New Larger Freight House." *Haverhill Sunday Record*, December 5, 1907.

Balfour, David with Joyce H. Koutsogiane. *Cumberland by the Blackstone: 250 Years of Heritage.* Virginia Beach: Donning, 1997.

Barrett, Richard C. *Boston's Depots and Terminals.* Rochester: Railroad Research Publication, 1996.

Beaudette, Edward H. *Central Vermont Railway.* Newton, NJ: Carstens, 1982.

Beauregard, Mark W. *Railroad Stations of New England Today: Volume 1., The Boston & Maine.* Flanders, NJ: Railroad Avenue Enterprises, 1975.

Bedini, Silvio. *Ridgefield in Review.* Ridgefield, CT: Ridgefield 250th Anniversary Committee, 1958.

Benson, Esther Fisher. "A Small House Moves Again." *Green Light*, July 1991.

———. "History of the OCNRR Depot." *Green Light*, April 1991.

Blakeslee, Phillipe C.. *Lines West: A Brief History.* New Haven: Camm Associates, 1974.

Bond, C. Lawrence. *Houses & Buildings of Topsfield.* Topsfield, MA: Topsfield Historical Society, 1989.

Boothroyd, Stephen J. *Down at the Station:The Rail Lines of Southern New England in Early Postcards.* Watertown, NY: Cranberry Junction, 2002.

Borrup, Roger, and Carl L. Smith. *Transportation Bulletin: Hyde Park Division.* Warehouse Point, CT: Connecticut Valley Chapter, National Railway Society, 1976.

Boston & Maine Railroad Historical Society. *The Central Mass.* Boston: B&MRHS, 1975.

Brecher, Jeremy. *Cornwall In Pictures: A Visual Reminiscence, 1868-1941.* Cornwall, CT: Cornwall Historical Society, 2001.

Brittin, Robert P. *Central Vermont: The South End.* David City, NE: South Platte Press, 1995.

Brown, Joyce S. *The Line: A Story of the Providence and Worcester Railroad Company.* Worcester: United Offset Printing, 1999.

Brusic, Lucy McTeer. *Amidst Cultivated and Pleasant Fields.* Canaan, NH: North Haven Historical Society, 1986.

Buck, Sylvia G. *Warren: A Town in the Making, 1741-1991.* Warren, MA: S. G. Buck, 1994.

"Building Is Inspected After Joint Luncheon." *Meriden Daily Journal*, September 21, 1942.

Bye, Ranulph. *The Vanishing Depot.* Wynnewood, PA: Livingston, 1973.

Byron, Carl R., with Arthur E. Mitchell. *Trackside along the New Haven 1950-1956.* Scotch Plains, NJ: Morning Sun Books, 2002.

Campbell, Faith S. *The Housatonic Railroad from 1840.* N.p.: Falls Village-Canaan Historical Society, 1991.

Campbell, Susan, and Bill Heald. *Connecticut Curiosities.* Guilford, CT: Globe Pequot Press, 2002.

Cane, Ena M. *Whately, 1771-1971: A New England Portrait.* Northampton, MA: Town of Whately, 1972.

Care, Pearl B. *The History of Erving, Massachusetts, 1838-1988.* Turner Falls, MA: Pioneer Litho, 1988.

Champlin, Winslow S. *The History of the Town of East Longmeadow: Written to Commemorate the Town's Fiftieth Anniversary, 1894-1944.* N.p., 1948.

Committee for the Preservation of Hull's History. *Then & Now: Hull and Nantasket Beach.* Charleston, SC: Arcadia Publishing, 2001.

Cooper, Fletcher E. *The Shepaug Railroad, 1872-1948.* Litchfield, CT: F. E. Cooper, 2002.

Cornwall Historical Society. *Cornwall: A Sampling of Our Heritage.* Torrington, CT: Cornwall Bicentennial Committee, 1975.

Cornwall, L. Peter. *In the Shore Line's Shadow: The Six Lives of the Danbury & Norwalk Railroad.* Littleton, MA: Flying Yankee Enterprises, 1987.

Cummings, O. R. *Transportation Bulletin: Berkshire Street Railway.* Warehouse Point, CT: Connecticut Valley Chapter, National Railway Society, 1972.

Dawson, Devon. *Holyoke.* Postcard History Series. Charleston, SC: Arcadia Publishing, 2004.

DePasquale, Ron. "When Bigger Is Also Better: Two Projects That Exceed Housing Density Limits Put Westborough on the 'Smart Growth' Track." *Boston Globe*, November 4, 2006.

Devito, Michael. *Transportation Bulletin: Hartford & Springfield Street Railway Co.* Warehouse Point, CT: Connecticut Valley Chapter, National Railway Society, 1973.

Dow, George Francis. *History of Topsfield.* Topsfield, MA: Topsfield Historical Society, 1940.

"D.P.U. Notifies Selectmen R.R. Station to be Closed." *Auburn News*, October 21, 1964.

Dubiel P., Frank. *Union Station, Providence, RI.* Fall River, MA: D. P. Frank, 1974.

Eastwood, Brian. "Rail Trail May Be a Reality." *MetroWest Daily News*, August 1, 2004.

Eaton, William E. *History of Wakefield, Massachusetts.* Wakefield, MA: Wakefield Tercentenary Committee, 1944.

Eldredge, Andrew T. *Railroads of Cape Cod and the Islands.* Images of Rail. Charleston, SC: Arcadia Publishing, 2003.

"The End of the Line." *Worcester Daily Telegram*, November 28, 1976.

Fanning, Patricia. *Norwood: A History.* Charleston, SC: Arcadia Publishing, 2002.

Farnham, Elmer R. *The Quickest Route: The History of the Norwich and Worcester Railroad.* Chester, CT: Peqout Press, 1973.

Farson, Robert H. *Cape Cod Railroads: Including Martha's Vinyard and Nantucket.* Yarmouth Port, MA: Cape Cod Historical Publications, 1993.

Fisher, Charles E., and Dubiel, Frank P. *The Story of the Old Colony Railroad.* Fall River, MA: F. P. Dubiel, 1974.
"Fire Destroys Old B&M Railroad Depot." *Athol Transcript,* August 21, 1935.
Flynn, Cathy. "The Old Railroad Station: Historic Landmark Emerges From Retirement." *Boston Daily News,* May 8, 2002.
Forman, Ethan. "New Station Work Started, Work Begins on Rail Station." *Lawrence Eagle-Tribune,* June 18, 2004.
Foulds, Alan E., and Arthur E. Foulds, *Lynnfield: Two Centuries, 1782-1982.* Lynnfield, MA: Bancroft Press, 1982.
"Freight Agency K.O. Approved." *Athol Daily News,* December 15, 1960.
"Freight Yard on Hale St. to Be Extended." *Haverhill Evening Gazette,* February 24, 1912.
Gardner, Warren F. "History of Railroad from Opening in 1838." *Meriden Daily Journal,* September 21, 1942.
——. "Meriden's New Station Opened with Ceremony." *Meriden Daily Journal,* September 21, 1942.
——. "Public's Agitation Ends in Comfort." *Meriden Daily Journal,* September 21, 1942.
Greene, J. R. *Quabbin's Railroad, the Rabbit: Volume I, The Independent Years, 1869-1880.* Athol: J. R. Green, 2000.
Hall, Ronald, and Robert Wuchert, Jr. *Memories of the New Haven.* 2 vols. Wallingford, CT: Cedar Hill Production, 1985-86.
"Haverhill Put Ahead by B. & M." *Haverhill Evening Gazette,* August 8, 1914.
Hazen, Henry. *History of Billerica, Massachusetts, 1653-1883.* Boston: Williams, 1883.
Held, Bruce D. *Boston & Maine in the 19th Century.* Images of Rail. Charleston, SC: Arcadia Publishing, 2002.
——. *Boston & Maine in the 20th Century.* Images of Rail. Charleston, SC: Arcadia Publishing, 2002.
Hicks, Judith A. *A Mystic River Anthology.* Wickford, RI: Dutch Island Press, 1988.
History of the Old Colony Railroad: A Complete History of the Old Colony Railroad from 1844 to the Present Time. Boston: Hager & Handy, 1893
Hitchcock, Henry Russell. *The Architecture of H. H. Richardson and His Times.* Cambridge, MA: MIT Press, 1961.
Hulbert, Joanne. *Holliston: A Good Town.* Camden, ME: Penobscot Press, 2000.
Humphrey, Thomas J., and Norton D. Clark. *Boston's Commuter Rail: The First 150 Years.* Cambridge, MA: Boston Street Railway Association, 1985.
——. *Boston's Commuter Rail: Second Section.* Cambridge, MA: Boston Street Railway Association, 1986.
Images of America Series. Dover, NH: Arcadia Publishing, 1995-97; Charleston, SC, 1998-2005. *Abington; Amherst and Hadley: Through the Seasons; Attleboro; Belmont; Berlin; Bethel; Billerica; Boston in Motion; Boston: A Century of Progress; Boston's Back Bay in the Victorian Era; Boston's Red Line: Bridging the Charles from Alewife to Braintree; Boxford; Boylston; Bradford: The End of an Era; Bridgeport; Bristol (CT); Bristol, Rhode Island: In the Mount Hope Lands of King Philip; Brookfield; Burrillville; Cohasset; Concord; Connecticut Whistle Stops Greenwich to New Haven; Courtland; Dorchester (Vol. II); Dover; East Longmeadow; Easthampton;*

Falmouth; Farmington; Framingham; Gloucester and Rockport; Greenwich; Hamden; Hanson; Hartford; Harwich; Holliston (2 vols.); Hopkinton; Hyannis and Hyannis Port; Kingston [MA]; Kingston [RI]; Lancaster; Lexington; Littleton; Lost Hartford; The Lost Towns of the Quabbin Valley; Lowell (Vol. II); The Lower Blackstone River Valley; Malden; Marlborough; Methuen; Mystic; Natick; Needham; Newton; New-town; Northampton; Norton; Norwood; Peabody; Redding and Easton; Ridgefield; Ridgefield, 1900-1950; Rockland; Salem; Salem, Massachusetts, Vol. II; Shelton; Southbridge; Spencer; Springfield (2 vols.); Stamford; Stoneham; Stoughton; Stratford; Templeton; Thomaston; Wakefield; Wallingford; Warren; Warwick; Westfield (Vol. II); Weston; Weymouth; Windham and Willimantic; Windham; Windsor Locks; Worcester, 1880-1920; Worcester (Vol. II).

James, Frank. "Dudley Freight Office to Close Tomorrow." *Worcester Daily Telegram*, May 28, 1958.

Jones, Robert C. *The Central Vermont Railway: A Yankee Tradition.* 6 vols. Silverton, CO: Sundance, 1981-82.

Jones, Robert Willoughby. *Boston & Maine: Three Colorful Decades of New England Railroading.* Glendale: Trans-Anglo Books, 1991.

———. *The New York Central in New England.* 2 vols. Los Angeles: Pine Tree Press, 1997.

Karr, Ronald Dale. *The Rail Lines of Southern New England: A Handbook of Railroad History.* Pepperell, MA: Branch Line Press, 1995.

King, Mary Louise. *Portrait of New Canaan.* New Canaan, CT: New Canaan Historical Society, 1981.

Koch, Katherine. "New Restaurant Pulling into Old Railroad Station." *Kingston Reporter*, August 1, 2002.

Konig, Michael F., and Martin Kaufman. *Springfield, 1636-1986.* Springfield, MA: Springfield Library and Museums Association, 1987.

Kyper, Frank. *Philip Ross Hastings: The Boston & Maine, A Photographic Essay.* N.p.: Locomotive & Railway Preservation, 1989

Lafleur, Michael. "Every 'X' a Challenge: Fix It." *Lowell Sun*, August 21, 2006.

Lewis, Edward A. *The Blackstone Valley Line: The Story of the Blackstone Canal Company and the Providence & Worcester Railroad.* Seekonk, MA: Baggage Car, 1973.

———. *New England Country Depots.* Arcade, NY: Baggage Car, 1973.

Liljestrand, Robert A. *The New Haven Railroad's Boston Division.* Ansonia, CT: Bob's Photos, 2001.

Liljestrand, Robert A., and David R. Sweetland. *Railroad Cities: Providence, Rhode Island.* Ansonia, CT: Bob's Photos, 2002.

Lilyestrom, Betty. "Old P.W.S.R.R. to be Dismantled for Oxford Dam." *Worcester Daily Telegram*, May 28, 1958.

"Local Depots of the Eastern Railroad." *Lynn Daily Evening Item*, October 23, 1909.

Lord, Robert F. *Country Depots in the Connecticut Hills.* Riverton, CT: Paper Mill, 1996.

Lord, William G. *History of Athol Massachusetts.* Athol: N.p., 1953.

Lowney, Patrick. "Wheels Keep on Turning Print." *Newport Daily News*, February 2, 2004.

Lynch, Peter E. *New Haven Railroad.* St Paul: MBI Publishing, 2003.

MacDaniel. "Construction Puts Squeeze on Station." *Boston Globe*, October 29, 2006.

Malcolm Grear Designers. *Amtrak's High Speed Rail Program, New Haven to Boston: History and Historical Resources*. [Pawtucket], RI: Public Archaeology Laboratory, 2001.

"May Be Vacated." *Athol Daily News*, November 12, 1960.

"Meriden's 99 Years of Railroad History." *Meriden Daily Journal*, June 24, 1937.

Mitchell, Alexander D., IV. *Train Stations*. Philadelphia: Courage Books, 2002.

Moore, Christopher. "Jumping the Tracks." *Danvers Herald*, September 9, 2004.

Moran, Kate. "Union Station Takes Step Backward." *New London Day*, September 4, 2003.

Nelligan, Tom. *The Valley Railroad Story*. New York: Quadrant Press, 1983.

Nimke, Robert W. *The Central New England Railway Story*. 3 vols. Rutland, VT: R. W. Nimke, 1995.

———. "Rutland LCL." *Rutland Newsliner* 5 (Winter 1991): 3-6.

Ochsner, Jeffrey Karl. "Architecture for the Boston & Albany Railroad: 1881-1894." *Journal of the Society of Architectural Historians* 47 (June 1988): 109-31.

———. *H. H. Richardson: Complete Architectural Works*. Cambridge, MA: MIT Press, 1982.

Oleson, Ellie. "Caboose Makes Its Last Journey: Wooden Apple Signmakers Add Old Caboose to Their Shop." *Auburn News*, April 2, 1992.

Owens, David. "Fire Hits Historical Canaan Train Depot." *Callboy* 55 (November 2001): 20.

Pierotti, James, and Scott Wahle. *Postcard History Series: Hingham*. Charleston, SC: Arcadia Publishing, 2005.

"A Poem in Stone." *Worcester Magazine*, July 1911.

Potter, Janet Greenstein. *Great American Railroad Stations*. New York: Preservation Press, 1996.

"Rail Freight Cut at Auburn." *Worcester Sunday Telegram*, January 24, 1965.

"Railroad Comeback Effort On a Day to Day Basis." *Meriden Daily Journal*, April 27, 1973.

"Railroad Freight Agency Closes." *Athol Daily News*, January 6, 1962.

[Railroad Stations of Stafford]. *Stafford Press*, November 16, 1893.

Ravo, Nick. "Boos, Cheers and Yawns for New Station." *New York Times*, November 29, 1987.

———. "Rough Road to an Opening." *New York Times*, November 29, 1987.

———. "Stamford Rail Center Opens, Off Schedule." *New York Times*, November 23, 1987.

"Recollections of Old Freight Depot." *Haverhill Gazette*, July 15, 1949.

Rogers, David. "Housing Project Moves Ahead: 19th Century Downtown Buildings to Be Transformed." *Amesbury News*, January 31, 2003.

"Rosemont Not Going to Quit." *Haverhill Evening Gazette*, August 4, 1915.

Russell, Joseph. *Vestiges of the Lost Valley: Buildings and Bells from the Quabbin*. Palmer, MA: J. W. Russell, 1986.

Sherborn Historical Society. *Sherborn, Massachusetts: Images of the Past*. West Kennebunk, ME: Phoenix Publishing, 1999.

Smith, Jimi. "The Wayland, MA, Station." *Boston & Maine Railroad Historical Society Modeler's Notes* 92 (September 2004): 1-2.

Smith, Larry. "Train Station Analysis Completed." *Hartford Courant*, January 1, 2005.

Springman, Mary Jane, and Betty Guinan. *East Granby: The Evolution of a Connecticut Town.* Canaan, NH: Phoenix Publishing, 1983.

Stanley, Robert C. *Narrow Gauge: The Story of the Boston, Revere Beach & Lynn Railroad.* Cambridge, MA: Boston Street Railway Association, 1980.

The Stoughton Railroad Station. Stoughton, MA: N.p., 1988.

Sweetland, David R. *New Haven Color Pictorial: Volume Two, Central Connecticut & Rhode Island.* Charleston, SC: Four Ways West Publications, 2003.

Thorpe, Sheldon B. *North Haven in the Nineteenth Century: A Memorial.* New Haven: Twentieth Century Committee, 1901.

"Train Depot Was Pride of City." *Leominster Pioneer*, April 29, 1986.

Turner, Gregg M., and Melancthon W. Jacobs. *Connecticut Railroads: An Illustrated History.* Hartford: Connecticut Historical Society, 1986.

"Two-Station Depot War." *Lynn Daily Evening Item*, October 23, 1909.

"Union Railroad Station: New London's Gem." *Connecticut Preservation News* 27 (January-February, 2004): 1-2.

"Unite For New Railroad Depot." *Haverhill Evening Gazette*, August 2, 1915.

Waters, Martin J. "In Days of Old, the 'Ghost Train' Streaked through Wallingford." *New Haven Railroad Historical & Technical Association Bulletin*, September 2001.

Watkins, Lura Woodside. *Middleton, Massachusetts: A Cultural History.* Salem, MA: Essex Institute, 1970.

Wiehn, John, and Mark Heiss. *Waterbury, 1890-1930.* Postcard History Series. Charleston, SC: Arcadia Publishing, 2003.

Winget, Kelly A. "Methuen Considers Buying Depot." *Lawrence Eagle-Tribune*, December 12, 2001.

Wood, Squire G. *A History of Greene and Vicinity, 1845-1929.* Providence: N.p. 1936.

"Wooden Structure to Take Its Place Temporarily." *Haverhill Evening Gazette*, June 5, 1905.

Annual Reports

Boston, Barre & Gardner Railroad, 1872
New York, New Haven & Hartford Railroad, 1874, 1882, 1884-86, 1888, 1897-1917

Historical Society Periodicals

Ambassador (Central Vermont Railway Historical Society)
B&M Bulletin (Boston & Maine Railroad Historical Society)
Shoreliner (New Haven Railroad Historical & Technical Association)

Other Suggested Reading

Railpace Newsmagazine

Index to Architects

THIS INDEX identifies architects and architectural firms associated with the stations included in this book. There are fifty-two structures for which the architect or architectural firm is known. When applicable, the architects responsible for rebuildings and renovations are also listed, e.g. for Hartford and New London Stations in Connecticut, and Worcester and Athol Stations in Massachusetts. Separate listings are not provided for auxiliary buildings built as part of a station complex, such as those associated with the stations in Providence, RI, and Framingham, MA.

Finegold, Alexander & Associates

MA   Worcester Station

Fletcher, H. B.

MA   Methuen Station

Francis, H. M.

MA   Athol Station

Frink, Alden

MA   Athol Station

Gardner, E. C.

MA   West Brookfield Station

Gilbert, Bradford Lee

MA   Andover Station
      Beverly Station
      Bridgewater Station
      Canton Junction Station
      North Abington Station

Gilbert, Cass

CT   New Haven Station

HNTB Architecture

MA   Hyannis Modern Station (Appendix A)

Huckel, Samuel, Jr.

MA   Worcester Station

JCA Architects

MA   Millbury [P&W] Station (Appendix A)

Keller, George

CT   Hartford Station

Lev Zetlin Associates

CT   Stamford Modern Station

Longfellow, A. W., Jr.

MA   Natick Station (Appendix A)

McCrea, Duncan J.
MA   Worcester Modern Station

McKim, Mead and White
CT   Waterbury Station

Mellor, Fredrick W.
CT   Hartford Station
RI   Pawtucket/Central Falls Station

Meyer and Meyer
MA   Anderson RTC Modern Station
Lowell [B&L] Modern Station

Pitcher, F. J.
MA   Sharon Station

Richardson, Henry Hobson
CT   New London Station
MA   Framingham Station
Holyoke [B&M] Station
North Easton Station
Palmer Station
Wellesley Hills Station
Woodland Depot

Sheply, Rutan and Coolidge
CT   Hartford Station
MA   Allston Station
Ashland Station
Dalton Station
East Brookfield Station
Newton Center Station
Newton Highlands Station
South Station
Warren Station
Wellesley Farms Station

Stone, Carpenter, and Willson
RI   Providence Station

Stull and Lee
MA   Ruggles Modern Station
South Station

Sullivan/Jamieson

CT   South Norwalk Eastbound Station

Sykes, Henry A.

CT   Suffield Depot (Appendix B)

Wallace Floyd Design Group

MA   Pittsfield Modern Station

Waller, Frank

MA   Stockbridge Station

Waterman Design Associates

MA   Westboro Station

Watson and Huckel

MA   Worcester Station

Notes

Also available from Branch Line Press

Lost Railroads of New England
by Ronald Dale Karr

Fully annotated directory of abandoned rail lines throughout New England, 1848-1994. Brief summary of the rise and fall of New England railroads, with tips on finding "lost" railroads.

6"×9" • 168 pages • $12.95

The Rail Lines of Southern New England
A Handbook of Railroad History
by Ronald Dale Karr

"Provides brief yet thorough summaries on the predecessor rail lines of the region and tells what remains of them today. Keeping up with the discussion is made easy with dozens of maps." – *Railfan & Railroad Magazine*
    Considered by many readers to be the "bible" on railroads in southern New England.

6"×9" • 384 pages • 90 photos & illustrations • $22.95

The Rail Lines of Northern New England
A Handbook of Railroad History
by Robert M. Lindsell

"As complete and well-researched and organized a history of northern New England's railroads as has appeared in recent memory."
    –470 Railroad Club Newsletter
    Maps and capsule histories of 77 rail lines, with state locator maps for all lines.

6"×9" • 416 pages • Over 100 vintage & contemporary rail photos • $23.95

Available through your local bookstore, or order direct from:

Branch Line Press
30 Elm Street
Pepperell, MA 01463

978-433-2236
Email: books@branchlinepress.com
On line at **www.branchlinepress.com**